PASTORAL THEOLOGY;

OR,

THE THEORY OF THE EVANGELICAL MINISTRY.

By A. VINET.

TRANSLATED AND EDITED

By THOMAS H. SKINNER, D.D.,

PROFESSOR OF PASTORAL THEOLOGY IN THE UNION THEOLOGICAL SEMINARY OF NEW YORK.

WITH NOTES, AND AN ADDITIONAL CHAPTER, BY THE TRANSLATOR.

"Ἐγώ εἰμι ὁ ποιμὴν ὁ καλός."

NEW YORK:

HARPER & BROTHERS, PUBLISHERS,

329 & 331 PEARL STREET,

FRANKLIN SQUARE.

1853.

Let not thy heart be hasty to utter any thing before God; for God is in heaven, and thou upon earth.—*Ecclesiastes*, v., 2.

Quand on ne serait pendant sa vie que l'apôtre d'un seul homme, ce ne serait pas être en vain sur la terre un fardeau inutile.—*La Bruyère.*

PREFACE

BY THE TRANSLATOR.

We began to read this work for our own advantage; but soon received an impression of its excellence, which led us to wish that it might have the free circulation which a faithful translation and an American edition would secure to it. A further acquaintance with it deepened this impression, until at length this translation became almost a natural result.

The work of translation is generally thought to be irksome; but, in the present case, the communion which it has occasioned with the beautiful, earnest, and holy spirit of the author, has changed labor into the highest pleasure. The minute attention which must be given to every sentence and word in translating has this advantage, that it obliges us to perceive every delicate shade of thought and feeling which the author expresses; and as there have been very few as pure, as discriminating, as imaginative, as spiritual minds as that of M. Vinet, it could not but be that in a treatise on a subject which he had so thoroughly studied, and which was so congenial to his character and temperament, there should be found a rich, varied, and full exhibition of sentiment and feeling: Adding to this the intrinsic excellence of the subject itself, PASTORAL THEOLOGY, whose sphere is that which was filled by the Chief Shepherd and Bishop of souls, it afforded a fund of enjoyment and profit, to which it was truly an unusual privilege to have such familiar and intimate access.

M. Vinet, among the gifted men of his times, was in the first rank. The editor of his "Études sur Blaise Pascal," we think, with no more than justice, classes him, in the most important respects, with that great man. "The general direction of his labors, the nature of his mind and temperament, gave him ready access to this noble and astonishing genius. A penetrating analysis of the human soul, a strong attachment of heart to truth and an imperious demand for evidence, a natural melancholy, an inclination to serious irony, a strict and sometimes transcendent dialectic, passion in reason, a comprehensive and powerful imagination—these traits are common to the author of *Discours sur quelques Sujets Religieux* and the author of the *Pensées*. We may say, making due allowance for circumstances, that Pascal and Vinet resembled each other. Pascal, moreover, inspired the Protestant apologist of the nineteenth century, and served as his model. If natural affinity, sympathy, and interest are of any aid to the understanding, M. Vinet assuredly ought to comprehend Pascal. It was this, perhaps, which led an eminent critic, M. Sainte-Beuve, to say: 'If we should collect into one small volume the articles of M. Vinet on Pascal, we should have, I think, the most exact results to which we can arrive on this great controversy.' "*

The work before us is worthy of its author. It was not prepared for the press by M. Vinet, but the subject had received his closest attention, protracted through a series of years; and though it is substantially composed of notes, which served as a basis of instruction in the Academy of Lausanne, yet these notes were carefully prepared by the author, and, of course, embodied his best and strongest thoughts. M. Vinet's own manuscripts were sometimes complemented from the notebooks of his pupils; but these insertions, which, in the French publication, are included in brackets, and which, in a volume of four hundred pages, amount to about thirty, have the full force and vigor of the author's mind, and are quite equal in excellence to the other parts of his work. The slight imperfections of form, arising from the causes indicated by the French editors, do not impair the value of this book: After removing the brackets, as we have done in this translation, they will probably not be observed.

The work is distinguished by the following great excellences: by comprehensiveness and fullness of plan,

* *Études sur Blaise Pascal, par* A. VINET, p. vii.

embracing all parts of the subject in just proportion; by a deeply philosophical vein of teaching under the guise of the most beautiful simplicity; by thorough, various, and extensive learning; by a pre-eminently pure and holy spirit, which often subdues and penetrates the reader's heart, and leads him to look within himself with the profoundest self-scrutiny; and, whenever the subject permits it, by a peculiarly elevated, eloquent, and charming diction.

If we were to distinguish between the merits of the different parts of this work, we should assign the highest place to the third part, especially chapter second, which treats of the care of souls as applied to individuals; where we can not but think that this spiritual and faithful man has transcended all who have preceded him. As an example of the earnestness and tenderness of his manner in this part, we insert here a passage which refers to the case of a pastor at the bedside of a dying man who is not prepared for death: "There are, it is said, souls who perceive with despair that the principle of the spiritual life is extinguished within them, and who with terrible evidence are convinced that there remains nothing in them that can love or pray: Faith comes to them at the last moment, but it is the faith of demons, resplendent with brightness, but it is the brightness of lightning. God only can know, indeed, that this soul is dead: As for you who do not know, struggle, pant with it, fight its battle, unite with it in its agony; let it perceive that there is by its side, in its last anguish, a soul that believes, that hopes, and that loves; that your love is but a reflection of the love of Christ; and that Christ, through you, has become present to it: Give it a hint, a glimpse, a taste of the Divine mercy; let it be, as it were, forced to believe in it by seeing the reflection of it in you: Hope against hope: Wrestle with God to the last moment: Let the voice of your prayer, the echo of the words of Christ, resound in the dying man's ear, even in his dreams: You do not know what may be passing in that interior world into which your views do not penetrate; nor by what mystery eternity may hang on one minute, and salvation on one sigh. You do not know what may avail—what one ejaculation of a soul toward God may embrace at the last bound of earthly existence. Then do not cease: pray aloud with the dying man; pray for him with a low voice: Be a priest when you can no longer be a preacher. Let the office of intercession, the most efficacious of all, precede, accompany, follow all others."

But while we can not but regard the third part with peculiar interest, we have been compelled to think that there is an omission here which should not be passed over without notice; and, with the hope of increasing the usefulness of the book in our own country, we have endeavored to supply it by adding a chapter of our own.

Our author has distinctly stated (page 242) the principle which guided us in this chapter, a principle which admits of many applications; but the subject we have here considered seemed to us, from its great importance, entitled to peculiar attention.

It is scarcely necessary to say that, in editing this work, we do not hold ourselves answerable for every opinion of the author: On two points, of much importance, we have thought proper to indicate some difference of judgment from him, in notes which will be found in the Appendix.

In the work of translation we have had occasion, more than once, to lament the impossibility of retaining in English the exceedingly *naïve* and touching manner of the author; but we have endeavored, in every case, to report faithfully the views and movements of his uncommon mind. We have studied exactness in giving his meaning rather than rigid conformity to his manner; although we have endeavored to deviate from this no further than was necessary in order to render his meaning into good English.

We concur with the French editors in hoping that this book will be read not only by ministers of the Gospel, but by the religious community generally: Better than any work we know of, it is adapted to impart profound and just impressions of the pastoral office, in which all the interests of humanity are so deeply involved.

CONTENTS.

PART SECOND.

RELATIVE OR SOCIAL LIFE.

CHAPTER I.

SOCIAL LIFE IN GENERAL.

CHAPTER II.

DOMESTIC LIFE OF A MINISTER.

PART THIRD.

PASTORAL LIFE.

SECTION FIRST.

WORSHIP.

SECTION SECOND.

INSTRUCTION.

CHAPTER I.

PREACHING.

CHAPTER II.

CATECHISING.

SECTION THIRD.

CARE OF SOULS, OR PASTORAL OVERSIGHT.

CHAPTER I.

OF THE CARE OF SOULS IN GENERAL.

CHAPTER II.

OF THE CARE OF SOULS APPLIED TO INDIVIDUALS.

APPENDIX.

ADVERTISEMENT OF THE EDITORS.

THE volume which we give to the public was not prepared for the press by M. Vinet. It is composed essentially of notes which served as the basis of a course intended for the students of the Academy of Lausanne. These notes, most frequently written out with much care, often have the character of a simple sketch, which the professor proposed to complete in his lectures. Hence some imperfections of form, which would certainly have disappeared if the author had put his own finishing hand to his work. We have, however, thought it our duty to publish it such as we found it, without permitting ourselves to refashion it, in any of its parts, except that as we had, on certain portions of the course, more than one original manuscript, it often happened that we were obliged to complete some from others. Moreover, when it seemed to us necessary to illustrate or complete the thought of the author, we have inserted amplifications taken from the note-books of the hearers of M. Vinet. These extracts might have been multiplied, but we have confined ourselves to what was strictly necessary, and all the insertions of this kind have been placed between brackets,* that they might not escape the reader's attention. M. Vinet himself has translated many passages, taken

* These are omitted in the translation.

from ancient or foreign authors, which will be found in the course of the work. Those which were quoted in the original language we have rendered into French.

The Appendix at the end of the volume contains principally passages from authors to which M. Vinet simply refers, but which appear to have been read in his lectures, and which serve to illustrate his thought. Many of these have been fully transcribed by himself in his note-books. They appear, at the same time, too extended to be inserted in the course, and too necessary to be merely referred to. The *Thoughts of Bengel*, which will be also found in the Appendix, were translated from the German by M. Vinet, and published apart in a small pamphlet in 16mo.

There are here and there allusions to the National Church of the Canton de Vaud. It should be remembered that the greater part of the hearers of M. Vinet were to exercise the evangelical ministry in that church, with which he did not cease to be connected, so far as the worship was concerned, up to the moment when a free church was established in the Canton de Vaud, in consequence of the secession of a great number of pastors.

We hope that the course of Pastoral Theology will be well received, not only by ministers of the Gospel and students of theology, for whom it is more especially designed, but by the religious public in general. The fundamental idea of M. Vinet recommends his book to the serious attention of all the friends of the Gospel. The pastor is not, in his view, an isolated being, far removed from the community of Christians into the desert of a solitary dignity, to which ordinary believers must not aspire. He conceives of him as less above them than as at their head, and in the advance in the work of charity. Neither are his labors exclusive; on the contrary, all should associate themselves actively with him, and will do so according to the measure of their fidelity. The pastor is not essentially different from a Christian—he is the representative Christian—the model of the flock (1 Tim., iv., 12). All Christians will find in this book valuable lessons, which they should treasure up. If they receive it as we dare to hope, we shall soon publish also *Homiletics*, or, *the Theory of Preaching*, of which we likewise possess the manuscript.

PASTORAL THEOLOGY.

INTRODUCTION.

§ 1. *Definition of the Subject. What is a Minister of the Gospel? Ideal of a Minister.*

We have elsewhere defined Practical Theology. It is art which supposes science, or science resolving itself into art. It is the art of applying usefully, in the ministry, the knowledge acquired in the three other departments of theology, which are purely scientific. It appears, then, that we may very conveniently call *Pastoral Theology* that collection of rules or directions to which we have given the name of *Practical Theology*. But, although the idea of the pastor (*Seelsorger**) and of the pastorate controls and comprehends all the parts of Practical Theology, yet it may be abstracted and considered by itself as a moral element pervading each part of Practical Theology, but which, also, distinct from the catechetical and homiletical departments,† forms one of its own, an object of special study. Pastoral Theology, then, would

* One of the designations of a pastor in Germany; literally, he who has the care of the soul.

† We might add liturgical; but the small space we can give to this part induces us to include it in our course of Pastoral Theology, or Prudence. As to ecclesiastical law, the study of which may comprehend that of the different ecclesiastical legislations or constitutions, and which is in this sense a science, it becomes an art, and, consequently, a part of Practical Theology, in so far as it practically directs the pastor in the observance and execution of the ecclesiastical laws of his own denomination. What little we shall say of it will be found in its proper place in this course.

treat of all the duties, all the kinds of activity to which the pastor is called, except public preaching and catechising.

The expressions *duties of the pastor* and *pastoral prudence* are incomplete. They present the thing too much under the point of view of an art or a practice. But this point of view should not be exclusive. The speculative side should have its place. Action is the last end of speculation; but, whatever may be the nature of the action, it is not sufficiently provided for, if attention be confined to it in the practical point of view. It should be studied abstractly. We should study the theory of the evangelical ministry, not only to know what we have to do, but also as an objective fact, which simply, as such, demands our acquaintance. Abstract speculation is of high utility. He who regards the things of his profession only in the midst of action, will act neither with freedom, nor with intelligence, nor with depth. Hence, among other reasons, this course is called the *Theory of the Evangelical Ministry*.

Perhaps our distribution is not exactly right. Catechetics, homiletics, etc., are not, perhaps, different in substance from Pastoral Theology. Still, on account of the extent of these divisions, of the detail which they require, and of the disproportioned space they would necessarily occupy if they should be treated in all their breadth in a course of Pastoral Theology, we separate them, intending to pursue the study of them when we shall be more at leisure. We are far from supposing that the chief one of these categories represents a whole, or even a reality: the reality exists only in the assemblage of the three functions, Worship, Preaching, and Catechising. By the very idea of a minister, these all belong to him. He would not otherwise be a minister. Not that these functions may not be distinguished and even separated—but they never should be after an exclusive manner; that is to say, in such a manner that he who exercises one is not to exercise the others; for they mutually suppose and contain one another.

Nevertheless, the idea of this unity has its date; it is a Christian idea. All religions have not conceived nor realized it.

In the Old Testament the office of priest and of prophet formed two distinct offices. It accords with the Old Testament to distinguish, as it does with the New to blend these two. The two systems are characterized by these two facts. Perfect unity between the form and the idea did not yet exist, and could not enter except with the law of spirituality and of liberty. On one side and the other, as on two distinct planes, were represented the letter which kills, and the spirit which gives life. The economy which was to unite them in one whole, was also to unite in one and the same man the priest and the prophet.

On this point the primitive Church presents us a phenomenon analogous to the whole genius of its economy, which did not rudely repudiate all the traditions of the theocracy. It divides the ministry into many different ministries. It does not appear that all ministers did the same things, nor that all did all things. It would seem, from Ephesians, iv., 11, and 1 Corinthians, xii., 28, 30, that this division of labor* had been formally instituted by the supreme Head of the Church; but whether this was so, or whether we ought to regard it only as a providential dispensation—whether the distribution of extraordinary gifts (χαρίσματα) explains the thing to us, there is no evidence that this distinction, of which besides it is very difficult to form a just idea, ought to be maintained as an immutable institution. At any rate, to renew

* It does not appear that this division of labor was of an exclusive character. We see (Acts, vi., 10) that Stephen, the deacon (verse 3), was a preacher or a prophet. The rite and the word are separated by St. Paul (1 Cor., i., 17): "Christ sent me not to baptize." Besides, this is not a question of rite. Either it is altogether apart from religion, which can not be admitted, or it does not exclusively belong to one of these classes of officers. This, however, is not saying that all may celebrate it.

it, it is necessary to renew the *χαρίσματα*, "the spiritual gifts."

It is very manifest that they regarded as ministers of the Church men whose qualifications did not fit them for ministers, according to the sense which we now attach to the word. There were *deacons*, appointed to serve tables; there were *presbyters* (whence comes the word, not the idea, of priest), who did not teach; but it is clear, from 1 Tim., v., 17,* that those among them who taught were of the first rank, were reputed the first, since the word is the grand instrument, and the essential character of the evangelical dispensation; and it is, in fact, to this class of presbyters that the title of minister or pastor has, in the end, been exclusively attributed; and this class has absorbed in itself all the other classes, so as to constitute in itself alone the ministry of the Christian Church.

The evangelical ministry is essentially a ministry of the word; all the other ministries are in the service of that one; they are so many ways of speaking the Word of God. Christianity is a word, a thought of God, which is destined to become a thought of man. Now thought and speech are inseparable; thought is an interior speech, and in the ancient languages the same word signifies the two things (λογος). That great revolution, which we call the advent of Christ and of the Gospel, has not rejected worship and symbol, but has spiritualized it, has approximated it to thought, and thus even to speech. The minister is a man who speaks the word of God; he does not recite it. The priest was a slave, but the minister has free intercourse with God. And as, since the unhappy and forced exclusion of the laity, there are, for example, no more ministers of alms, of science, etc., the minister combines in himself all these offices, because he is the minister par excellence.

* "Let the elders that rule well be counted worthy of double honor, especially they who labor in word and doctrine."

The minister, in this way the inheritor of all the diverse ministries of the Church, has taken, in the plenitude of his qualifications and of his activity, the name of *pastor*. It is remarkable that this name, of all others, is the most rarely applied to the minister in the New Testament.

What is a pastor ?

His name tells us : he *feeds ;* he nourishes souls with a word which is not his own (as the shepherd nourishes his sheep on grass which he does not make to grow). But he feeds them by means of his own word, which reproduces and appropriates to their various wants the Divine Word, and becomes, in turn, a word of instruction, of direction, of exhortation, of reproof, of encouragement, and of consolation.

The word is, then, his instrument ; but it is not every thing ; the pastorate should be regarded as a *paternity ;* and, after the example of Jesus Christ, the minister should sympathize in all the interests and all the afflictions of his flock. He ought to be at once almoner, justice of the peace, and schoolmaster.

Such, in our Church, is the idea of a pastor. The Catholic Church regards it altogether otherwise. It was impossible, because of our sinfulness, that the Christian Church should not have been tempted to forsake its first steps. We all have a propensity to backslide : nothing is so active in us as a tendency to return to what God has abolished. As early as the time of Chrysostom, the essence of the pastor's office was regarded as consisting in the administration of the sacrament. This was his own view.* It was a return to the ancient law, and it was one of the first traces of the exclusive importance that the Catholic Church afterward gave to this part of the duties of a minister.

In the number, and at the head of the Jewish ideas, of which Catholicism is full, we must place, without doubt, *the*

* A beautifu passage, *De Sacerdotio*, lib., c. iv. See *Appendix*, note A

real presence. God is as *really* present in the Catholic worship as he was in the Levitical. I venture to say, that, assuming the spirituality of Christianity, this resemblance itself condemns Catholicism. "Yea, though we have known Christ after the flesh, yet now henceforth know him no more." —2 Cor., v., 16.

By this means alone we are carried back to *caste;* for according to this, any individual whatever of the priesthood may properly celebrate rites; so that the personal character is as nothing. In the communities where the idea of priest reigns, the individuality being of small importance, the corporate power must proportionately prevail.*

With us a minister is essentially a minister of the word, so far from the word's becoming a rite, the rite becomes the word. We take, in the fullest acceptation, the sense of the apostles, who refer the work of the Gospel to the incarnation of the word; and we find nothing too strong in these expressions of Erasmus: "*Diabolus concionator: Satanas, per serpentem* LOQUENS, *seduxit humanum genus. Deus, per filium* LOQUENS, *reduxit oves erraticas.*"†

This ministry (essentially moral, since the word constitutes its essence) does not suffer the word to materialize itself, and turn itself into a rite. It aims to be the action of soul upon soul, and of liberty on liberty. Before all, after all, it remains a *virtue.* The Catholic Church, while it appears to give more of authority and more of action to the pastor, really contracts the pastoral office, by stereotyping the first forms under which it exercises itself,‡ and in prescribing as rites what ought to be suggested on each occasion by charity and

* See LAMENNAIS, *Affaires de Rome.*

† The Devil is a preacher: Satan, speaking by the serpent, has seduced mankind. God, speaking by his Son, has brought back the wandering sheep.—*Ecclesiastes,* lib. i.

‡ It has given one fixed form for each of the inspirations of pastoral love.

by wisdom, according to man's wants and circumstances. In the one case there is a real library; in the other, a library imitated in wood. In both communions there is confession; but in one it is a confession of the heart, in the other a prescribed confession; a confession which, of course, ceasing to be moral and true, amounts to nothing. Here is the abuse of Catholicism; but let it not be exaggerated: Catholicism, as it has the cross, is also acquainted with the spirituality of the Gospel. Moreover, among the Catholics, strong protestations have arisen against the exclusive predominance of rite, especially from the Jansenists, who attach to preaching a very great importance, considering it as the greatest and the most awful of mysteries.* This idea would lead us far from St. Augustine, who saw in the eucharist the only awful mystery. It is thought that there is no mystery in the action of soul on soul, through the word, because this is an ordinary affair; as if that which is ordinary was not often most mysterious and unsearchable. The same word acts in one manner on one, in another manner on another. Without doubt, the character of the individual has much influence on the result; but whence comes it that an ardent preacher often produces no effect, while a feeble preacher often ploughs the deepest furrows in the souls of men? How many who have been untouched by the one have been saved by the other! How often, by a single word, is the hearer converted! Is not the dispensation which moves one soul, a single soul in a whole crowd that remains cold, one of the greatest of mysteries? Preaching is, indeed, a mystery the profoundest of all; one which embraces a multitude of other mysteries. In fact, it is God who preaches, and man is only his instrument.

The form of the ministry, then, is the word. The design of the ministry is to subject to the discipline of Christ, "to lead captive to his obedience," souls which are appointed to

* See the quotation from St. Cyran, in the *Appendix*, note B.

it. It is to perpetuate, to increase, to establish continually the kingdom of God on the earth.

To unfold this idea in its different aspects, let us recall with Burnet* the different names given in the New Testament to the ministers of the Gospel. And let us first remark, that in the ecclesiastical as in the political sphere, all the names of functions, of dignity, etc., have, in their origin, an altogether different sense, an altogether different force, from that which usage has at the same time consecrated and enfeebled. It happens to them as to proper names, which are no more than arbitrary signs, after having been truly significant. At the beginning of an institution truly original, the names of offices express duties, affections, hopes ; it is the soul that gives the name—and the name which it uses expresses less a power, exactly defined, a legal qualification, than a virtue to be exercised, an idea to be realized. All true names are adjectives, which become substantives by the lapse of time.

1. Deacon (a word which we translate by minister) signifies *servant*, joining with it the idea of liberty.† The word *deacon*, like all words which pertain to an institution, has had the fortune of naming, instead of what the thing ought to be, instead of the ideal of the thing, that which it has become, that which it has been made by accident, at a certain time and in certain circumstances—a form of the thing rather than the thing itself; the ideal sense gives place to the historical, and the historical becomes the law of the idea. The word *deacon* has received a special meaning ; but it was at first general; and it designated, without distinction, any minister or servant of the Gospel. "Who then is Paul, and who is Apollos, but ministers (deacons) by whom ye believed, even as the Lord gave to every man."—1 Cor., iii., 5. "Giving no offense in any thing, that our ministry (deaconship) be not

* Burnet : *A Discourse of the Pastoral Care*, p. 44.

† *Of Commission:* Committed to a certain office—Commissary.

blamed."—2 Cor., vi., 3. "Whereof I have been made a minister (*a deacon*) by the gift of the grace of God, which he hath given unto me by the effectual working of his power." —Eph., iii., 7. "Christ Jesus our Lord hath enabled me, for that he counted me to be faithful, putting me into the ministry (*the deaconship*)."—1 Tim., i., 12. "The Gospel of which I, Paul, was made a minister (*a deacon*)."—Col., i., 23. For the special and later sense, see 1 Tim., iii., 8: "The *deacons** must be grave."—1 Tim., iii., 12. "Let the *deacons* be the husbands of one wife;" and, Romans, xvi., 1: "I commend to you Phebe, a deaconess, of the Church of Cenchrea."

We are struck with the title of *deacon*, as a special title, because a particular institution has appropriated this name; but in the first series of passages that we have cited, it is not more special than is the word *δουλος* (slave, servant), in Philippians, i., 1: "Paul and Timothy, slaves or servants of Jesus Christ." And how has it happened that the members of the clergy do not bear the name of douli (*δουλοι*), and the ministry that of *döuleia* (*δουλεια*), as some of the members of the clergy have taken the name of deacons, and their function, that of the *diaconate?*

2. *Presbyter* (elder). "Let the *elders* who rule well be counted worthy of double honor."—1 Tim., v., 17. "They sent to the *elders* by the hands of Barnabas."—Acts, xi., 30. Acts, xv., passim. "He sent from Miletus to Ephesus, and called the *elders* of the Church."—Acts, xx., 17. "I left thee in Crete, that thou shouldst ordain *elders* in every city." —Titus, i., 5. "Is any among you sick, let him call for the *elders* of the Church."—James, v., 14.

Our versions commonly render *πρεσβύτερος* by *pastor*, which we scarcely find applied to ministers except in Ephesians, iv., 11: "Some pastors and teachers."

* The New Testament of the Vaudois ministers, Lausanne, 1839, translates, *Servants of the Assembly*.

3. *Bishop* appears to be the synonym of *elder*, in Titus, i., 5, 7: "That thou shouldst ordain *elders*." "Now a bishop must be without blame;" and in Acts, xx., 17, 28, Paul calls the elders of Ephesus, and commends to them the flock over which the Holy Ghost has made them *bishops*. See also Philippians, i., 1: "Paul and Timothy to the *bishops* and deacons," etc.; and, 1 Tim., iii., 2: "A *bishop* must be without blame."

This does not forbid that there should be bishops over other bishops—inspectors of inspectors: "Against an elder receive not an accusation, but before two or three witnesses."—1 Tim., v., 19; and Titus, i., 5, cited above. But this does not suppose an institution, it was only an expedient.

4. *Apostles* or *Delegates*.—"Our brethren—they are apostles of the churches,* and the glory of Christ."—2 Cor., viii., 23.

It must, however, be remembered that the word is applied *κατ' εξοχην* (par excellence), to the immediate envoys of Jesus Christ, in Acts, ii., 42: "They persevered in the doctrine of the apostles."

Our intention is not to determine the work, the particular function, which each of these names designates.† We believe that the words *elder* and *bishop* denote officers of churches, whether they were or were not charged with the function of teaching, a function attached to a gift or a grace, which does not appear to have determined the designation of *elders* or *bishops*, since neither the one nor the other of these words appears in the famous passages, Ephesians, iv., 11, and 1 Cor., xii., 28–30. And as for the word *deacon*, it has a sense much more general, and also a sense much more spe-

* Messengers of the Assemblies.—Translation of the Vaudois ministers.

† Consult NEANDER on this: *Geschichte der Apostel*, i., 1, p. 37–47. VILLEMAIN: *Mœurs des Chrétiens pendant les trois premières Siècles*, p. 178, *et suiv.*

cial than the two others, designating either any kind of Gospel work, or a very particular function in a church. Our object, without stopping to distinguish the different applications of the ministry, is solely to explain, by means of words, characters common to all—characters of the evangelical ministry, in whatever department it may be exercised. What we have found in the three first words, that is to say, without going beyond the proper terms, and before approaching figures, are the ideas of *voluntary service*, of *authority* (founded in one case on age), and of oversight.* But it is probable that figurative expressions will instruct us further ; for their purpose, in every subject, is to descend to a greater depth in the idea than the expression strictly conveys. We proceed then to cite figurative expressions, which unquestionably are applied, by anticipation, to ministers of the Gospel.

1. Pastor is not, as we may be inclined to think, the synonym of *elder*, but that of *teacher*.—See Ephesians, iv., 11. We have already said that the office of elder or administrator is not embraced in that solemn distribution of powers or virtues (*χαρίσματα*), of which we have before spoken. Moreover, the passage in Ephesians, iv., 11, is the only one in which the title of pastor is directly applied to ministers of the Gospel ; but, without doubt, it is applied to them indirectly when Jesus Christ is called the Shepherd (pastor) and bishop of our souls (1 Peter, ii., 25), and when Jesus Christ said to Simon, "Feed my sheep."—John, xxi., 16, 17.

The word pastor, taken in a figurative sense, occurs in the Old Testament, but it is there applied indifferently to prophets and to magistrates.† Besides, in the sense of the Theoc-

* M. Vinet did not add, until after a revision of his lecture, the word apostle to this first series of names, which no doubt is the reason that he does not here present the idea of *mission*, which is included in the fourth.

† *Ποιμένες λάων*. "It has almost come to pass that religion and justice keep pace in the republic, and that men are consecrated by

racy, magistrates were pastors, even as pastors were magistrates. They were two forms of the same employment. Nevertheless, in Ezekiel, xxxiv., *passim*, it is admirably applied to a pastor, in the actual sense of the word.

2. *Steward* or *Dispenser*.—"Let a man so account of us as stewards of the mysteries of God; moreover, it is required of stewards that a man be found faithful."—1 Cor., iv., 1, 2.

3. *Embassador*.—"Now, then, we are embassadors for Christ."—2 Cor., v., 20.

4. *Angel* or *messenger*.—"The seven stars are the angels of the seven Churches."—Apoc., i., 20.

5. *Ruler*.—"Obey them that have the rule over you" (*πείθεσθε τοῖς ἡγουμένοις ὑμῶν*).—Hebrews, xiii., 17.

6. *Builder*.—"I have laid the foundation as a wise master-builder."—1 Cor., iii., 10.

7. *Workman*.—"We are workers together with God; ye are God's husbandry, God's building."—1 Cor., i., 19. "A householder hired laborers into his vineyard."—Matt., xx., 1. "The harvest is great, but the laborers are few; pray, then, the Lord of the harvest to send forth laborers into his harvest."—Matt., ix., 37, 38. "I have planted, Apollos watered, but God giveth the increase."—1 Cor., iii., 6.

8. *Soldier*.—"Epaphroditus, my fellow-soldier."—Philippians, ii., 25. "Endure hardness as a good soldier of Jesus Christ."—2 Tim., xi., 3.

Let us first remark that, of all the designations by which we might expect to see the minister of religion defined or characterized, only one is wanting in the New Testament. It is that of *priest*, although it is the Christian word *presbyter* which has furnished the word *priest*. There may be priests in those religions which wait for the true and sovereign Priest; there are none in that religion which has re-

the magistrate as well as by the priesthood."—La Bruyère, *Les Caractères*; the chapter entitled *De quelques usages*. See Burnet, *A Discourse of the Pastoral Care*, page 45.

ceived and which believes in him. In this no one is priest, because every one is priest; and it is remarkable that in the Gospel it is only to Christians in general that this word is applied. See 1 Peter, ii., 9: "Ye are a chosen people," "a royal priesthood,"* etc.—the fulfillment of the prophecy of Isaiah, lxi., 6: "Ye shall be called the *priests* of the Lord, and ye shall be named the ministers of our God."

It was necessary to have a sacrifice perpetuating the only and once accomplished sacrifice, in order to recover the idea of the ancient priesthood, which was absorbed in the supreme and eternal priesthood of Jesus Christ.

For us, who do not receive the real presence, what remains in the minister when once the supernatural gifts have ceased? The Christian, only the Christian, consecrating his activity to make others Christians, and to confirm in Christianity those who have embraced this religion. He does habitually what occasionally, and in a special manner, all Christians should do. He does it with a degree of authority proportioned to what we may suppose a man has of knowledge and fitness, who has consecrated himself exclusively to that work. But he has no revelation peculiar to himself. In announcing the wisdom of God as a mystery (1 Cor., ii., 7), in giving himself to be a steward of the mysteries of God, he does not profess to be more inspired than the humblest believer. He is a steward, a manager of the common interest; he does not take, like Jesus Christ, of that which is his own (John, xvi., 15), but of that which belongs to all. If he thinks it is right, according to the word of St. Paul, that believers should obey him as their spiritual ruler, the sense in which he understands this leaves intact the liberty and responsibility of those who obey. He protests against the idea of domineering over the heritage of the Lord, 1 Peter, v., 3, compared with 2 Cor., i., 24: "Not that we have dominion over

* *Βασίλειον ἱεράτευμα.* See NEANDER, *Geschichte der Apostel*, i., 162, 163.

your faith." He opposes, also, the individuality and independence of a Christian to the servile credulity of the idolater: "Ye know that ye were Gentiles drawn away toward dumb idols, even as ye were led."—1 Cor., xii., 2.

The idea of service* covers all the titles which he gives and the authority which he attributes to himself: He rejects every idea of his own power: "Who, then, are Paul and Apollos but *servants?*"—1 Cor., iii., 22. And remark that these rulers, these embassadors, call themselves servants not only of God, but of believers themselves. If they say, "Let every one so account of us as servants of Jesus Christ" (1 Cor., iv., 1), they also say "Ourselves your servants for Jesus' sake."—2 Cor., iv., 5. "Whether Paul, or Apollos, or Cephas . . . . all is yours, and ye are Christ's, and Christ is God's."†—1 Cor., iii., 22.

Examine all the titles, all the names which are given to ministers in the Gospel, you will not find one which goes beyond the limits of this idea, the servant of humanity, in its great interest, from the love of God. All is noble in this institution, which rejects every force except of persuasion, has no other end but the reign of truth, and is not distinguished except by a more absolute devotion.

Still, all these words, all these metaphors, all the additional passages, do not attain to the complete sum of the elements of the ministry—to the ideal of a pastor. We have need of a type, a model, a personification of each idea. Where shall we look for it? If any one has been the type of man, he has been, at the same time, the type of a pastor;

* *Δουλος* is a name more than once applied to apostles.—See Rom., i., 1; Gal., i., 10; Phil., i., 1; Col., iv., 12; 2 Tim., ii., 24; Tit., i., 1; James, i., 1; 2 Peter, i., 1; Jude, i.

† As to the speedy appearance of the contrary principle, or the personal authority of the priest, see Schwarz, *Katechetic*, p. 11, 12. Soon after the apostolic age appear the *clergy* and the *hierarchy*. Note C, *Appendix*.

for it is impossible that the pastor should not make a part of the ideal of man—impossible that he, in whom the perfection of human nature was fully represented, should not have been a pastor.

This new man, this second Adam, could not have been such except by love. The first object of love is that which is immortal in man: It is, then, upon the soul that love will chiefly exercise itself; and as we can not do good to the soul except through its regeneration, and as it can not be regenerated except by the truth, to impart the truth, to nourish the soul with truth, to feed it thus in green pastures, and along tranquil waters, was necessarily the office of a perfect man, of the type of man: He must have been a pastor.

Christ also has said, "I am the good Shepherd" (John, x., 11); and again, "I am come to serve, and not to be served."* —Matt., xx., 28.

Also, his immediate disciples have named him "The chief Shepherd (pastor) and Bishop of our souls."—1 Peter, ii., 25.

And he himself has given the most sublime commentary on this word shepherd in this passage: "The good shepherd gives his life for his sheep."—John, x., 11. Here the metaphor is insufficient; it is not in the idea of a shepherd to give his life for the sheep.

And what he said he has done. He not only watches the sheep, but he goes after them. He goes from place to place. John the Baptist remained in the desert.

And at last, from a pastor he makes himself a lamb, substituting himself for the lambs: He was immolated: He is "the lamb slain from the foundation of the world."—Apoc., xiii., 8.

* "Summus Ecclesiastes Dei Filius, qui est imago Patris absolutissima, qui virtus et sapientia genitoris est æterna, per quem Patri visum est humanæ gentis largiri quidquid bonorum mortalium generi dare decreverat, nullo alio cognomine magnificentius significantiusve denotatur in sacris litteris, quam quum dicitur *verbum*, sive, sermo Dei."—Erasmus, *Ecclesiastes*, lib. i.

This divine pastor, who behooved to be, according to Saint Bernard, the pastor of the worlds in the heavens, and who has made himself that of humanity, has embraced in his solicitude all the interests of humanity; for which he accomplished, during the days of his flesh, both the good which it desires, and the good which it does not desire.

In conclusion, for we have reserved this trait for the last, he has, of deliberate purpose, without external necessity (in every thing, indeed, circumstances concurred with his will), symbolized the spirit of the ministry in washing the feet of his disciples; nor did he by silence permit this symbol to remain obscure.—John xiii., 5, 14, 15, 16. If, as he said himself on that occasion, "the servant is not greater than his master," we have found the idea of a pastor. We ought to be servants; but the notion of service, in its plenitude, contains that of sacrifice. The minister is, as he ought to be, a permanent victim. It may be said that the Christian is already a victim; this term expresses no more as to the pastor. The objection only gives force to our assertion; for if the Christian is a victim, much more the pastor, who is a Christian by office.

On the whole: The pastor is nothing more by name than a steward of the word of God. He is a man who has consecrated himself to break to the multitude the bread of truth. He is a man who has devoted himself to apply—to appropriate to men the redemptive work of our Lord Jesus Christ,* since God has determined to save men by the foolishness of preaching. As Jesus Christ is sent of God, he is sent by Jesus Christ. He comes, on his part, to do from gratitude all that Jesus Christ did from pure love. He reproduces every thing of Jesus Christ except his merits. As to the obligations imposed on him, he is neither less nor more

* "God was in Christ reconciling the world to himself, and has committed to us the word of reconciliation."—2 Cor., v., 19.

than his master. He does, under the auspices of divine mercy, all that Jesus Christ did under the weight of the divine wrath. By word, by works, and by obedience, he perpetuates Jesus Christ.

HYMN.

King of glory and man of sorrows! whoever has loved thee has suffered, whoever loves thee consents to suffer. He commits himself at once to glory and to sorrow.

On thy account he suffers even in dreams; so suffered, without knowing thee, the wife of the judge who delivered thee up. Whoever feebly loves thee, or whoever laments thee, can not but find himself on thy road. Like Simon of Cyrene, he becomes a partaker of the heavy burden of thy cross.

Men curse those who bless thee; humanity excludes them from its universal communion; and in that place of exile from the human family, they are themselves twice in exile.

All those who have loved thee have suffered; but all those who have suffered on thy account have loved thee the more. Grief unites us to thee, as joy does to the world.

Like a generous wine, grief intoxicates those whom thou invitest to thy mysterious banquet, and from their contrite heart it draws hymns of adoration and love.

Happy he who, like the Cyrenean, has abased himself to take his part of the cross which thou bearest! Happy he who would endure in his body that which remains—that which will remain till the end of the world, to be borne of thy sufferings for the Church, thy body!

Happy the faithful pastor, who, in his flesh, partakes of thy sacrifice and thy conflict! While he struggles and groans, I see him, in my visions, hidden in thy bosom, as on the day of the funereal banquet, him whom thou lovedst.

While love bears him, bruised and bloody, from place to place, and from suffering to suffering, he himself, unknown to the world, reposes upon thy bosom in an august retreat, and tastes in silence the sweetness of thy words.

Happy the faithful pastor! His love multiplies his sacrifices, and his sacrifices multiply his love. Love, which is the soul of his labors, is also his exceeding great reward.

Happy the faithful pastor! That which every Christian would be, he has been. That cross, which each one endures in his turn, he bears without ceasing. That Jesus, with whom the world incessantly divides our regards, is himself his world, and the object of his assiduous contemplation.

Happy, thrice happy, if all his desire is to add some voices to the concert of the blessed, and to remain concealed in the universal joy, only keeping in his heart the invisible regard and the everlasting *Well done!* of the Master and the Father!

§ 2. *Necessity of the Evangelical Ministry.*

It concerns candidates for the holy ministry to know whether this office be necessary.

At the first glance this inquiry appears very superfluous. Facts precede proofs: we are convinced by instinct. Still, we may ask (and a whole Christian community, that of the Quakers,* has replied to the question in the negative), Whether a particular class of persons, consecrated to the administration of worship, and to instruction in religion, is necessary.

The almost universality of the institution would be, in the eyes of many persons, a sufficient proof of its necessity. It is, however, only a very strong presumption, after which there remains an open question.

We make two kinds of replies: one, applicable to all the analogies of the ministry; the other, to the ministry immediately.

I.—1. Every important office, relating to one of the chief

* With Quakers, even, some persons from the whole are invested with a kind of ministry.

necessities of society, to one of the essential elements of life, requires special men exclusively devoted to that office.*

2. Every community requires and supposes officers, a government. That government may be composed of only one class of persons, or of many; may be more or less rational, more or less perfect. It matters not, the principle remains: and a society without government, a society having rules, and no one to maintain or represent them, is perhaps more inconceivable than a government without a rule which limits and directs its own action.

II.—1. The office of the ministry can not, in general, be carried to its true perfection except by men who are exclusively devoted to it; and, in general, many things can only be accomplished by such men.

2. In times when religion, cultivated scientifically, has become itself a science—when, having formed a multitude of relations to private and public life, it is charged with a mass of details and applications, it is difficult for the ministry to be well and completely discharged by a man who is not exclusively a minister.

3. There is, in the work of the ministry, a limit at which each one, or the greater number, will stop, if positive duty does not oblige them to proceed; each one will take only what is convenient to him, and many even will think that they have done too much in going so far.

When a single person has to decide a thing, he will bring all his conscience to it; when forty persons, each one will bring the fortieth part of his conscience. When one does not consider his responsibility as entire, it is to be feared he will do little, if any thing at all. It would then be in a superfi-

* The *jury* is not an exception. It does not exclude the office of judge. It is only the indication of an idea (which religion reproduces in other forms), that a society commits to special men only that which all can not do, and that the commission ceases when those who give it can act for themselves.

cial, irregular, and intermittent manner that the work would be done, if we could not always rely upon certain men.

Zeal for the advancement of the kingdom of God, and faith in a universal priesthood, were certainly not less, than they are now, at the time when the Holy Spirit said, in Antioch, to a college of prophets and teachers, already separated and called by him, " Separate me Barnabas and Saul for the work unto which I have called them."—Acts, xiii., 2.

It may, perhaps, be said that one can not judge by what is now done as to what would be done if believers would not cast upon ministers the burden of a ministry which belongs to all. We believe that what they would first do would be to make ministers. For if it be said that general zeal would be greater in the absence of these special men, that zeal, even at its greatest height, not meeting precisely all the wants for which the minister is appointed, would lead Christians to do that which, we think, indifference and idleness might make them do ; that is to say, to make sure, by the creation of a special office, the satisfaction of those wants for which they themselves would no longer suffice. The more the zeal, the less would they be disposed to leave great interests to suffer, for the want of special men to take care of them.

Hüffell* regards ministers of the Gospel as depositaries and guardians of the principle of life deposited in the Gospel. Christianity is essentially a life which transmits itself; but if chosen men do not transmit it,† if that transmission of life is abandoned to the life itself, it will soon cease. Without the

* HÜFFELL : *Wesen und Beruf des Evangelisch-christlichen Geistlichen*, t. i., p. 28, third edition.

† *Vitai lampada.*—These words, which we throw into a note, and which, in M. Vinet's manuscript, are in the text, between parentheses, are probably transferred from this verse of Lucretius :

Et, quasi cursores, vitaï lampada tradunt.

—*De Rerum Natura*, lib. ii., v. 78.—*Ed.*

ministry, according to Hüffell, Christianity would not last two centuries.

This is, perhaps, too positive and too absolute; but it can not be said that it would, in general, be doubting the truth and power of a work to make its duration depend on certain means. Nothing is done without means; and when it is the institution itself which creates its own means, when it draws them from itself, and chooses them conformably to its nature, we can not say that it must be precarious because it employs means. We should rather think it precarious if it did not employ them. If it employed in the ministry its own best elements, the best part of its substance, to propagate itself, would it not grow?

No one doubts but that the life of the Church supposes and requires a perpetual testimony, an uninterrupted tradition; and it is necessary that this testimony, this tradition, should be sure. A Church would be wanting to itself if it did not make sure not only the perpetuity, but the just perfection of this testimony, this tradition.—Rom., x., 14, 15.

Herder* defends the institution, but thinks it may not be always necessary. We shall not pursue this inquiry; let us keep it as long as it shall be necessary, and not abandon it until it shall be no longer needed. We are convinced that this time will never come.

§ 3. *Institution of the Evangelical Ministry.*

Besides the necessity resulting from the nature of things, is there not a necessity of another kind, a positive duty; in other words, is not the ministry a divine, or a canonical institution?

Did Jesus Christ himself, or the apostles in his name, ordain that the Church should, in all ages, have special men

* HERDER: *Provincialblætter*, iii., tome x., *des Œuvres Théologiques*, p. 334–341.

charged with the administration of worship and the conduct of souls? Strictly speaking, no. Jesus Christ instituted but little; he inspired much more. It is his cross, and not his institutions, which separates the Old World from the New. What remained he left to the Holy Spirit, who was to come after him. He abolished virtually, rather than formally. He preferred the insensible but infallible action of the Spirit to the less sure and less delicate action of the letter. His reign is a spiritual reign. His disciples understood this, and were in no haste to abolish or to overthrow. And it was not always given them to see at once what in the old economy was consistent with the new. God did not impart to them at once all they were to know, but gave them a light which was gradually to chase away the darkness. The entire development of Christianity has been thus made, and we have yet to hope for a new world of discoveries. This progressive march, however, relates only to secondary points in the Gospel; for, as to doctrine, the apostles, from the beginning, were of the same mind, and they have told us every thing. It is not the same with institutions; these have been provided, little by little, as the want of them has been felt.

Jesus Christ called around him a few men from among his followers, and intrusted them with a message, and with functions resembling his own, and said to them (to *them*, and not to others), "As my Father hath sent me, even so send I you." —John, xx., 21.

St. Paul says that Jesus Christ gave some apostles, and some prophets, and some evangelists and teachers.*—Eph., iv., 11. Here Jesus Christ appears as the guide of the Church, of its first messengers; the organization and government of the Church are ascribed to Him; and it was evident, according to St. Paul, that it was his will that the Church

* Bridges remarks how the form of these words shows grandeur in the institution (*The Christian Ministry*, p. 5). See Calvin, commentary on this place, t. vi., p. 129, Berlin edition, 1834.

should have ministers. The apostles, as they had been sent, sent in their turn; the ministry continues of itself, without having been formally instituted—once for all.

But as Jesus Christ said to his apostles, "Go and preach the Gospel to every creature" (Mark, xvi., 15); and since those to whom he directly spoke could only begin the execution of a command, for the entire fulfillment of which centuries were necessary, he addressed himself also, in their person, to their successors: He has thus implicitly instituted the ministry, unless it may be said that the continuation of the work did not require special men, such as had been needed at the beginning.

This leads us to our second reflection, which is, that, unless the circumstances in which Jesus Christ conferred the apostolate have essentially changed, his order stands for all ages, and is equivalent to an institution. For not to renew, in similar circumstances, that which he himself founded, would be, in some sort, to condemn the first foundation, which never would have been made if it had not been intended to be continued forever.

It has been objected that ministers should be interpreters of the Holy Spirit, that consequently the Spirit, which has been given to all the faithful, would set apart for each want the ministers that would be required, and move them to speak at the given moment. This is the opinion of the Society of Friends. From a true principle they have drawn a false consequence. For a special ministry does not bind the Spirit, does not prevent the Heavenly wind from blowing where it listeth.

We must, by all human means, endeavor to have ministers through whom the Spirit speaks. If, notwithstanding this, unworthy men are found among them, while we deplore the evil, we must confess that the same thing might happen in those churches where all have a right to speak, and all wait for the Spirit to inspire them. Might they not deceive themselves? and those who have the gift of speech, might they not speak in order to gain power? The danger would be greater than with us; for these preachers, not being prepared by special study, would have less security against it.

It has been said that there can not exist a ministry, because there is no Church; that a Church is not possible in this world. This is true, if one speaks of the ideal of a Church. This ideal has never been realized, not even in the time of the apostles; but now, as then, Christians meet to hear the word preached; to be consoled, to be confirmed; they need to pray together, to give thanks together; and for this a minister is necessary, a servant of God who puts the word within their reach, and who, under the guidance of the Holy Spirit, comes to the aid of their weakness.

At least missionaries will be needed: For in our day we may say with St. Paul, "How shall they call on Him in whom they have not believed? And how shall they believe in Him of whom they have not heard? And how shall they hear without a preacher? And how shall they preach, unless they be sent?"—Rom., x., 14, 15.

But all the ministers Jesus Christ gave to the primitive Church were not missionaries, in the special sense we attach to the word. Many were pastors, and provided as such for wants that exist to-day, and always will exist: And, after all, are not all pastors half missionaries? Are there not in the bosom of their churches, and all around them, souls which must be sought after, as one seeks after pagans and idolaters a thousand leagues distant? Does the work of conversion ever cease? Must we not always throw the net far and near? The circumstances, then, which in the beginning led to the institution of the ministry, are they not the same to-day, and do they not require the same measures? And would it not be disavowing Jesus Christ himself, not to do in his name to-day what he himself would do if he were in the midst of us?

Let us also observe, that whatever may be said to-day in favor of the abolition of the ministry might have been said at that time against its institution. One might have said then that every faithful person is a minister, which is true; that no believer should be exempt from the duty of "*showing forth* the praises of Him who called him out of darkness into his marvelous light" (1 Peter, ii., 9), which is also true; that the Christian life is a system of preaching; that faith begets faith, etc. All these things are true; but with them there are others not less true, which make the ministry as necessary to-day as it ever has been.

Let us observe, finally, that the apostles have never spoken of the ministry as an accidental, transitory thing, or as a temporary institution. In short, on this subject we think, that to strike out the word institution would scarcely be more than taking away a word; since, if Jesus Christ has not formally, and in some way by letters patent, instituted the ministry, we can not doubt as to His will in respect to it? It is no departure from truth—no exaggeration to say that the ministry is a divine institution.

§ 4. *Does the Ministry constitute an Order in the Church?*

A discussion has been raised on the question, Is the ministry *an order?**

This may appear idle, after the solution of the former question, from which it can hardly be distinguished. Theologians, however, who agree as to the divine institution of the ministry, are divided on this point. It is, then, worth while to examine it.

If the ministry, that is to say, the consecration of certain special men to the management of the Church, has been instituted, these men, distinguished among all others, form nec-

* In German, *Stand.*

essarily an *order*, at least in one sense. If there is controversy, it is without doubt on the greater or less latitude of meaning, of which the word order is susceptible ; for the disputants are agreed to acknowledge the institution.

It is certain that the word *order* may awaken in different minds very different ideas. Some incline to the notion of a *Levitical tribe*, of a sacerdotal caste, separated into a religious society, exercising exclusive functions, proceeding less from the community than the community proceeds from it, existing by itself, imposed upon the flocks by an authentic divine institution, or by Providence ; *legitimate*, in a word, in the sense which political parties have given to that expression.

Others, who, in a certain sense, would be disposed to accept the ministry as an order, having received it as an institution, refuse to see in the clergy an order, if that word necessarily imports all the ideas which we have just expressed. With these the ministry constitutes, indeed, a particular class of persons, a kind of functionaries of which Jesus Christ would have his Church never deprived ; but, in their view, the similarity of their functions no more raises them to an order, than the grade of captain or officer makes an order of all the captains or all the officers of an army, who are nothing, in fact, but soldiers of a more elevated rank. Ministers are, in their view, only officers of the Christian army, with this important difference that each may become an officer of his chief, as soon as he shall find soldiers prepared to accept him as such, and to march under his direction.

Each of these opinions has, again, degrees and shades. With the greater part of the defenders of the one and the other, there is less a reasonable conviction than a habitude or tendency : As to their origin, they are less two systems than two different spirits. But when circumstances have induced lively manifestations of these two spirits, and have brought them together, it has been necessary to explain them ; and habit on one part, and tendency on another, have become formally systems, which have had to give account of their foundations, discovered perhaps too late.

Those who admit that the ministry is an order look to the past as their support ; the others rest on speculation. At the Reformation they did not systematize; they felt that they lived, and method and form were neglected. Afterward came a season of repose ; the clergy in certain places formed an order. Now we have to choose ; Catholicism urges us ; we ought to be openly Protestants. We have kept many Catholic rags ; we should now decidedly dress ourselves anew.

Among the more eminent defenders of the second system, in these later times, we should distinguish Neander.

Neander* notices the tendency, which discovered itself early in the Church, to make pastors a caste. He notices the resistance of Clement (i., 217) and of Tertullian (i., 245) to this return toward Judaism. These fathers valued (and Neander did after them) the idea of a universal priesthood, according to 1 Peter, ii., 9, and Apoc., i., 6. Neander and his authorities did not admit the institution of priests, except in the sense of a useful division of labor.† See Acts, vi., 4, the institution of deacons.

Harms replied to Neander‡ that the language of St. Peter is figurative, and that the Hebrew people were denominated priests : "Ye shall be to me a kingdom of priests and a holy nation."—Exod., xix., 6.

But this is passing from side to side with arguments, of which one destroys nothing, and the other constructs nothing. For the idea of universal priesthood does not contradict that of special priesthood ; and Harms has reason to allege on

* NEANDER : *Denkwürdegkeiten*, i., 64–69, et 179. *Geschichte der Apostel*, i., 162. See also SCHWARZ, *Katechetik*, p. 11. Notes C and D, of the *Appendix*, give the translation of these passages.

† NEANDER : *Allgemeine Geschichte der christlichen Religion und Kirche*, i., 277. Note E, of *Appendix*, gives the translation of this passage. See also RETTIG, *Die freie protestantische Kirche*, p. 87.

‡ *Pastoraltheologie*, ii., p. 11.

the subject Exod., xix., 6 ; and, on the other side, a special would not be inconsistent with a universal priesthood.

It appears to me useful to remark, for the advantage of both these truths, that those who spoke in the Bible of a universal priesthood were themselves clothed with a special priesthood, and maintained that character in opposition to those to whom they addressed themselves : In their idea the two priesthoods, or the two ministries, were not inconsistent.

Besides, in the new economy, it is certain that, in one respect, the universal ministry is the only real one ; not that it excludes the other, but because in this new economy the other ministry, I mean to say the priesthood properly so called, no longer exists : No one is specially a priest, and each is one in proportion to his union to the Head, Jesus Christ. There only remains the ministry of the word, which is, at the same time, special and universal. And here we repeat our observation : inspired men who received this ministry as universal did not cease to exercise it in a special manner ; they did not dream of annulling either the one or the other.

They also acknowledged that the believer is directly taught of God, and that consequently he has his sovereign pastor in heaven : They insisted much on the immediate relation of every believer to Him who is at the same time the object and the author (the beginner and the finisher) of his faith. This is, in effect, the essence of true religion ; the spirit of the true worshipers of the Father, the character of worship when God is revealed as Father. Even in the Old Testament we find vivid traces of this idea.—Jer., xxxi., 31, 34. But these same men who preached the immediate intercession of the believer with God, and who gave mediators no place or part with the Holy Mediator, did not less exercise the ministry of the word, which has precisely for its object and its last end to produce that immediate intercourse. Are they inconsistent with themselves? Not in the least. We must not, then, oppose either the universal ministry to the special ministry, or the special ministry to the universal ministry; but as they are of the same nature, as in no one of their elements are they different; as the one has no efficacy or light which has been refused to the other, we must truly acknowledge, with Neander, that the special ministry exists only by virtue of a division of labor, and for divers reasons which we have indicated above. To inquire for the reason of an institution, the idea which gave it birth is not to nullify the institution, nor to overthrow the authority of Him who founded it.

The truth on this question finds its limit on one side (that is to say, on the side which tends to a strict distinction of ministers), in the words already cited (1 Peter, ii., 9: "Ye are a royal priesthood," and Apoc., i., 6); on the other side (that is to say, on the side opposed to the distinction), in the words of St. Paul: "Paul, separated to the Gospel of God." —Rom., i., 1.

There is, then, an order only in the sense of a class of men indispensable in the Church, co-ordinate and set over each Church, the living centre of each Church, "for the perfecting of the saints, for the work of the ministry, for the edification of the body of Christ."—Ephesians, iv., 12.

This order can be a *caste** only in the following cases:

1. In the case where it is hereditary, as in the Mosaic institution; or transmitted, as in the Romish Church. Now the first does not exist; and, as Protestants, we deny the second. Transmission in the Romish Church has sense and reason only by virtue of the mystery of the real presence, and infallible interpretation; take away these two dogmas, make the pastor to be a simple administrator of worship, without mystery, and a simple preacher of the word, which the Holy Spirit may explain to any other as well as to him, and what

* *Caste* is a term applied to certain classes of persons, to distinguish them from the rest of the nation to which they belong.—*Dictionnaire de l'Academie.*

rational, psychological foundation remains for succession? And reciprocally, if you admit the dogma of succession, you are constrained to find for it a reason, a ground, in one or the other of the two forecited dogmas, or else in both. The historic, or legal foundation, never suffices to preserve an institution which does not subsist, except by interior reasons, founded in human nature. Reduce the transmission of ecclesiastical powers to a historic base, and you take away from them, whatever may be the solidity of that base, all sufficient reason of existence, all means of perpetuating them. In our national Protestant churches our ministers are consecrated by ministers, and this is well; but still it may be, that, in ascending from consecration to consecration, we may arrive at men who consecrated themselves: The right is then acquired by all others to do the same thing.

2. In the case where the minister is not a citizen in the full extent of the term. Now it may be that here and there civil institutions may restrain his quality of citizen; but that restriction is not of his doing, and is not required by any of the elements of the institution. It is otherwise with respect to the Romish priest, who can not be a citizen and retain his character as priest. As to constitutional power, which, in certain countries, may appertain to his *order*, it is a very different thing from civic individual fitness: It is the intrusion of the Church, or of the clergy, into the department of civil affairs.

3. In the case where his functions are exclusive. Now a society may very well agree to recur, as a society, to this man or this order; but, apart from this, the functions of the ministry may be exercised by simple believers.

The ministry, then, does not form a caste. It does not even form a body, except accidentally. The accident is certainly frequent, but still it remains an accident. Existence as a body is not essential to the ministry.

To conclude in a word: the ecclesiastical ministry is a consecration, made under certain conditions, of particular members of a Christian flock to be occupied specially, but not to the exclusion of others, in the administration of worship and the care of souls. A religious society may, moreover, direct that the solemnities which bring it together shall be presided over exclusively by those special men whom it calls ministers or pastors.

It seems easy to hold a position between the two limits now indicated. If either should absorb us, it would be at the expense of evangelical truth. But it is certain that we could not lose one of these things without losing the other also. There is no choice left to us. We must preserve or lose both at once.

This discussion is not idle. It is true that the attack and defense pass from side to side without an encounter, each part maintaining that which the other does not reject, and rejecting what the other does not care to defend. But this discussion, which would have been out of place at another time, indicates a disposition of mind which should not be unobserved, and, moreover, it leads us to determine well our position in the Church and in society.

The disposition of mind is singular. It implies a contradiction. We do every thing that we may become a caste, and yet we are afraid that we shall be a caste. It is not considered that it is in the nature of a body in exile to make itself an empire, and that it will not even recognize equals, when it has no opportunity of comparing itself with others. We create, or, at least, strengthen the *esprit de corps* by this fear of the *esprit de corps*.

The clergy itself is undecided between the remembrance of its ancient authority and the sense of its actual situation.

Religious interest revived, not yet in the masses but in a certain number of individuals, tends to give importance to the clergy; this same interest approximates the laity to the functions of the clergy, and more or less effaces the distinction.

This state of things should teach us this, at least, to remain or to enter on the terms of the Gospel. These terms we have defined.

Thus in every Church, organized according to the word, and according to the spirit of Jesus Christ, there will be ministers, forming or not forming a collective body, I would say never a *caste;* entering, in every thing which does not exclusively concern their official functions, into the category of other citizens and other Christians, and not having any inalienable qualification, except in the interest of the order, and within the limits of that interest.

§ 5. *Excellence of the Ministry.*

The ministry, necessary to Christianity, partaking of the necessity of Christianity, and also instituted or ordained by Jesus Christ, can not but be, according to St. Paul (1 Tim., iii., 4), *an excellent office.*

Let us, nevertheless, study it in itself, and indicate the principal characteristics which should exalt it in our view.

At the first glance, and according to secular views, the art, par excellence, is that of governing minds (*Ars est artium regimen animarum*); and although others besides the preacher undertake this, and succeed in it, it is certain that when he does succeed in it, it is in a manner more definitive and more profound, because of the nature of the motives which he employs. He awakens and strengthens in man thoughts which must determine and control his whole life.

Rising higher in our point of view, we see that it is the preacher's great prerogative or great mission, to maintain faith in invisible things and in a spiritual world, in souls, which earthly things are always seeking to absorb; to be among men, a spiritual man and a man of eternity.

Those who are devoted to the social interests of mankind regard the minister as the chief instrument of civilization, inasmuch as he is the chief agent in advancing general morality—asserting and diffusing as much as lies in his power the maxims of virtue. Magistrate of consciences, counselor of benevolence and of peace, he represents the element of the highest social life. Religious instructor of the people, he can not be a stranger to the care of their intellectual culture; he is its promoter; he is every where at the head of popular teaching, as well as of the Church; and in that respect, also, the minister of the Gospel is a minister of civilization.* The prophet and the priest of the middle ages, as are now the missionaries among savage tribes, were ostensibly and openly the chiefs of society. All society was more or less theocratic at its birth. That was a time when second causes were little observed, and when, in all things, there was a direct ascent to the first cause. Afterward, men did not take the trouble of ascending so high. The same, also, as to the conduct of society. It was only indirectly, and by its influence, greater or less, that religion controlled civil order. Since then the minister has been placed in an analogous position. Society has not recognized him as its head. But it could not but be that the gravest and most solemn affairs of individual life and of public life, should be assigned to religion, and of course to him; that a multitude of great interests should, of necessity, be confided to him; that the last depth of the human soul should be surrendered to him by religious preoccupation, the strongest of all. His hour always returns, and religion with him penetrates into the midst of interests which are surrendered to him. Where religious institutions are fee-

* All this applies especially to the Christian ministry, for, Christianity apart, the minister is often, and particularly in these times, the representative of the anti-social element and of anarchy, the minister of darkness. But even in false religions, at their commencement, this was not so. Whatever may be the delusions which are mingled with religious traditions, truth has always its place, and civilization has had the advantage of it. The necessity for Religion is a noble necessity: she has always been the cradle of society.

ble, where the Church is no longer a reality, the pastor only remains; it is to him that we look. It is with the pastor as with the Sabbath. Happy he to whom all days are Sabbaths; happy the time when the importance of the ministry shall diminish because all Christians will be ministers.

His every-day life, instead of being trivial, like that of the greater part of men, is serious. His functions pertain to the foundations and roots of human life. He is brought into contact, by his ministry, with all that life has, which is serious and most affecting. Its great pauses or halts, its great concerns, appertain to him—birth, marriage, death.

His life is a life of consecration, without which it has no meaning. His career is a perpetual sacrifice, which includes all that belongs to him. His family is consecrated; it belongs to the ministry, and partakes of its privations: Even as Jesus came into the world not to be served, but to serve, so of the ministry; and this is its glory: "To serve God is to reign." He seeks the glory of God directly; he seeks it again in serving men; for to serve men from love to God, is to serve God. A minister is a man of benevolence and compassion. And this is every one's impression; every one, even the natural man, demands charity of the minister. No one will observe cruelty, avarice, coldness, the want of kindness in him, without reproaching him with it. Benevolence and kindness belong essentially to Christianity. In nations not Christian, even among the Jews, the priest has not at all this character, and sometimes he is considered as a terrible and wicked being. But now the most unbelieving person thinks that Christianity is the religion of kindness. A minister is a man to whom God hath said, "Comfort ye, comfort ye my people." He is among men the representative of the idea of mercy, and he represents it by transferring it into his own proper life. To impart succor, that is his ministry, that is his life.

In short, the ministry, at least in the Protestant Church

and among Presbyterians,* can not at its outset present an object of ambition, though possibly it may end in this. One pastor can be distinguished from another only by a more commodious post, more agreeable circumstances. It is a noble thing to see his ambition definitely arrested, his desires imperatively restricted. Man is but too much harassed by his desires. He is as a sick person agitated by fever, who knows not on which side to turn. Nothing can tranquillize him but that which shuts the door against his desires. A minister is no more confined to his ministry than another man to his profession, and he may satisfy the demand of his nature for development, which is one of the privileges and characteristics of humanity. But what distinguishes him is, that, once a minister, he is all that he can be externally; his place is taken, and he must never forsake it.

Let us now take a higher point of view, that of Christian faith. The dignity and excellence of the ministry proceed,

1. From the excellence of the doctrine which it teaches. This is a "wisdom among them that are perfect" (1 Cor., ii., 6); that is to say, a wisdom which renders men as perfect as they can be; not giving an appearance or a part of the truth, but the truth itself and the whole truth. Nothing is greater than this mission. He who on any subject has infallibly the truth, is already a great personage. Jesus Christ, in the presence of Pilate, associates the royalty of truth with the testimony he rendered to it. His business, in fact, is with truth, with supreme truth, with that which explains and governs life, with truth as pertaining to the relations of man with God. What more exalted work than that of preaching it! And this is the pastor's mission.

2. From the fact that its doctrine is a Divine revelation.

* The context seems to require this designation to be understood here in its comprehensive sense, or as embracing all denominations that hold the parity of the ministry.—*Tr.*

Oracles have been confided to it. "These are things which eye hath not seen, nor ear heard, neither have entered into the heart of man, and which God hath prepared for them that love him."—1 Cor., ii., 9. The minister is then the direct messenger of God himself. "He that receiveth you receiveth me, and he that receiveth me receiveth him that sent me."—Matt., x., 40.

3. From the fact that "the minister is a laborer with God" (1 Cor., iii., 15), who makes himself one with him; becomes surety for him, promises to work for him and by him.

4. From the fact that he announces and offers salvation. If the ministry was one of condemnation, if the pastor preached on God's behalf the law only, though he would fulfill his work with anguish and terror, it would nevertheless be an excellent one. But as God has made his glory to consist in pardoning, so he has put glory on the ministry of pardon. Hence St. Paul, speaking not only of the two economies, but the two ministries, says, "God hath made us able ministers of the New Testament; not of the letter, but of the Spirit; for the letter killeth, but the Spirit giveth life. But if the ministration of death, written and engraven in stones, was glorious, so that the children of Israel could not steadfastly behold the face of Moses for the glory of his countenance, which glory was to be done away, how shall not the ministration of the Spirit be rather glorious? For if the ministration of condemnation be glory, much more doth the ministration of righteousness exceed in glory. For even that which was made glorious had no glory in this respect, by reason of the glory that excelleth."—2 Cor., iii., 6–10. It is, moreover, very manifest, that as the glory of the mercy of God consists of two inseparable elements, mercy itself and the fruits of righteousness, the glory of the Christian ministry is also composed of these two elements. This is what Isaiah had in view in these words: "How beautiful upon the mountains are the feet of him that bringeth good tidings,

that publisheth peace; that bringeth good tidings of good, that publisheth salvation, that saith unto Zion, *Thy God reigneth!*"—Is., lii., 7.

These two elements are embraced in the power to loose and to bind conferred on the apostles, and after them on all Christian ministers.—Matth., xviii., 18. The minister can not bind without loosing, nor loose without binding. He binds, when he binds the conscience, by adamantine chains and mystic ties, to a perfect law; he looses in detaching us from the law of commands, in proclaiming abolition of servitude, and amnesty from God. These two things are two poles which always correspond to each other.

It is true that the minister is a *savor of death* to him to whom he is not a *savor of life;* "the chief stone of the corner is also a stone of stumbling and a rock of offense" (1 Peter, ii., 7); and the condemnation of him who hears without believing is so much the greater; but this necessary consequence of the nature of the ministry which he exercises detracts nothing from its excellence.

To say all in a word, let us transfer to the ministry all the excellence of Christianity; let us impute to it all the benefits of Christianity, since it produces and perpetuates them; or, if we choose, let us measure its excellence by that of Christianity; we shall have said enough.*

§ 6. *The Difficulties and Advantages of the Evangelical Ministry.*

After having established the excellence of the ministry, it may seem idle to adjust the balance of the advantages and disadvantages which it may offer as a profession, or as a state, to those who may consecrate themselves to it. But, although

* See Erasmus, on the dignity of the ministry. This passage has been translated by Roques, in the *Pasteur Evangélique*, page 190. *Appendix*, note F.

this excellence removes, as to him who recognizes and feels it, the entire question, and although, as to him who does not perceive or recognize it, the question of the advantages or inconveniences of a state which he should not embrace, has not even the interest of curiosity, I think I ought not to place myself in a point of view so absolute, and ought to reason as if the second question had an interest independently of the first.

Let us begin with the difficulties, the troubles, and the dangers. It is a very different thing whether we contemplate the ministry at a distance or near at hand, and it is important to bring it close to us. At a distance, though we may have a general view of it, it is impossible to have a true knowledge of its duties. "For which of you, intending to build a tower, sitteth not down first and counteth the cost, whether he have sufficient to finish it."—Luke, xiv., 28–30. Without doubt, it is necessary to be a Christian, cost what it may, and of that necessity I conclude that the expense is too great for no one; but the quality of the pastor is not identical with that of a Christian; it adds itself to it, it makes an increase, and it is this increase which must be supported. We should examine whether the cost is too great for us. We shall thus avoid painful and discouraging surprises.

There are two ways of conducting this examination. The first is to examine all the extreme positions, the extraordinary situations, the most perilous cases. If there is any thing tragic in the life of a Christian, there is much more reason to expect it in that of the pastor, who is the Christian by eminence. The second way is to examine the ordinary cases. The difference does not lie in the nature of these cases, but in their frequency.

The extraordinary cases are so called because, by the goodness of God, they are rare; but it can not be superfluous to speak of them. There are times when "those who build a wall work with one hand, and with the other hold a sword."—Nehemiah, iv., 17. Perhaps the present is such a time. It is not that which stands forth to the eyes that makes times ordinary or extraordinary ; in reality, the times are more or less what we make them. We may make all times sublime, even as we may render the most extraordinary ones common. The ministry is always extraordinary. There is a heroic way of conceiving of it, and that alone is the true way. The minister, by office, is a devoted man ; and to avoid mistake, we must elevate the office to its greatest height, and see it in its most difficult positions. We are always prone to take low views, and how fatal the consequences of seeking one's ideal at mid height, instead of at the summit ! If we would not, then, have inferior views, we must take the most uncommon cases, and ask ourselves whether we are ready to accept the ministry of missionaries in savage countries, the ministry of the martyrs. It is necessary, at the outset, to suppose almost impossibilities, if we would have the idea of the ministry. In any position in which it is exercised, the ministry is always what it is ; nothing will change it—neither easy nor difficult times. For a moment God may leave us in an easy position ; but the ministry implies the most dangerous situations ; it is always a complete sacrifice of body and soul to the service of the Church. It is necessary, then, to place before us the greatest difficulties, not only that we may have an extraordinary spirit in ordinary times, but because that which appears impossible to us is not so.

The history of the Church is composed of a succession of troubles and of peace ; and these periods are unforeseen. The deepest perturbations are not always announced by sure, and especially by distant presages. The sky is serene in the evening ; the next day a storm bursts forth, and the stormy weather can not be anticipated. It is still as it was in the time of Noah : " Until the day when he entered into the ark, they married and were given in marriage, and knew not till the flood came and took them all away."—Matt., xxiv., 38, 39 ; Luke, xvii., 27. Our age depends very much on institutions and on their force ; and, without doubt, they are of vast power ; but meanwhile evils are of rapid growth.* In the midst of civilization, human nature remains always in a savage state ; it is only tamed by society. There are passions which only sleep in the heart of man; and in spite of the security procured by social institutions, we are never secure against the hatred of the Gospel, which is always living in the heart of man, and which shows itself all the stronger as Christianity advances. We must, then, regard as probable, revolutions and persecutions, even as we do natural calamities. Storms will beat, especially upon Christianity ; it will draw to itself more of hatred and more of love ; its normal condition is neither of absolute affliction nor absolute peace. It is not essentially dependent on peace ; God gives it peace to temper it anew. But a long calm might be fatal to it ; it must have trouble and tempest.

Every one, then, before he enters into the ministry, ought to represent vividly to himself these critical periods, and to ask himself, What shall I do ? It will perhaps be necessary that, in a pestilence or time of war, I should give my life for my flock, as Jesus Christ laid down his life for us. Shall I be able to do it ? In our time there is no persecution, except that we are sometimes ridiculed. This time may change ; we may be persecuted, that is to say, menaced in our goods, in our families, in our persons. Such a situation is as normal as any other. It is not more natural or more regular to go tranquilly to church, and to worship in peace, than to go to the stake, to be persecuted in our wives and children, to encounter the wrath of the great of the earth, and to perish under their strokes ; to be exiled, or to exercise the ministry in extreme poverty : we may even say that peace is the exception. There are, moreover, other crises besides external ones. There are times as difficult as those

* In the French, *les ongles repoussent vite.* This figure can not well be retained in the translation.—*Tr.*

of persecution; such are times of heresy and error, when the greater part of the clergy do not preach the Gospel. Then we must contend for the truth, and not fear sacrifices. Even now we see error and heresy raising their head; we have to combat those who would weaken the Gospel; we ought, of course, to expect calumnies and the hatred of the multitude.

In our country the ministry may be exercised now in a position substantially independent; but is it certain that this will last, and that we shall not one day be called to exercise it in poverty? The time of *suffraganship** is already somewhat severe; but, though evil in one sense, it has nevertheless its blessing; the calling is purified by these trials.

We must not fear to bring before us the gloomy view of the ministry. Let us say to ourselves that in this career heroism is necessary. All pastors ought to be heroes, for Christianity even in the people is heroism; a Christian is in spirit a hero, a hero potentially. The right of Protestant ministers to have a family does not change their position; it only renders their self-consecration more difficult. The priest is by himself. The Protestant minister unquestionably is not exempted from any sacrifice. He must, if necessary, surrender his life; and all his sacrifices must be the more severe that his family must partake of them. To devote himself is his business. Why should this devotion be more painful to him than to the physician, for example, about whom no one asks if he be married?

We will now consider the evangelical ministry in ordinary times, no longer in those of conflict and persecution. Without excluding any situation, our observations will apply to the greater number of cases; to that which is the most ordinary, the situation of a country pastor.

The ministry, according to Gregory Nazianzen, "is a tempest of the spirit." Chrysostom says, that "a bishop is more

* Fr., *suffragance*. See Part IV., chapter iii.

agitated with cares and storms, than the sea with winds and tempests."*

1. *The difficulty of governing by purely moral means* a multitude of very different minds and dispositions. There are combined in this multitude many elements which do not agree among themselves. It is his work to govern them, and to secure not only an external, but an internal obedience. He must subjugate not only acts, but thoughts, and reduce them to unity, and all this by persuasion; "for the weapons of our warfare are not carnal."—2 Cor., x., 4. Political government is, in one sense, more easy; there are material means, there is opinion, for government is more or less the expression of society. It can do no more than society in its best elements decides, it follows society. The pastor has to conduct men where they would not go; he has to induce them to receive unlooked-for ideas which man is not disposed to receive, and which he regards as foolishness. We hence see the immense difficulty of pastoral government. The Gospel unquestionably contains the elements of humanity, of true humanity. It corresponds to the interior man, the conscience, which it reaches by traversing the outward man, which intercepts the light. The inward man, in his darkness, stretches out a hand toward the Gospel; there is in him a secret intelligence. But what obstacles are to be surmounted! how difficult is it to tie the two threads!

St. Gregory, in developing the idea of the diversity of sentiments and characters, remarks, that the truth is one, but that it is now meat, now milk, according to different individuals. Now we must give to each the nourishment which agrees with him.† Certain truths repel some, attract others,

* *De Sacerdotio.*

† "The art of arts, the science of sciences, appears to me to be that of directing men, the most varied and the most changeable of beings."—Gregory Nazianzen, *Apology*. In the same book, man is represented (*ἑνος ζώου συνθέτου και ανομολου*). See the passage on dif-

smother some, and save others; we must give the same truth under different forms to different individuals. Pastoral government is that of individualities; the civil law does not embarrass itself with differences of character.

Thus the first characteristic of ministerial excellence is also its first difficulty.

2. *Much Labor.*—The poor, the sick, schools, good offices of charity, pacific interventions, official correspondence, sermons, catechisings. The multitude and the weight of these offices does not authorize the neglect of the sermon, which is the only means of reaching certain individuals, and the catechism, which in some degree gives us the guidance of each generation. But this enumeration does not express all, for where the ministry is not perfectly fulfilled, it must gain in depth what it loses in breadth. The smallest parish should become, by the zeal of him who cultivates it, as onerous as the largest; this work has no limit, no spot where the material fails.* And he must seek for remoter occasions when nearer ones are wanting. He is not a true follower of the first of ministers who is not eaten up by the zeal of God's house. To give an idea of the extent of pastoral labor, let us say, that all the extension which, in another profession, the highest enthusiasm, or the most boundless ambition might suggest to the man who exercises it, is but the exact meas-

ferent wants, according to different degrees of intelligence and culture: "Some need to be nourished with milk, with the most simple and elementary lessons; but others with that wisdom which is entertained only among the perfect, a nourishment more strong and solid. If we should give to these latter milk to drink and pulse to eat, food for the feeble, they would be dissatisfied, and certainly with reason, not being strengthened according to Christ," &c.

* A single soul is enough to occupy a priest, for in the ways and works of salvation each soul and each man is as a great world, though very small as to his natural qualities. Thus a priest can do the more for a soul the fewer he has to govern.—SAINT CYRAN, *Pensées sur la Sacerdoce.*

ure of that which is contained in the simplest idea of the pastoral office.

3. *Uniform Labor.*—There are labors more uniform, but the kind of work compensates for its uniformity. The evil effects of uniformity are especially perceived in delicate matters, and matters of feeling ;* they are much less serious in other professions where there is less to lose, a less delicate point to be blunted. Functions which rest upon feeling at length become insupportable, if the Spirit of God does not incessantly revive it. If uniformity is any where to be feared, it is in the exercise of the ministry. How can one but fear when a solemn duty presents itself, and when all is frozen within ; when around him all is great, and within his soul all is little ! Before a scene of death, for example, habit may leave your heart cold. Here is great danger, and if there were no remedy, it would be necessary to renounce the ministry. But there is one.

This uniform work is without the prospects and chances of other professions ; we can not ascend in the social hierarchy. We must say to ourselves, I must all my life be doing the same thing, without any change—without any extension of my worldly horizon.

4. *Work ill appreciated.*—It is so by the greater part of people, at least in respect of its intensity and its weight. Country people, in particular, regard as an idler him who does not work with his hands ; they do not understand how the work of the mind can be work. Still, the work of the understanding finds those who appreciate it ; but the work of the heart, prayer, spiritual care for one's flock, who sees labor in that ? The pastor must consent to be but little understood.

5. *Many sorrowful and sad functions ;* for the principle occasion of religion and the ministry is suffering. What sad

* *Corruptio optimi pessima.* There are few examples such as that of the priest, cited by Marmontel.

discoveries in this circumnavigation of human misery! The Gospel is a moral pharmacopœia. There is a Gospel, because there are evils to be cured. The minister goes to those who are spiritually sick, but also to those who are sick in body, or suffering from affliction of any kind. Sickness or sorrow is often the only porter that can open a house to him. What a sorrowful entrance! One more readily participates in the miseries of the body, in the dissolution seen every day by the physician, than in the miseries of the soul. The view of moral evil, and especially its analysis, withers and corrupts, if one has received the fearful gift of knowing man without knowing God. The true minister certainly knows God, but the fiery darts of the wicked one sometimes find a defect in his armor. One may, in this way, become a misanthrope, and see the fire of charity quenched in himself.

In short, the minister has pains of heart, as little understood by the greater part of men as the pastor's work is little appreciated. Thus, when he finds a hard but hypocritical heart, which has eluded all the efforts of his charity; that a soul has not been saved, on account of circumstances which, perhaps, he might have foreseen, no one can understand what he suffers; and yet to be understood is the greatest compensation of our sorrows.

6. *The sacrifice of many even innocent Tastes.*—He must often renounce things innocent in themselves, but which would scandalize the weak. The measure of this interdiction varies, but still it exists.

7. *Talents lost, rusting in Obscurity.*—It can not be that every man of talent should be placed in a situation in which he will be appreciated. This business is not an indulgence of self-love, but an exercise of activity. It is a sacrifice, but he must make it. And, at any rate, the world is full of hidden talents. This is the divine arrangement; we are not responsible for it, and must accept it without murmuring.

8. *Painful isolation to him who has known the charms of Social Life, and the intercourse of kindred Minds.*

9. *A species of Defiance and of Fear which the Pastor inspires.*—For many people he is the representative of the sorrowful side of human existence. The minister seems to wear the mourning of life. His own life is grave, and gravity always borders on sadness. This exiles him into a kind of solitude, which still more increases that which he is obliged to make for himself on account of the nature of his position.

10. *The double Danger of pleasing and of displeasing the World.*—If we please it, we cling to this success, and wish to make sure of it for the future: it is hard to see one's self deserted after having been caressed: Apart from all self-love, it is painful to give up the good-will of one's equals, and not to live at peace with all men. If we displease it, it saddens or irritates us, and we do every thing to displease it still further.* We may abuse the idea that truth offends; we may wish to add to this unpopularity of the truth, before it has subjugated the heart. The minister should conciliate the affection of the members of his flock; and if he is unpopular, he should examine his conduct, to see if the unpopularity does not proceed from himself. However that may be, the two dangers exist; we coast along two abysses.

11. *Self-love is very active in a Profession which exposes us to Observation, and which is Intellectual, and conversant with Art and Literature.*—The minister may assemble the people to hear him on any subject he chooses. It would not be surprising if for this reason many had embraced the profession. The flock then becomes as the public, the auditory a tribunal. The position of the minister is false; his noble independence and his authority are compromised; he imposes a yoke upon himself. He no longer preaches God, he preaches himself; and by a sacrilege, of which it is difficult

* See John Newton, *Omicron*, vol. i., p. 142, 146, Letter xiii., On the Dangers to which the Minister of the Gospel is exposed.

to measure the extent, the pulpit becomes a theatre, a stage for his vanity. This word seems hard; and yet, in examining ourselves, we find it is often only too just. At the close of triumphant orations the pastor may receive praises; at each praise a reproach will resound in his heart. Happy for him if he preferred to these praises the silent respect of one faithful soul, that has listened to him in retirement, and whose heart he has touched! a victory how much greater than to have excited a fruitless admiration!

Self-love is our most terrible enemy, because it is our nearest. Every one covets praise; but there is a strong self-love that has no bound, which is vanity; as there is also a feeble self-love which is moderate. We baptize the latter with the name of modesty. This is not a virtue, it is a natural quality, a simple mark of good sense. There is a great distance between modesty and humility: True humility is a miracle. A supernatural grace is necessary to impart it to a minister. Nothing but love can remove self-love from the throne of his heart. Love is an ardent, passionate preoccupation, which withdraws from every thing that is not allied to itself, from blame and from praise alike. Conversion essentially consists in love. We must love the flock in order to preach to it well.

There is one form of self-love which manifests itself more in the ministry than in any other profession: it is the love of authority. The pastor in his parish is the only one of his class; he is called to command. In public, at least, no one may dispute with him; he has the monopoly of the word. Often he has to do with the poor, who show a great respect for him because they are more or less dependent on him. This habit of command, so easily formed, narrows and falsifies his view, and alienates those who can not sacrifice their tastes to his. Chrysostom has developed with admirable force the dangers of self-love in the ministry.*

* CHRYSOSTOM: *De Sacerdotio*, p. 270, 281, 287, lib. v., 1, 4, 7, 8.

The danger of self-love is greater with the Protestant than with the Catholic, who speaks much less. It is difficult for the Protestant minister not to give himself up in some measure to the idea of being a good orator. At all events, a good preacher is a good orator. And in seeking perfection for its own sake, it is very difficult not to seek to please, were it only one's self. This leads us to regard in the ideas which are presented only a neutral *substratum*, which has no value except from the form which is given to them.

12. *Internal conflicts between Faith and Doubt* (*in German, Anfechtungen*) perhaps more frequent and more profound with the pastor than with the private Christian, and in the midst of which he must pursue the work of the ministry. Doubt, as a psychological fact, has been little studied. There is philosophical doubt, and the doubt of ignorance ; we have nothing to do with these. But are there only these ? Is there not a state in which the best proofs leave us in doubt? The intellectual proofs are present, but the soul is not convinced. Christian assurance is a different thing from the assurance of the understanding. Doubt is a negative state, a state of temptation through which all have passed. When life is feeble, faith is feeble. Faith increases life, but life sustains faith. Faith is a vision ; when it is not so, it descends to the rank of believing. Faith is one thing, but it has its degrees ; and if, in such a situation, one might retire, withdraw himself, interrupt works which all imply faith, he would not be so unhappy ; but he can not ; he must always preach. Every one may find himself in the state into which Richard Baxter fell, and perceive himself all at once in an absolute void, where every thing vanishes, not excepting fundamental beliefs. This state is frightful. To come out of it, we must stir up ourselves to try anew all the powers of the spirit in fervent prayer.

Gregory Nazianzen expresses himself thus : "In every spiritual function the rule is, to neglect personal interest for that of others."

13. *Internal Humiliation on perceiving in ourselves the Man at so great a distance from the Preacher.*—Has not the most faithful man sometimes become weak, and felt himself reproved by these words: "What hast thou to do to declare my statutes, and to take my covenant into thy mouth, seeing thou hatest instruction, and castest my words behind thee?"—Ps. l., 16, 17.

14. *The agonizing Thought, that one bears in his Hands the Destinies of so many Souls, and that he exercises a Ministry which kills, if it does not give Life.*—It kills, in aggravating the condemnation of those who might, but do not profit by it. Thus it is with a faithful ministry. As to him who exercises it without fidelity, and whose life does not correspond to his word, it kills in another manner.* And this thought, that the scandals we give are the greatest of all, and that the least unfaithfulness in us has the gravest consequences, is enough to frighten us, and make us say, "Lord, send by whom thou wilt send." Let us hear Massillon: "The Gospel, to the greater part of the people, is the life of the priests of which they are witnesses." And this will always be so in the bosom of Protestantism. "They regard the public ministry as a stage designed for the exhibition of the great maxims which are beyond the reach of human weakness; but they regard our life as the reality, and the true standard to which they should conform." And further, "We are pillars of the sanctuary, which, if overthrown and cast about in public places, become stones of stumbling to passengers."†

15. The most deplorable case is when these wounds, which

* "Par fois li communal clergié,
Voi-je malement engignie,
Icil font le siècle mescroire."
La Bible Guyot (Troizième Siècle).

† Massillon: *Discours sur l'excellence du Sacerdoce.* First Reflection, near the end.

the consolations of God alone should heal, become healed by habit, and by a false resignation—a case which too often occurs. As it has been said, "repeated repentance wears out the soul,"* and puts it, so to speak, out of humor with itself. All these troubles are painful, but there are many of them which it is more hurtful to avoid than grievous to submit to; and all need to be foreseen, and, as it were, tasted beforehand.

To this enumeration, perhaps incomplete, and of which no trait, perhaps, is presented strongly enough, we may with confidence oppose, as a compensation, the following advantages:

Religion, which is the most excellent thing, and the whole concern of man, is the minister's office and duty for all days and all hours; that which mingles itself with the life of other men constitutes his life.

He lives in the midst of the loftiest and sublimest ideas, and of occupations of the highest utility.

He is called to do nothing but good; nothing obliges him, nothing entices him to do evil.

He occupies no rank in the social hierarchy, belongs to no class, but serves as a bond to all; representing in himself better than any other, the ideal unity of society. The minister, it is true, is not so well situated in this respect as the unmarried priest. But yet he may have this privilege when he wishes it.

This life, unless circumstances are very unfavorable, is the most proper realization of the ideal of a happy life. It has a great regularity, a sort of uniform calm, where, perhaps, is to be found the true place of earthly happiness. The predilection of poets and romancers for the character of a country pastor is not without foundation. All this is true only on the supposition that the pastor is faithful, and filled with the spirit of his profession. If he has this spirit, all is counterbalanced, corrected, transformed; and it suffices him, with-

* Allusion to a passage from *Corinne*, book x., c. v.—*Editor*.

out minutely weighing the inconveniences and advantages, to make one reflection : " Jesus Christ assigns to his ministers painful trials, internal and external, to the end that they may sympathize with their flock, and know, from their own heart, the seduction of sin, the infirmities of the flesh, and the manner in which the Lord sustains and supports all those who trust in him.* So that, in a certain degree, one may transfer to the minister what has been said of Jesus Christ : " We have not a high-priest who can not be touched with the feeling of our infirmities, but was in all things tempted as we are."—Heb., iv., 15.

In short, the word of God, directly or indirectly, blesses peculiarly his labors and his estate.

It declares (remark the gradation) that "those who are wise shall shine as the brightness of the firmament, and those who turn many to righteousness as the stars forever and ever." —Dan., xii., 3.

In promising to the immediate ministers of Jesus Christ that, in the renovation of all things, "they shall sit upon thrones, to judge the twelve tribes of Israel," it presents to their successors proportional honors and rewards.—Matt., xix., 28.

It so honors and blesses the ministry, that even to those who aid it special promises are given : " He who receiveth a prophet in the name of a prophet, shall receive a prophet's reward."—Matt., x., 41.

§ 7. *Call to the Evangelical Ministry.*

But the advantages of the present life which we have mentioned, and the promises of the life to come to which we have referred, will be, the first wholly deceptive, the second without effect, for the minister who becomes one without a call to the ministry. We must put a call into the balance as a

* John Newton : *Cardiphonia*, vol. iii., p. 12.

weight, to raise that other scale, so full of griefs and fatigues, which the want of a call not only does not mitigate, but fearfully aggravates. Apart from a call, all the advantages vanish; some also of the disadvantages will disappear, and there remains a life the most false, and, consequently, the most unhappy, that can be imagined.

It is always unhappy to be unequal to the business which we have to perform, or to feel ourselves out of sympathy with it; but this unhappiness is inexpressible in the case of the ministry, and nothing can save us from it but insensibility or degradation; while, though every thing be adverse, and the trials of the ministry be carried to the highest degree imaginable, a call corrects every thing, renders every thing agreeable, and makes these troubles themselves an element of happiness.

But it is not only under the aspect of happiness or unhappiness that we must contemplate the subject. The minister without a call is not only unhappy, he is guilty; he occupies a place, he exercises a right which does not belong to him. He is, as Jesus Christ said, a hireling and a robber, who has not entered by the door, but by a breach.

The word call has, when applied to professions of a temporal order, only a figurative signification; at least, we only so understand it. It is equivalent to *talent, aptitude, taste.* It has been natural to represent these terms as voices, as calls. But, applied to the ministry, the word approaches its proper sense. When conscience commands, and obliges us to discharge a certain task, we have that which, next to a miracle, merits best the name of a call. And it must be nothing less. To exercise legitimately the ministry, we must have been called to it.

I do not wish, however, to draw too strictly the line of distinction between the ministry and temporal professions in respect to a call. Wherever there is responsibility, wherever one may do injury in charging himself with a work which is not his, there is room for inquiring whether he is called to it. And even between two occupations, to one of which he is better suited than to the other, and in one of which he may be more useful than the other, there is one to which, in a Christian point of view, we may say he is called.

This idea is consecrated in the Old Testament, all the parts of which, provided they are spiritualized, may be transferred to the New. No one was a prophet to his superior, at least in the special sense of the word *prophet;* for there is another sense in which prophesying belongs to all, as forcibly appears from the beautiful words of Moses, "Would to God that all the Lord's people were prophets."—Num., xi., 29. He fulfilled an extraordinary vocation because it conferred extraordinary powers. Whatever may be the authority of the pastor, in one sense, it will always remain inferior to that of the prophet.* Now prophets could not be invested with such an authority without an express call; and we understand, in this view of the case, the threatenings denounced against those who should prophesy without a call: "If a prophet shall presume to speak in my name a word which I have not commanded him to speak, that prophet shall die."—Deut., xviii., 20. "Say thou to them that prophesy out of their own heart, Woe to the foolish prophets that follow their own spirit, and have seen nothing!"†—Ezek., xiii., 2, 3. "I am against the prophets that steal my words." —Jer., xxiii., 30.

Mutatis mutandis, the necessity of a call remains, and on this point, as on others, we only need to translate the Old Testament in the language of the New. The ages are destined to replace one another, but the foundation of eternal truth remains always the same. It is ever true, then, that

* See Isaiah, xxxix., verse 3, *seq.*

† This same idea is symbolized in Numbers, i., 51, "When the tabernacle is to be pitched, the Levites shall set it up, and the stranger that cometh nigh shall be put to death."

in one way or another, to do the work of God, we must be called of God.

Now that the voice of God is not directly and sensibly addressed to an individual, to call him to the office of a prophet, we distinguish two sorts of vocation, the one external, the other internal; but it is clear that both, to be true, must be of God; for in either case it must be God who calls.

Now the external or mediate vocation can have this character, in our view, only as we regard the men from whom it comes, as having full power, either conferred *in casu*, or conferred once for all on a few, by whom it was conferred on others, and so on. This is the Catholic system or pretension: we shall not discuss it.*

In the Protestant system, which denies the Catholic succession, and does not pretend to begin a new one, there is nothing parallel to this transmission of full powers; of which, moreover, we do not see the object, as this legal transmission

* In the sixteenth and seventeenth centuries, the question of the succession gave rise to many disputes. On this question the Catholics, with a fixed, absolute doctrine, had a better and a more exactly defined position than the Protestants, who, though they discarded the priesthood, contended for the succession. Dumoulin earnestly maintained that all the Protestant ministers had been consecrated by Catholics. This was an error, and it was needless. By the progress of time, this pretension has been dropped. The Archbishop of Dublin, an Anglican, has shown, with resistless force, that the succession is a chimera. According to him, one instance of irregular vocation breaks the chain.[1] This idea, however, is of no moment to us: It was opposed by Claude, though not always with good arguments. He thinks *that it is the Church and the pastors* united who confer the outward call. He is not in favor of having the pastors act alone in this case, for they may not be believers; while in the Church there always are believers and saints. There is, then, an uninterrupted succession in the calls given by this universal and everlasting Church. Still, he admits that a flock may sometimes call a pastor without the concurrence of other pastors.

[1] See WHATELY: *Kingdom of Christ.*

meets no want which can not be satisfied without it. To maintain the necessity for such a transmission, is to displace the Holy Spirit. But as our wants are met by a transmission of spirit and of life, as we do not need a communication of oracles, or the administration of miraculous power ; the ordinary agency of the Holy Spirit suffices. The external call then, if it exists, occupies only a subordinate rank, and remains in the sphere of humanity.

Moreover, as soon as we compare it with the internal call, as soon as we give the latter its proper place, it at once assumes the superiority. Catholics have not been able to deny this ; but not to give it all the ground, and let it absorb the external call, they have assigned to this latter extraordinary reasons, which we, for our part, can not give to it. And yet without these it is not, and can not be, on the one side, more than a measure of order ; and, on the other, more than a subsidy or complement to the internal call. In our system, the external call recognizes, as far as possible, the internal, which it always presupposes. The judgment respecting what is outward is here connected with a judgment as to what is internal, and always assumes the internal as a reality.

Besides, this whole question may be dismissed. The necessity of the internal call, acknowledged by the Catholics as well as the Protestants, is all that we are concerned with. The point we have to establish is, that without at least an internal call from God, one can not with safety or innocence put his hand to the work of the ministry ; or, to speak better, take a place in the Church as a minister of the Gospel. The question as to being called or not called by others, I do not discuss. This question, on which there is division, and which also does not belong to my subject, I waive, to treat only of one on which there is agreement, and which does belong to my subject.

As it is in the name of another, that is, of God, that a minister officiates, he must be sent. The prophet does not say, I will go; he says, "Here am I, Lord; send me."—Is., vi., 8. The spontaneity in this matter does not exclude the mission or the call. The charge of a pastor is a *charge*, a ministry. This implies sending or vocation. One can no more be a minister without a call, than a magistrate or a judge.

It also follows that we have no warrant for relying on the divine aid and favor unless God has sent us.* A minister without a call does not, it is true, concern himself as to this; but we are not now considering the extreme case of a minister who has no sense of the object of his mission, and no desire to gain it—one whom the Gospel names plainly *a thief*. A minister without a call may desire to act consistently with his title, at least in a negative way; to avoid scandal; to honor his profession; not to profane the ministry. But how can he be sure even as to this? how venture to expect even this measure of favor, when he occupies an office to which he has no right, and when the first means of securing the divine favor would be to resign the office?

We must, then, be called of God. A call to a ministry which is exercised in the name of God, and in which he is represented, can emanate only from him.† The business here, in fact, is not our's; it is another's, and that other is God: In a word, it is a *ministry*. Whether external or internal, the call ought to be Divine; and speaking of it in this view, we name it *mediate* or *immediate*.

Men *mediately* called by God must have received full powers, either from God, or from other men through whom God confers them. If these full powers be denied, the external or mediate call becomes but a conventional affair, regulating the internal relations of a religious society; not implying necessarily, but only assuming a general fitness for the ministry; and as to the candidate, it is only one more

* See MASSILLON: *Discours sur la Vocation à l'état Ecclesiastique.*

† Ezekiel, iii., 2; Jeremiah, xxiii., 21.

means of establishing his vocation. We shall defer the consideration of the subject under this point of view.

As the ministry is purely moral, not sacramental, the qualifications for it are purely moral, and an *immediate* call should be sufficient.*

Accordingly, in one system this call is sufficient, as in both it is held to be necessary. In any ecclesiastical system which has its basis in Christianity, it can neither be overlooked or lightly esteemed. In only one form of government might it be superfluous, namely, that of a theocracy supported by miracles.† Missions like that of Jonah can not be conceived under the evangelic law. But where the external call is declared indispensable, the internal or immediate necessarily suffers.

Catholic writers have always felt embarrassed in explaining themselves on this point. Saint Cyran, for example, manifestly inclining to the interior call, and not well knowing how to dispose of the exterior, thus expresses himself: "As he who has not been called to the priesthood by the external call of the Church can, in the Church's judgment, do nothing useful for her, although he performs the same external works, administers the same sacraments, and preaches

* Immediate vocation is external or internal. External, when God immediately, by himself, causes his voice to be heard, and his will to be known. Such was the miraculous call addressed to the prophets by a voice, in apparition or in vision.

† But even here it has not been represented as superfluous. It is not, in every case, necessary to the accomplishment of the divine purpose, but to him who accomplishes it it is in every case necessary. Jonah and Balaam, in spite of themselves, and not of their own choice, executed the will of God. "Send me," said Isaiah (vi., 8); and the qualification of the messenger has almost always, even under the old law been regarded of some, and even of much importance, to the success of the mission. Many things seem to have been left at the option of the prophets. Even the Levite, in the fulfillment of his duties, was permitted, in a small measure, to use his own discretion.

the same Gospel as the other priests who have been regularly called and ordained by the Church, so he who has not the interior call of God to the ecclesiastical estate—to the priest's office, or to a curacy, can do nothing good for himself in the judgment of God, although he does the same good works and administers the same sacraments as the priest whom God has called to it."*

Those who maintain the sufficiency of the internal call may be content with the second part of this paragraph; and the first can not give them much trouble, since they hence learn that, although not ordained by the Church, they may *preach the Gospel.* We may, then, do all, for all is included in this, unless the administration of the sacrament implies miraculous power; which certainly no one on his own authority can ascribe to it, and for which the immediate call is not sufficient, unless it has in itself a miraculous character.

But a question presents itself: The immediate call being no longer addressed from God to man by a miraculous voice, may it not be said that there is no longer an immediate call?

This might be said if, in truth, man, apart from supernatural communications, has no means of assuring himself concerning the will of God in respect to a particular case; and in respect to a choice among many determinations, of which each one accords with the general principles of morality.

For it is here, and here only, that the word call is applicable. There is no place for a call to the practice of the general duties of morality. There is place for one when we have to choose between two courses of conduct—two employments of our faculties, equally sanctioned by morality and by the spirit of the Gospel.

Now, as the sensible, direct call, expressly from God, is wanting, by what can this be supplied? In other words, how may we know that we are called? Not, certainly, by

* SAINT CYRAN: *Lettre à M. Guillebert sur le Sacerdoce,* c. 25.

finding ourselves in an agreeable and tranquil position in the exercise of the ministry. Nor from our having been devoted to the ministry by our parents. The vow of parents, if it be serious, may be blessed, and in respect to many pastors it may be, in some sense, a preliminary call. A child devoted by his parents to the ministry may hence derive a certain preference for it; but this is not a call to it. Still less is constraint. This had influence in the early days of the Church: even in the time of Chrysostom the idea of priest and of sacrifice was prevalent, which explains how it was that constraint itself made an indelible impression. The same may be said of signs, which with many persons are decisive. They first select and then interpret the signs, and thus determine their own lot. This with Christians is a sort of spiritual sloth—to desire the whole truth, without being at the trouble to seek for it, by prayer, labor, and application. While we have conscience and the Word of God, we need no other guide. Finally, no one, surely, will say that interest may be taken instead of that direct call from God of which we are now speaking.

But what are the decisive indications? The call to the ministry evidences itself, like every other, by natural means, under the direction of the Word and Spirit of God. In vocation, the general rule is to satisfy ourselves as to the course of life for which we regard ourselves as best suited, and in which we think we can be most useful. And in this matter, if we would attain to clearness and firmness, we should combine in our view circumstances and principles which have been established by good sense and God himself.*

* "I have never conceived of a divine call (*goettlicher Beruf*) as any thing more than an external occasion which has presented itself for doing or realizing something good, under a religious impulse, and, of course, through the divine agency."—PLANK, *Das erste Amtsjahr*, page 8.

But when we have to do with a moral action, in which the soul is the instrument with which we act, we must have regard to the state of the soul, which, indeed, is the principal element in the call. In respect to an ordinary profession, we sometimes must abstract the sentiments we have toward it, hold ourselves aloof against the attractions of taste, and follow it uninfluenced by taste.* This is not the general rule; it is rather an exception which is more or less frequent. In respect to the ministry, however, the rule is absolute: there is no exception. The soul's conformity to the object of the ministry is necessary; and this conformity embraces these elements: *faith*, *taste* or *desire*, and *fear*.†

As to *faith* or belief in the reality of the object—the truth of the message we bear as ministers—there is no need either of explanation or proof. As to *desire*, this must be added to faith, in order to constitute a call; for if faith were sufficient, every Christian ought to be a minister. We must not say that faith includes desire. It does, indeed, include the general desire of living as far as we can to the glory of God, but not the particular desire of having the ministry as our work, and of consecrating to this work our whole life. The institution of the ministry supposes, as its ground, that every one is not called to the work of the ministry. But, when fitness for the ministry exists, will not this supply the place of desire, and be sufficient evidence of a call? Fitness, we reply, does not exist when the desire does not. When the desire is wanting (and we have seen that it may be wanting in a true Christian), there is not that harmony of the man with his duties, that intimate understanding of the matter, that undivided heart, which are so essential to the success of the work. We do not say that a Christian will do no good who engages in this work without a taste for it; we only say that he has no call, and that he ought to leave this office to others, except

* In this sense there may be a *vocatio ab* as well as a *vocatio ad.*

† "Rejoice with trembling."—Psalm ii., 11.

when the peculiarity of time or place may, as it were, providentially impose it on him. In the absence of all proper instruments, God seems to say, as in the prophet, "Whom shall I send?" and seems to expect from every or any one who has the requisite ability the reply of the prophet, "Here am I; send me."*

But, though desire is the first sign of vocation, it is an equivocal sign. It is necessary to ascertain well its object. It is necessary to know whether it be the ministry itself, or something in the ministry, which suits our taste. The taste, the inclination, we feel for the ministry may be superficial, carnal, erroneous as to the object. It may be that what we like in the ministry is a respectable and honored profession, or the sphere and the occasions which it offers for the exercise of talents with which we may think ourselves endowed; the power of public speaking,† moral views which are not strictly religious;‡ or a vague religious sentimentalism; or an unreflecting enthusiasm, an ideal image, the poetry of the thing. The imagination, in these questions, is apt to take the place of the conscience and the heart.

Newton gives an excellent rule for deciding whether we have a true desire for the ministry. "I hold it," he says, "a good rule to inquire whether the desire to preach is most fervent in our most lively and spiritual frames, or when we are laid in the dust before the Lord. If so, it is a good sign. But if, as is sometimes the case, a person is very earnest to be a

* Isaiah, vi., 8. The absence of taste is not repugnance, disgust for the ministry, which can not exist in a Christian—it is often but a taste for something else.

† An object of ambition to one class of minds far above the command of armies or civil empire. The pulpit, as a means of gaining it, is not surpassed by the forum or the senate-house.—*Transl.*

‡ The ministry favors all the interests of general morality, of temperance, honesty, industry, frugality, chastity; and these are higher in the regards of some men than the interests of spiritual religion.—*Transl.*

preacher to others when he finds but little hungerings and thirstings after grace in his own soul, it is then to be feared his zeal springs rather from a selfish principle than from the spirit of God."*

We give a rule included in Newton's, when we propose to the candidate to inquire if the impulse which induces him to devote himself to the ministry is the same with the object of the ministry as made known to him by the Gospel. If his ruling motive can express itself in the terms which define the institution of the evangelical ministry, it is a good one.

Can you, we would say to him, adopt, as expressing your self-consecration, these words of St. Paul: "And all things are of God, who hath reconciled us to himself by Jesus Christ, and hath given to us the ministry of reconciliation. To wit, that God was in Christ, reconciling the world to himself, not imputing their trespasses unto them, and hath committed to us the word of reconciliation. Now then we are embassadors for Christ, as though God did beseech you by us: we pray you in Christ's stead, be ye reconciled to God."—2 Cor., v., 18–20.

Have you in your heart any measure of the feeling which St. Paul expresses when he says, "My little children, of whom I travail in birth till Christ be formed in you?"—Gal., iv., 19.

With your whole heart do you receive this precept of the apostle: "Let the same mind be in you which was also in Christ Jesus, who, being in the form of God, thought it not robbery to be equal with God, but made himself of no reputation, and took upon him the form of a servant."—Phil., ii., 5–7.

Do you enter fully and freely into the thought, "I fill up that which is behind of the afflictions of Christ, in my flesh, for his Body's sake, which is the Church."

In a word, a desire springing from love; from ambition, but for God only—the desire of God's glory; love for, or at

* Newton: *Cardiphonia*, vol. ii., p. 45.

least ready submission to, whatever in the ministry is laborious, painful, humiliating, diminutive ; do you recognize these traits in the inclination of your mind toward this excellent office, and do you esteem it excellent regarded in this point of view, and as involving such inconveniences ? If you do, you may rest assured that in this first respect, desire for the ministry, your call is genuine.*

This touchstone would be infallible, if any thing could be in our hands ; but we may easily be mistaken : Let us then enter further into this inquiry.

In order to be fully assured that we have a true call, we must possess in some degree, or, at least, must desire, three excellent and inseparable qualities : the love of man, the love of God's glory, and the love of our own spiritual welfare. We shall begin with the glory of God, where ordinarily we do not begin. The motive which inclines us to do good to our fellows is excellent and necessary, but is often rather a natural than a Christian sentiment. Common benevolence may be easily mistaken for charity, or the love of souls. A desire to do good to mankind may be regarded as a call to the ministry. We must have a more elevated spiritual affection, of which we can only become conscious by perceiving in ourselves a love of the Divine glory. But one may have a sort of logical, reasonable affection for God, and say to himself, for example, God has done all things for us, we ought to do every thing for him. This is not true love, for love does not reason. Our love for God should be like the infant's love for his parent, a wife's for her husband. Nothing is more strange to the heart of man than this desire for the glory of God ; nothing marks more decisively our birth to a new life. When one perceives unfolding in himself this strange desire, so chimerical to the natural man,

* On the purity of motives, see MASSILLON, *Discours sur la Vocation à l'état Ecclesiastique*, the paragraph beginning with these words : " Le dernier témoignage que doit vous rendre votre conscience," &c.

this necessity that God be honored, glorified in the world, then may he think himself called to the ministry ; and even when it may seem that souls may be saved otherwise than by his means, he must proceed.

It is not necessary to insist on the love of men. The love of our own spiritual welfare is only a secondary consideration. We may seek, in the ministry, a spiritual asylum ; we may desire to put ourselves under the covert of the sanctuary ; but this should not be our determining motive.

As to *fear*, desire does not exclude it ; these two feelings regulate one another, and constitute that "joy with trembling" of which the Psalmist speaks. The fear to which we refer results from a view of the greatness of God, and of our own weakness. The Christian who, before his conversion, had no fear of offending God, finds himself exercised with strange fears. The minister has yet more of feeling and of fear from his own unworthiness and weakness. Fear hence arising is not groundless or unnecessary ; and it may repel, at least for the moment, a candidate who has the deepest consciousness of being called. Not after a fall, but at the highest degree of Christian strength, may this momentary repulsion take place. At no time should this fear be wanting, though other elements should counterbalance it ; and thus should it be with us, even to the end of the pastoral career. Indeed, since the more deeply we enter into the ministry the more awful it appears, this feeling should be constantly increasing. "Who is sufficient for these things ?"—2 Cor., ii., 16.

After this, it is almost needless to put *conversion** in the number and at the head of the elements of vocation. Various meanings may be given to the word conversion, yet there can be no question as to the legitimacy of a call such as we have characterized. In our apprehension, conversion is included in *desire* such as we have defined. This desire is

* "When thou art converted, strengthen thy brethren."—John, xxii., 32.

conversion itself, and something more; whence it was that, to avoid confusion and repetition, we did not speak of the conversion of the candidate before speaking of an inclination to the ministry.

If, however, we take conversion as including love to Jesus Christ and his interest, it is unquestionably the first seal of vocation. Though we may love Christ without being called to the ministry, we can not be called to the ministry without loving Christ. When Christ demanded thrice of Saint Peter, "Lovest thou me?" and thrice said to him, on his answering in the affirmative, "Feed my sheep, feed my lambs," he did not mean to signify that whoever loved him ought to be employed in the evangelical ministry* (Saint Peter's call, in Christ's view, had a more particular ground); but he certainly did mean to say that no one ought to be his minister who does not love him. "We ought," said a pastor cited by Burk, "to subject all aspirants to the ministry to the same test to which Saint Peter was subjected, and ask of each one of them, "Simon, son of Jonas, lovest thou the Lord Jesus?"† This appendix to a confession of faith would certainly not be superfluous.

Love to Christ supposes many things. It supposes intercourse with Christ, an intimate relationship to him. He who has no personal reminiscences of Christ, who knows him only as the Savior of men, not as his *own* Savior; as the teacher of men, not as his teacher, does not know enough of him, and should not begin his work until he is qualified for it. Faith, in order to become sight, must be exalted as to its degree; and thus it must be elevated in a minister who can speak from experience. This personal knowledge is necessary as a qualification for the ministry, and as a means of fulfilling it in a useful manner.

Reducing the idea of conversion to this simple and touch-

* *Sermon de Consécration.* By M. le doyen CURTAT.

† BURK: *Pastoraltheologie,* tome i., p. 56.

ing notion, love to Jesus Christ, we can fully subscribe to the maxim that, to preach the Gospel and exercise the ministry we must be converted ; and we cordially unite with the writer in Herrnhutt's *Practical Observations* in the following remarks : " Though the Gospel, apart from the instruments by whom it is presented to men, is, to believers, the power of God unto salvation, and may be such, of course, by means of the writings and discourses of men who themselves have never felt this power, it is still most certain that a forcible and lively exposition of the Gospel, and especially its application to the wants and the condition of individuals, which, properly speaking, is the care of the soul, is not to be expected with confidence, except from one who has felt and who continues to feel the power of the Gospel. This experience, then, is essential, is indispensably requisite to a truly evangelical preacher. No one can well show to others the way of salvation until he can say with entire truth, " I believed, therefore have I spoken."—Ps. cxvi., 10.

Thus, then, conversion, or, if you please, love to Jesus Christ, is, as an element in vocation, on two accounts necessary ; first, as a seal, which legitimates the call ; next, as a means of carefully exercising the ministry, or a condition, without which it can not be so exercised.

This desire, nevertheless, which, in its purity, we have made essential to a call, and which we have affirmed to be the first sign of a call, does not suffice without fitness ; and as there is a way, and a very serious one, of " stealing the words of God" (Jer., xxiii., 30), namely, by taking them into one's mouth without sincerity and without love, so may they, in our judgment, be stolen, by undertaking the ministry of the word without possessing, in some measure, certain *aptitudes* for it.

Some of these are *physical*, as the voice and the health. This latter may be delicate, and may give rise to questions which are to be resolved *in casu* rather than *in specie.* It is needless to inquire whether, with health too feeble to sustain the fatigues of the ministry, one may decline a weight which would crush him. This is so evident, that even if he exaggerated the weakness of his constitution, he should be permitted to withdraw ; for this exaggeration would indicate the absence of a desire to exercise the ministry, and where this desire is wanting there is no call. To disregard this indication or this objection would imply that all Christians are under obligation to enter into the ministry, and we should thus blot out even the institution of a special ministry. Rather should we question, if one manifestly in such a state of health should yield to desire, and undertake a ministry which in a short time would terminate his life. I would apply to a minister, as a general rule, the advice given to poets: " *Sumite materiam vestris, qui pascitis, æquam viribus.*"* Be useful in a sphere somewhat different, and simply as Christians, as long and as much as you can, instead of obliging yourselves to pursue a course of labor in which you would be constantly impeded by bodily weakness. This rule, however, may, I admit, be modified by circumstances, which should be always well considered. There are times and places in which this sacrifice, which can never be commanded, may be approved and admired. Although I do not believe in works of supererogation, or think that we may do too much, and that God may be restricted in his requirements from us, yet I hold that there is not only a difference between unbelief and faith, but that there are degrees in faith, and that of two true Christians, one may have more or less zeal or love than the other. It may be well to be rash, and imprudence,

* HORACE says (*Art of Poetry*, v. 38), "Writers, choose a subject to which your strength is equal."

Sumite materiam vestris, qui scribitis, æquam, viribus.

By substituting the word *pascitis* for *scribitis*, M. Vinet makes this verse an advice to those who would feed souls, to inquire whether they are fitted for this work.—*Ed.*

or what men call by that name, is very often true prudence. Circumstances, in short, may create duties, which in other circumstances would not have existed.

As to *intellectual* aptitudes, they comprise *talents* and *acquirements*. What these should embrace, or how far they should extend, it would be improper here to define. Besides, there is more than one sort of ministry; or, rather, the ministry is not always exercised in the same circumstances. Although instruction and knowledge can never be superfluous, one may, in certain situations, exercise a very useful ministry without much knowledge. Still, certain measures of knowledge, certain talents, are always necessary, and perhaps in a higher degree, where science, in the strict sense, is wanting. Absolutely speaking, zeal without science (without any true mental discipline) creates only phantoms, and makes converts only to fanaticism. "Add to your faith knowledge" (2 Pet., i., 5): Knowledge, and not talent only; for talents without knowledge make us presumptuous and imprudent, and discover to us obstacles only by bringing us into collision with them. The first good effect of knowledge is to teach us our ignorance, to make our darkness visible. In general, the ministry ought to have all the knowledge which may be necessary to defend religion against its adversaries; to edify, to instruct, to render their teachings as useful as possible. It is always desirable that a minister should be a sound teacher, should be doctrinally acquainted with religion, should know the world, and especially should know human nature. The idea is a most unhappy one, that pastors have no need of much knowledge. They ought, as to acquirements, to be at least equal to any oppositions which they may have to encounter. Still, we must avoid that frivolous knowledge which is pursued with a view to no end ulterior to itself.

The power of acquiring knowledge depends on talents. These are necessary as a means both of acquiring knowledge and of power in the application of it, in the pulpit and the ministry. But the ministry does not require extraordinary talents; piety, to a certain degree, takes the place of them. Piety is a great talent. Not more, perhaps less talent is necessary to be a good minister than to be a good judge, a good advocate, a good physician, &c. That which is necessary should not be rare. What all to some extent ought to be, many should be able to carry to some degree of perfection.

As the ministry does not generally require very great talents, neither does it require very special ones. One may be an excellent minister with talents which in every other profession would succeed but passably. Fitness for the ministry is not a particular and exceptional fitness. In general, there are fewer than we think of those imperative calls of which we like so well to speak, and it is a kindness of Providence that there are so few.

Finally, if piety may to a certain extent supply talent, talent can not supply piety, and the most special talent (eloquence, knowledge of the heart, ingenuity, government of minds) will not constitute a call. A man may be eminently suited to describe a minister without being called to be one. Neither can talent take the place of instruction. There is no hope more treacherous than that which a man has from the consciousness of talent. No one may fail sooner, if his talent do not rest upon a just foundation. Many distinguished talents are lost, while moderate talents arrive, by labor, at results which appear reserved only for genius. Talent, like labor, can only inspire a relative and subordinate confidence. Both, though necessary, do not in any way supply the essential condition. They do not of themselves confer a mission. It is an armor which only injures us, if God himself have not put it on us. It is necessary that God should speak to our heart. "He alone," said J. Newton, "who created the world can make a minister of the Gospel." This is true, not only because he alone gives the talents and the acquisitions, but especially because there is something more profound, which he alone can give. It is the right neither of the greatest talent, nor the greatest labor, nor the most extended science, to "steal" this mission. There is more than one kind of simony. A man makes himself guilty of simony when he would buy the ministry as a venal thing, at the price of talent or of labor. This price pays very well for every other business; it pays very badly, for it "steals," the ministry; and for one who has thus usurped it, the anathema of Peter is ready: "Thy *talent* perish with thee, because thou hast thought to purchase the gift of God with talent."—Acts, viii., 20.

"The error of Simon Magus," says Bishop Saunderson,* "was that he thought the gift of God might be obtained for the price of money. It is another error to think that it may be obtained by labor. In vain will you rise in the morning, go late to bed, study hard, read much, devour the marrow of the best authors; if God do not add his blessing to your enterprise, you will not be less lean and meagre in respect of knowledge, I mean true and useful knowledge, than the kine of Pharaoh were lean after having eaten the fat ones. It is God who gives the harvest to the sower, and it is God, also, who multiplies the harvest: the beginning and the increase come from him."

All that we have now said is an admonition against assuming talent as sufficient, but in no way does it tend to exclude it. There is, however, a certain measure and a certain sort of talent, of which the absence is almost incompatible with the exercise of the ministry, and to the feeble it may perhaps be the occasion of scandal. Not only are we excused from the ministry, we are not authorized to assume it when an absolute want of memory, or of facility in speaking, or of presence of mind, does not allow us to fulfill in a suitable and edifying manner the ordinary duties of this office.

Sometimes the measure or the kind of talents which a man

* Cited by BRIDGES, *The Christian Ministry*, p. 39, 40, in a note.

has received from God may suffice for some other profession, in which he may zealously work to the glory of God. Why should one who has talents for government wish to be only a minister? It is a sad error to think that one manner of serving God will please him more than another, when we are not fit for it; and the idea of being attached more directly, as it is said, to the propagation of his kingdom appears to me to have already done harm enough. Our views of the universal ministry, or of the call to all to perform, in their respective positions, the function of ministers, offer compensation and comfort sufficient to those to whom the weakness of their talents denies the exercise of a special ministry. One class, especially, have cause to fear this illusion, and the more so in certain seasons. The class I refer to is that of men uneducated in youth, and the seasons I have in view are those of much religious interest. With these persons the care of souls is every thing; with others nothing is thought of but preaching. The whole work is to be kept in view.

Among the number of aptitudes, we may reckon the *natural character*, which is not to be effaced by principles, nor even by a religious change, though, to a certain extent, affected by the influence of Christianity. It is in some points so closely connected with temperament, that it yields to principles and convictions scarcely more than temperament. Timidity, irresolution, fickleness, may abide in conversion, and remain to such a degree that the ministry may be obstructed by them, or may fail to secure that respect by which it ought to be attended. We should carefully consider this matter.

It has been asked whether *past sins* may not annul a call, otherwise complete, and as well substantiated as possible. The question does not relate to every kind of sin; it would imply, if it did, that none are worthy of the priesthood. It has respect to sins of a gross character, both as to nature and form; aberrations of conduct—faults which, if known, would compromise our reputation in the eyes of the world; not only sins, but serious faults, even in the view of natural men Have we, with or without the knowledge of the flock, com mitted such faults; and may they destroy a call otherwise well founded?

It is interesting to know the manner of thinking on this point among the Catholics. Catholicism, which petrifies truths by depriving them of their fluidity, secures them, in doing so, a durable existence. That petrifaction preserves for ages the form of the thing. It is a dearly-purchased benefit of Catholicism. A religion in which the external form is not so unchangeable has an advantage, but by the side of it there is a danger. It may have phases in which the change of form affects the foundation; in which case the truth is lost. It is hence important to study Catholicism.

By certain Catholic doctors, perhaps by Catholicism itself, the question has been resolved by an exaggeration. Massillon excludes from the ministry those who have been given up to sins which have acquired over them the power of habit. "Mourn," he says, "for your crimes in the position of a common believer—that is your place; but do not, by receiving a sacred character, put a seal upon all your iniquities: do not defile the sanctuary, and add not the profanation of a holy place to that of your soul. You may repent, return to God, move his mercy, and save yourselves among penitent believers; you would die hardened and impenitent should you become priests. It may be that this rule has had some exceptions—that a great sinner, after being purified by a long life of mortification, may become a holy priest; but when an exception to a rule is concerned, the utility of the infraction must compensate for the inconveniences. Now it is yours to say what great advantages the Church may promise itself from your promotion to the priesthood. For my part, all that I can say to you is this, if faith still remains to you, it can not but seem terrible to you to enter into a state of which the general rule declares you unworthy, and in which we must have recourse to a solitary exception, to a rare, singular case, to one of those prodigies of which a century scarcely furnishes an example, if you are not to be a profaner and an intruder."*

This rigor may seem inconsistent with other Catholic views, which tend to make the personality of the pastor too insignificant an element. But there is no contradiction—there is agreement. The priest, a neuter substance, from whom the Spirit has retired, ought, at least as a victim led to the altar, to present no spot externally; and it is of these external defilements that there is a question in the passage from Massillon. Besides, in the case he supposes, when the obstinacy of the disorder has effaced from the soul all feelings of modesty and virtue—when the habitude of crime has put into it a disgust for heavenly things, it is very evident that one should be excluded from the ministry; for he can not have a call to it. But this is not the question. It relates to our knowing whether, in respect to a true call, the memory of grave faults should exclude us from the ministry. Besides, it is not here a question of general, universal sin, but of great and deep iniquities—of faults against honor and morals.

I respect conscience, and in certain cases I may approve the motives of him whom the memory of old sins restrains from the ministry, whether the public partakes with him in these painful remembrances, or whether he has confided them to no one.

In the first case, there is a fear on the one side that the public—I mean the mass of the flock—will oppose to the exhortations of the pastor, and to his reprimands, the image, always vivid, always ready to revive, of his ancient disorders, even when excess of virtue and devotedness have disallowed and effaced them.† And on the other side, the thought that the public knows them may intimidate the preacher,

* MASSILLON: *Discours sur la Vocation à l'état Ecclesiastique.*

† According to the rule of the Church, public penitence is incompatible with the priesthood.—(ST. CYRAN, *Pensées sur le Sacerdoce.*

and entirely take away from him that holy boldness, without which he can not usefully exercise the ministry. Massillon lays down a principle, that we must not impose ourselves on a people who will not accept us.* This is true; and if it be true that, although ecclesiastical authority, which, however, is supposed to be delegated by the people, will admit us, the people or the public, on account of our known faults, will not admit us, if we have the feeling that they do not admit us with good-will, we must wait to be reinstated among them, or seek a ministry far from places where the remembrance of our faults will envelop and smother us. It is easy here to draw a conclusion as to the young Levite who is exposed by his very youth, that his youth will not be sufficiently respected.—1 Tim., iv., 12. If his youth has been not at all scandalous, but too noisy, too little serious, even that is an evil. It is necessary not only that the candidate should be exempt from those faults which society will not pardon, but more, that from the moment in which his life belongs to the public, he should be surrounded with an atmosphere of sanctity, of seriousness, of innocence in morals and manners.

In the second case, the memory of his sins pursuing the minister even into the pulpit, and overwhelming him, perhaps the more that he has not made reparation for them by means of a public avowal, may cause him extreme difficulty and trouble. It is not certain that God intends in all cases, in taking away the guilt of sin, to take away also the weight of its remembrance. Perhaps this hard discipline he imposes on certain persons who have need to be held, even to the end, in humiliation and in terror. Perhaps such a man will feel that it is not for him, polluted as he is, to exercise a ministry of which even angels are not worthy; perhaps his respect for the ministry will hold him aloof from the ministry; and if it should be so with him, I should not dare to oppose these scru-

* MASSILLON: *Discours sur la Vocation à l'état Ecclesiastique.* "The suffrage of the people is the second mark of a canonical vocation," &c.

ples; I should not dare to advise their suppression, unless I should see a germ of self-righteousness, and discover in the individual's sense of unworthiness the idea of man's worthiness in general.

This painful sacrifice might be blessed, and if I saw that it was made from the proper principle, I should hope that this man has renounced the ministry only to exercise it under another more humble, more simple form; that he will preach the Gospel at the foot of the pulpit as he would have done higher up; that he has denied himself the official priesthood to exercise another, and that he will do by a good example (which he is the more required to give, because he has given a bad one) what he would not venture to do by his words.

It is difficult, in cases like these, to interpose between a man and his conscience. The question must be settled between them: At least we must enter only as we are invited; we must use precaution, and not force any thing. But while it is difficult to solve particular cases of this kind, it is less so to lay down a general principle according to which they should be solved, and which each one may apply to himself as it may suit him. The principle is this: It is not, we would say in each case, it is not what you have been, but what you are, that is to be considered. If it were absolutely unlawful for you to enter into the ministry on account of the sins of your youth, no one could exercise it; for all have sinned, all have been dead (Eph., xi., 1), and in death there are no degrees. If these sins, after you have abjured and utterly renounced them, render you unfit for the ministry, they also render you unfit for heaven. To preach the Divine forgiveness, you must have believed in it, you must have received and accepted it; and if you have accepted it, you are, according to the terms of the Gospel, as if you had never sinned. Between you and others there is no difference; since "all have sinned and come short of the glory of God."—Rom., iii., 23. As you believe, then, in the Divine forgiveness, you have, neither more nor less than any other man, a right to preach the Gospel. Has not that grace which has cleansed you as a man cleansed you also as a minister? We can not disown these truths without disowning with them the elements of the Gospel, which make no difference between the laborer of the first and the laborer of the eleventh hour, the publican and the strict pharisee, the prodigal son and his elder brother, who by supposition remained always with his father. In the work of grace, which is a new creation, the things which are past are no more remembered.—Is., lxv., 17. The new man's relations toward God date from his renovation; what he now is effaces what he has been, though what he now does can not efface what he has done. "What greater change can a man experience," says St. Cyran, "than from a child of Adam to become a child of God? We may say it is a less change to pass from nothing to a mortal man, than from being a mortal man to become a child of God."*

This is the truth, in its abstract and absolute form. It is not affirming that, because God's mercy takes no account of our former conduct, we ourselves should take no account of it; nor that those should not who may have to decide concerning our call to the functions of the ministry. It is not enough that repentance separates our past conduct from our new life; it is necessary that there should be a test of sufficient devotion to assure others and ourselves that the poisonous germ is dead, and the man is no longer the same one that sinned and gave cause for scandal. Thus past sins will present no obstacle to our entering into the holy tribe; it may even be that those sins which we deplore, and because we deplore them, may impart to us a prudence, a seriousness, a force, and a compassion, which do not always belong to those whose lives have been passed in comparative innocence.

* Saint Cyran: *Pensées sur le Sacerdoce.*

On this subject, the Abbé de St. Cyran has a thought which deserves attention : "I do not fear to introduce into the priesthood, on urgent occasions, a man who has repented of his public or known sins, though they may have been gross and against the Decalogue, provided I find two qualities in him. One of them is firmness of mind (something beyond mere good sense), which, with the aid of Divine grace, may be of much avail to him in resisting his other sins, and also the temptations arising from the exercise of the priesthood. The other is an entire freedom from cupidity, whether as to wealth or as to honor and praise. For, not unfrequently, a man loses his innocence by only one kind of mortal sin, springing from strong inclination and favored by the ardor of age ; and a passing occasion may prevail against a nature good in every other respect, and endowed in body and mind with many acquired and gracious qualities. This sometimes is enough to displace every fear of making a man a priest, supposing him to be truly penitent, and that he has passed some years without falling again, and in striving perpetually to cure his sinful habits. We may have more assurance in this case, if, while living in a city, he foregoes intercourse with persons not easy to be avoided, such as relations, friends, and others whom it is difficult to keep at a distance from us in cities. Of those who have fallen from innocence, some have more strength and resolution than others who have never fallen."*

May *doubts* annul a call ?

We reply, 1st. That there would be few ligitimate calls if doubt might annul them.

2d. That there would be few Christians even on this sup-

* Saint Cyran : *Lettre à M. Guillebert sur le Sacerdoce*, chap. xviii. "God himself has chosen as ministers men who had grievously sinned ; and many holy bishops and pastors of whom ecclesiastical history speaks, had been exceedingly dissipated men." — *Augustin, Rancè.*

position; for, though it is possible to be in a state where all is light, they who never doubt are graceless beings.

3d. That the study, the life, the exercise of the ministry, will raise new doubts.

The question to be settled is, Do we believe? Is Christianity a reality with us? Are we able to give a reason for our faith to ourselves and others? Have we that experience of the truth, that inward certitude which, without resolving doubts, sweeps them away?

But it is objected—can a man who is sent to remove the doubts of others doubt himself? Not absolutely. But we are not now speaking of skeptical or unbelieving ministers, but of a man who is not clear on all points, and who sometimes must know it.

May certain *inclinations* annul a call?

The inclinations which we have in view are like the doubts of the soul, and the difficulty is resolved on the same principles.

We do not speak of tastes, innocent in themselves, but which a pastor can not indulge. These do annul the call, if the call do not annul or overcome them.

We refer to evil inclinations—inclinations which are as incompatible with the Christian profession as they are with the ministry. As a minister, in yielding to them, is more culpable, and will do greater harm than a simple Christian, the question presents itself, Should he not begin to conquer them as a man? If he say that he can do so better as a minister, this would be playing high game, doubling the difficulty in order to surmount it. If the Church is an hospital, ministers are not the sick, but the overseers of them. They ought to enter it in a good state of health. They may doubtless do themselves good here, but there is something repulsive in this calculation. There is danger, however, that, instead of being purified by the ministry, a stain will be brought upon it.

I regard *ascèse*,* or *spiritual exercise*, as an important preparation for the ministry. I mean by this not the arbitrary exercises of certain Christians and certain sectaries, but a system of moral life, resting on Christian principle, but acted on in anticipation of the ministry afterward to be exercised. We may suppose ourselves in the most difficult position, and live as if we were there. Doubtless there will be many differences. What is a privation to one is not to another; so that we can not enter into details. Our concern is, by the aid of Divine grace, to become masters of ourselves. This is the essential point.

Most manifestly are these questions referred, for decision, directly and definitively to ourselves. And on the whole, no man, nor body of men, can know with entire certainty that we are called; as, on the other hand, they can not in every case declare with certainty that we are not called. In short, there are times and places in which a man can not be sent, except by himself, and in which he who ought to be called is the last that would be called. A case of this kind is that in which one sets himself in opposition to a general error. Pastoral order should always be maintained; but the Church, in certain times, is the offspring of the pastor, as in ordinary times the pastor proceeds from the Church. In general, however, an external call, which is not necessary *in right*, or, in an absolute sense, is necessary in fact: It is so,

1. To the minister himself, who, though the sole judge of his own intentions, is judge of nothing more; and on his own account needs a testimonial from others as to his tact, talent,

* Ασκησις.—M. Vinet has adopted this word, which the Germans before him (*christliche Ascese*) had introduced into theological language. It is borrowed from the Greek, as formerly were borrowed ascete, asceticisme, and ascetique.—*Edit.* The French word has been retained, as there is no English word corresponding to it.—*Transl.*

and knowledge. It is very true that, even when we are called by a Church, we may think we are not called ; but if a Church does not call us when we think we have been called, there is then room for doubt as to our call. It is the duty of every man, even though drawn to the ministry by very lively convictions, to doubt his call when he sees that he is unacceptable. There should, at least, be delay before we refuse to submit to the scientific and ecclesiastical authority which resists us. Neither can we understand well the undertaking beforehand ; and, in respect to its nature, its extent, its difficulties, its true character, we should rest upon testimonials which may well, in this case, be called *authority*. They who are acquainted with the work have a means of knowing, which we have not, whether we are qualified for it.

2. To the flock. Unless, from particular circumstances, the flock are able, and in a condition to judge of the capacity and worthiness of the minister who presents himself, they will always ask : " Whence do you come ? Are you he that should come ?" Wherever there is a Church, it will provide an established rule, according to which those are to be judged who pretend to pastoral functions, and an institution which forms and selects them. This is but a moral security, but it is the only one which is possible. And in the Romish Church, though they have greater pretensions, have they essentially any thing more ?

As regards the minister's personal satisfaction as to his call, the external call is equivalent to a consultation. But this consultation, it should be said, is very imperfect, and will always be so, compared with that which we may hold, no longer with a collective body of men, but at our own request, with tried friends and our brethren in the faith. A collective authority can not judge of inward sentiments, of the reality of faith, of the degree to which imagination may have place. A friend can do this much better. Let him be consulted, then, but with entire sincerity, without any mental reserve. We often think we have said every thing, when the important word remains unuttered.

I should also have indicated exercise* as a means of assurance, if it were generally possible for a man to exercise himself sufficiently before consecration; that is to say, in a manner which shows well the nature of the work to which, as a minister, he is to be devoted. Without attaching too much importance to this means, I think it would be well, within the limits of prudence and modesty, and under a wise direction, to make trial of some of the labors of the ministry. It would tend to give seriousness to the life of a student, provided these exercises be in their own nature serious; and would throw in advance the light of practice on theory. Thus young physicians not only read and attend lectures, but visit the sick. Let young ministers do likewise. There is a *clinique* also of the ministry. The departments of theology and of the ministry present but too many theorists who have not been instructed by practice, and but too many practitioners who care nothing for theory. Bengel advises young theologians who have finished their studies to go into the country for a year, and there exercise the ministry, and then to pass some time at a new university. Without making this a rule, it is an excellent precept.

In general, a serious and well-directed young man would do well, at the outset of his theological studies, to take his resolution intelligently, and at the end of a year's study he may find his call confirmed or annulled. At the end of this period let him put the question to himself again, or let it be put to him. If he has no call, he may then know it. He can not beforehand so well assure himself that he truly has a call; but his impressions may determine him to begin his studies. Let him have the courage, if he find that he has obeyed an imaginary call, to retrace his steps, however late it may be.

* Preliminary practice.—*Transl.*

A young man should have regard to the wishes of parents, who may prefer this office, and often see in it the door of safety for their child; but let his parents and himself well understand that it is not absolutely the place of safety, that the ministry in itself alone does not secure ministers, and that to enter into this profession with a call to a very different one may one day result in seeing nature grown the strongest, and inclining us to pursuits, subjecting us to habits, which, out of the ministry, may appertain to a Christian, but which, in the ministry, are as so many instances of disloyalty and scandal.*

* What follows is extracted from the note-books of M. Vinet's auditors, and is only another form of the thought of which the original expression is reproduced in the text. We think the reader may be interested to see both versions.

"This question concerning vocation is a great question. But it does not always arise out of itself. In order to resolve it, it must be well considered, and considered before entering into the ministry. Often, nay always, should the candidate be questioning himself; but especially at two periods; one at the beginning, and the other at the end of his special studies. That he should examine himself on this point at the beginning of these studies is natural, but is that the proper time for deciding it? Some may be under a powerful impression, but this is not the case with the greater part. And even with the smaller number such an impression is not a sure sign of a call. Age may have great influence; but the common case is rather one of indecision, a conflict between tastes and tendencies. Should we exclude from the novitiate those who do not find themselves under a lively impression? By no means; we should try them; they may perhaps prove themselves sincere, faithful—may appreciate the beauty of the ministry, may not be urged by merely external influences. It is true that there is great danger in a candidate's entering on his studies in such a state of mind. Afterward, when he is more unimpressed, when the course of his life may take a different direction, he may rather persevere in than renounce his present dispositions. This is a danger, but no one should be excluded on account of it. At the end of his studies he should interrogate himself in a more decisive manner. He will then be no longer doubtful as to the general agreement between his profession and his heart. He should exam-

But he who shall have made use of all these means will not feel less, but more than any other, that they are insufficient in themselves; for they profit only the upright and sincere soul—the soul which is free from all foreign preoccupation. And how can one assure himself on this point, how secure himself against every illusion, if he do not first obtain that single eye, that pure eye, without which the light itself is but as darkness? How can he perceive in himself a spirit in which objects appear as they are, in which nothing irrelevant mingles itself, in which we know and judge ourselves with all possible certainty, and in which, to say all, no serious and irreparable error can have place? This isolation, this chosen and pure medium, is prayer. Truth has its dwelling with prayer.

No object was ever more worthy of it. We are "to beseech men in the name of God, and as though God besought them by us" (2 Cor., v., 20); and how can we venture to do this without his leave? and how can we be sure of having his leave, when we may directly ask him, and fail to do it? I do not attribute to prayer any supernatural or magical effect; God does not mean to exempt or deprive us of the use of our faculties by inviting us to prayer; he does not promise to say "Go" directly, without the use of means, to the question which we address to him, "Shall I go, Lord?" But besides this intrinsic virtue attached to prayer, it is in the power of God, the Lord of our spirits and of circumstances, to combine every thing in such a manner that we shall see what we ought to see, and not think we see that which is not. His Providence does not exercise itself at the expense of our liberty, which always remains perfect.

We shall never call upon God, if we do it not in this time

ine himself thoroughly: if he find that he has no call, let him have the courage to retrace his steps. Finally, a minister who, after some period of practice, learns that he has not been called, has indeed made the discovery very late, but not too late to abandon the ministry."

of the greatest danger. For thus truly we must name the chance of entering into the ministry without a call to it. No reading, example, or company; no influence of education and authority; no temptation from without or within, neither excessive riches nor excessive poverty; nothing can corrupt us so profoundly or so irrevocably as a ministry exercised without a call; that is to say, without the convictions and sentiments which are its only legitimate ground; and the Abbé de Saint Cyran has reason to say, "that no men are more irreclaimable than those who, not having been called to the priesthood by the vocation of God, do nothing which appears worthy of a priest all their life."* Thought terrible, but true! For, on the one hand, it is certain that the one, without a call, will do himself exactly as much evil as the other will do himself good by a legitimate ministry; that whatever moves and edifies a true pastor hardens him in the same proportion; that each word of truth which he pronounces shuts his heart somewhat more to the sentiment of truth; and that he perishes by that by which others live: And on the other hand, it is easy to understand that the crime of usurpation, and consequently of hypocrisy, is such that the scandal of morals adds sensibly nothing to it, and that flagrant scandals, reproachful as they are to the ministry, less compromise the ministry. These scandals are, in our view, the mark of a slave who struggles in his chains; they are as an abdication of the ministry; the minister who gives them is a robber, but not an impostor; and he corrupts himself less, perhaps, by these excesses than by hypocrisy. The other does much more evil; he undertakes the function of a minister of the Gospel only to weaken the Gospel, to retain under empty and dead forms the souls that are committed to him, to make them sleep a sleep still more profound. Strange, but true; scandals which he might cause by irregular conduct would be comparative benefits. They admit of

* SAINT CYRAN: *Pensées sur le Sacerdoce.*

no illusion; they give notice that truth is elsewhere, or, at least, that it is not there; but decency of manners, regularity in purely external duties, all without conviction, are the most admirable means of keeping souls far from the living waters, and near the stagnant and putrid pools of legalism, of formalism, or of indifference. I do not inquire whether he be more or less culpable than a scandalous minister, but I doubt not that he does more evil.

In presence of a danger so terrible, what is the stupidity that would not tremble, that would defy appearances, that would not suspect the wishes, the invitations, and the counsels of those by whom we feel ourselves most and best loved; who, in a word, would not resist all combinations of impulse, and who would not seek to raise himself by prayer so high above the illusions of imagination and all human influences, that he would find nothing between himself and the truth? What he desires is a call which comes from God himself. He will not be satisfied with less; he will not rest until he has drawn from God the solemn word, Go! or, Go not! This word God without doubt will not articulate, but God will make all the objects, the consideration of which ought to determine him, to reflect themselves purely in the mirror of his conscience, and he will have, if we may so speak, the conscience that it is conscience which has spoken—the new man, and not the natural man.

DUTIES OF THE PASTOR.

The plan which I have adopted is not, perhaps, the best; but we may tolerate any classification of things which excludes nothing essential and embraces nothing false.

I trace many concentric circles around the soul of the pastor, which is my centre and my point of departure. I first give rules relating to the purely individual and interior life of the pastor; a life particular and distinct, by which all the other spheres of his existence are determined.

I pass afterward to his social life, and, first, his domestic life (always considering him as a pastor).

Finally, I come to his pastoral life properly speaking, in which I distinguish the *pastor*, the *conductor of worship*, and the *preacher*.

PART FIRST.

INDIVIDUAL AND INTERNAL LIFE.

I ASSUME a holy vocation and a regular entrance, a pastoral and even a zealous spirit.

The pastor, even as the Christian, must fortify, must confirm his vocation (*βεβαίαν ποιεῖσθαί*, 2 Pet., i., 10). In this there is a mystery, the profound, invisible concurrence of the human will which is excited with the Divine will which excites it. It is with vocation as with conversion. In one sense, we are called but once, as we are converted but once; in another sense, we are called and converted every day. Analogy here should suffice, and even be an *à fortiori* argument; but the Gospel is explicit: St. Paul says to Timothy, "I put thee in remembrance, that thou stir up the gift of God which is in thee."—2 Tim., i., 6.

I dismiss the question whether there are not many whom it concerns to make to themselves a call, while they are already engaged in the work.

The exercise of the ministry, will not this of itself suffice for the confirmation of the call?—It should contribute to it, but it may also have the opposite effect. The exercise of the ministry endangers the spirit of the ministry, if it be not sustained from within. If there be not this balance, if the internal does not exert itself sufficiently on the external, the external injures the internal, as the internal no doubt would fail without external action. There is danger that function may become a substitute for feeling.* Our first impressions have in them much of imagination; when this is once exhausted, and without further aid from it we are made dependent for feeling on the heart and the conscience, it is much to be feared that we shall have too little feeling.†

We must not depend on the vivacity of our first impressions; that which affects us most to-day will leave us cold soon: For the influence of things on our sensibility we shall have to rely on their direct relation to our heart and con-

* "The first time the priests and Levites saw in the desert the holy tabernacle which Moses was directed to construct, the miraculous cloud which went before it, the glory of God which covered this holy place, the oracles which proceeded from the inner sanctuary, the magnificence and the august solemnity of the sacrifices and ceremonies, they could not but approach them with a holy dread. Of the purifications, and all the other preparations which were prescribed to ministers by the law, they omitted nothing. But gradually the daily sight of the tabernacle made them familiar with this holy place; the precautions ceased with their awe; the prodigy of the pillar of fire, which God continued there every day, became contemptible by long custom; profanations soon followed; rash ministers ventured to offer strange fire; others usurped the functions which belonged exclusively to the high-priest; at last the daughters of Midian soon became to them a stumbling-block and a scandal, and hardly in the entire tribe of Levi could a Phinehas, a holy and zealous priest, be found, who dared to avenge the honor of the priesthood and the sanctity of the law, which had been shamefully dishonored before an unfaithful people."—MASSILLON, *Discours sur la Nécessité où sont les Ministres de se renouveller dans l'Esprit de leur Vocation.*

† In the first fervor of the Christian and of the minister, imagination easily, and even necessarily, intermingles. In all life imagination has its part. It is a kind of vehicle without which many ideas could not reach us. And how far does its power extend! even to making us conscious that we have a life within us to which we are entire strangers. It enters into all our moral acts, and in some in a very high degree. When it leaves us, every thing it has created disappears with it as a phantom, leaving within us the net product of the work it has wrought in us. This often is little. The lees only remain at the bottom of the cup—the cordial of imagination has been drunk.

science, and, from being apparently full of zeal, we may become mere men of office. There must, then, be a renewal of our call, and in proportion as the charm of novelty is effaced, the moral element must be strengthened.

Now the first means of renewing our vocation as pastors is to renew our vocation as Christians. The Christian is not to be forgotten in order to dream only of the pastor; the one can not of itself, and all alone, do the work of the other. Even as pastors, it is important to remind ourselves that, of the souls which have been confided to our care, our own are the first; that toward these first our ministry should be exercised; and that, first of all, we should be pastors to ourselves.

Whether it be that, to advance the salvation of others, we must not neglect our own, or that justice requires each one's charity to begin with himself, St. Paul, in addressing himself to ministers in the person of Timothy, speaks to them first concerning themselves: "Take heed to thyself and to thy doctrine, for in so doing (in doing these two things, and not the last only) thou shalt save thyself and those who hear thee."—1 Tim., iv., 16. "Take heed to yourselves, and to all the flock over which the Holy Ghost hath made you overseers."*—Acts, xx., 28.

Nevertheless, we are also required to renew *directly* our

* "To observe the order of St. Paul (Acts, xx., 28; 1 Tim., iv., 16), a minister must begin with himself, fulfill his own duties, and care for his own salvation before all things. Before going abroad from love to his neighbor, let him withdraw into the secret place of the divine holiness. Before compassionating the misery of others, let him be sensible of his own ills and of his own weaknesses. And, before urging others to obey the law of God, let him first obey it himself. The first duty of a bishop is to be holy."—DUGUET, *Traité des Devoirs d'un Évêque*, art. ii., § 1. Gregory of Nazianzen expresses himself thus on the subject: "We must first be pure, and then purify others; be taught, and then teach others; become light, and then enlighten others; draw near to God ourselves, and then induce others to approach him; sanctify ourselves, and then make others holy."

vocation as pastors, which means that we must be always renewing in ourselves the disposition which was decisive in respect to our vocation.

If, therefore, the exercise of the ministry do not of itself suffice for this constant renovation, we must seek the means of it externally, apart from the ministry.

The first of these, which is rather the condition of all, is *solitude.** Let us not exaggerate ; let us not attempt to recommend solitude to the exclusion or detriment of social life. For the advantage of this, and as a means of better preparing himself to improve it, must the pastor sometimes withdraw himself from society. In a solitude too profound, too protracted, there are peculiar dangers, and greater ones, perhaps, than those of the world. When habitual, solitude is contrary to the will of the Creator, who said it was not good for man to be alone ; and against the mind of Jesus Christ, who prayed to his Father not to take us out of the world, but to keep us from the evil. As an exception, then, and not as a rule, is solitude to be recommended. But so regarded—regarded as an exception or as a remedy (we do not nourish ourselves with remedies), it is of great value.

We do not mean to say that solitude is good in itself: It is not, except with certain qualifications. It has often been spoken of with the unqualified enthusiasm which we have for what has once charmed us. Poets,† moralists, philosophers, have vaunted it ; and this concert of praise, surely, is not without some foundation. But we must not be indiscriminate. What we have intended to recommend is, internal solitude, or the spirit of solitude. We must discipline ourselves to being alone in the midst of the world, to tranquillity

* See, on this subject, a discourse of M. Vinet, entitled *La Solitude recommandée au Pasteur.—Edit.*

† See, among others, LA FONTAINE, *dans Le Songe d'un Habitant du Mogol, le Juge arbitre, l'Hospitalier et la Solitaire.*

in the midst of tumult, to stillness in the midst of excitement. Having made ourselves capable of this kind of solitude, we may hold ourselves quit of the other. When external solitude is denied to us, we think that the other, carefully cultivated, may be relied upon as sufficient.

External solitude is evil if it be not good. If we have the world in the heart, we shall take it with us into the closet. To an unsocial, envious, irritable man, who feeds upon his resentments or his hatreds, solitude of this kind is very injurious. And to men agitated by passion, we can, in many cases, recommend nothing better than intercourse with others who are pursuing some useful occupation. Solitude is good or evil according to the use we make of it.

But solitude can not fail to be useful to him who seeks good from it, precisely because he seeks it; and even, previous to experience of it in ourselves, we can easily understand that what makes outward things vanish, and silences the noises of the world, favors the interviews which we wish to have with ourselves; that, except in these circumstances, we can but partially hold these interviews; and, in particular, that the truths which concern the conscience here detach themselves better from all those foreign accessories with which they are overloaded and darkened in the discussions which are carried on respecting them.*

Life, in our day, is made up of so many elements, is cut into so many surfaces, that it produces a kind of bewilder-

* Saint Gregory calls the occupations of the ministry a tempest of the spirit. Saint Bernard wrote to Pope Eugene thus: "Since all possess you, be one of those by whom you are possessed. Why should you alone be deprived of the gift which you make of yourself? How long will you not receive yourself, in your turn, among others? You know that you are debtor to the wise and the unwise, and do you refuse yourself only to yourself? All partake of you, all quench their thirst at your breast as at a public fountain, and do you hold yourself at a distance athirst!"—Saint Bernard, *Traité de la Considération*, liv. i., ch. v.

ment, and the eye needs to repose itself in the quiet and sweet light of solitude.*

We must not, then, despise external means : Jesus Christ did not despise them. How often is he represented in the Gospel as withdrawing himself, and passing long hours away from men and noise ! Would a means which was necessary to Jesus Christ be useless to us ? "I learn from Saint Augustine," says Bossuet, "that the attentive soul makes a solitude for itself : *Gignit enim sibi ipsa mentis intentio solitudinem.* But let us not flatter ourselves ; if we would keep ourselves vigorous in the inward man, we must know how to avail ourselves of seasons of an effective solitude.†

Moreover, it is only as giving opportunity for action that solitude is desirable. The peace, the repose which it offers, are but a frame-work which we have to fill up. Vagrancy of thought is always hurtful. Christianity makes us think, not dream.

Solitude, on account of its general influence as now set forth, is most valuable to a minister who can employ it in these three ways.

1. It enables him to take an estimate of his modes of life, external and internal. This self-examination should be often made, for the progress of evil is no less rapid than insensible. We are worse to-day than we were yesterday, if we are not better. As diligent stewards, let us settle our account every evening, for the thief may come during the night. A too minute manner of examining ourselves may, however, open a door to selfishness : Let us then, even here, be on our guard,

* See, on the Catholic Institution of Retreats, Massillon, third Synodal discourse, *De la Nécessité des Retraites pour se renouveller dans le Grâce du Sacerdoce;* and Bourdaloue, *l'Avertissement de la Retraite Spirituelle.*

† Bossuet : *Oraison Funèbre de Marie Thérèse d'Autriche.* For the quotation from St. Augustine, see *De divers. Quaest. ad Simplic.*, lib. ii., Quaest. iv., t. vi., col. 118.

for the enemy glides in through every inlet. Some, with too little caution, have advised us to keep a minute and daily journal; we must not record too much about ourselves, even though we record evil. We shall find it useful, however, to take note of the most important occurrences of our life.

2. It assists him in gathering up the results of his experience. Experience is properly a reaction upon things which have been done; it does not suffice to have seen them, to have assisted in them; we must reflect upon them, detach them, separate them, classify them. "One might pass," says Argenson, "the whole of a long life in working without principles, and thereby learn nothing. Experience is rather the fruit of reflection on what we have seen than the result of a multitude of transactions to which we have not given the attention they deserve."

3. It aids him in consulting God. The holiest occupations can not prosper without this; how necessary, then, to the minister! Let him regulate his remoter conduct, form resolutions, deliberate with himself; he will make many false steps, especially at the outset, if he does not settle his plans of procedure: But let God be called to the consultation, and never let Him be away when the deliberations are going on.

In solitude PRAYER finds its natural place, but we shall consider it apart as the second means of renewing vocation. It is not only a duty and a privilege; it is not only a preparation for the ministry, it is one of its labors for the accomplishment of which the first ministers of Jesus Christ demanded a discharge from certain secondary functions: We must, said they, *give ourselves* to this.—Acts, vi., 4.

Prayer is necessary to keep us at the proper point of vision, which is always escaping from us; to heal the wounds of self-love and of feeling; to renew our courage; to anticipate the always threatened invasion of indolence, of levity, of dilatoriness, of spiritual or ecclesiastical pride, of pulpit vanity, of professional jealousy. Prayer resembles the air of certain isles of the ocean, the purity of which will allow no life to vermin. With this atmosphere we should compass ourselves about, as the diver surrounds himself with the bell before he descends into the sea.*

But the prayer of a pastor is *sacerdotal prayer*, and as such it is a function. It has been said that he who works prays; how much more true is it that he who prays works! Prayer is a work like that of Moses in the mount. Intercession is what remains to the ministry of the priesthood.† It was practiced immediately by the Great Pastor and by his apostles, who, without ceasing, made mention of their flocks in their prayers, at the same time that they claimed intercession from their flocks.‡

Another mode of employing the hours of a pastor's retreat, and a third means of renewing his vocation, is STUDY.

First, the study of the Bible. This, even when divested of every thing scientific, is inexhaustible, and leads to new discoveries, even to the end of life. For the pastor it is both *obligatory* and *necessary;* obligatory, since his business is nothing other than preaching the word of God, or according to this word; and thus his ministry will be interesting and fruitful in proportion as his word is penetrated with the substance, and even with the letter,§ of the Divine word.

* Frequent prayer is recommended to the pastor by HARMS, *Pastoraltheologie*, tome i., p. 25.

† Not intercession only, but prayer for the coming of God's kingdom. See Isaiah, lxii., 6, 7. "Ye that make mention of the Lord, give yourselves no rest, and give *Him* no rest till he establish, and till he make Jerusalem a praise in the earth."

‡ The prayer of Bacon before his study, reported by M. DE VAUZELLES, *Histoire de Bacon*, tome i., p. 107. That of Kepler (*Semeur de* 1838, p. 245). See these prayers, and two passages from Massillon, in *the Appendix*, note G.

§ See 1 Tim., iv., 13, "Give attendance to reading," etc.; and 2

I need not enlarge on the richness and the interest of the preaching of a minister who does not confine himself to knowing certain parts of the Bible, but who understands and cites every part.

The Bible is still more necessary for the care of souls. We run the risk of being often unprovided for occasions as they arise, if we are not familiar with the word of God. What power has a profound knowledge of the Gospel given to certain missionaries. They doubtless have not learned it by heart, but they have heart-knowledge of it. This is the best knowledge, which belongs only to those who have felt its power. Let the minister read the Bible as a pastor and as a Christian ; there is danger of reading it chiefly as a preacher. He should seek in it, not passages and texts, but powers, virtues, inspirations ; otherwise he will consult it no longer as a book, but as a collection of verses.

The holy men, as well as holy words of the Bible, are to be studied. We too much neglect this ; lives are the words of God. Christianity, in its greatest depth, is not a book, though it has a book for its foundation and support ; it is a fact and a moral fact. The lives of saints, the lives of pastors, the lives of missionaries, should generally be studied. They tend to keep us at the highest point in our ministry. We shall not be kept there if we look only to what is customary.

The Bible should be studied in the original. Even for the country-pastor this study is necessary, for it concerns him to be imbued with the spirit of the Holy Scriptures. We may doubtless conceive of preaching as attended with the Divine blessing, where this means is not used ; but the knowledge of the sacred languages is a privilege not to be despised.

Together with, or rather subordinate to, the study of the

Tim., iii., 15, 17, "From a child thou hast known the Holy Scriptures," etc.

Bible, there are other studies which the pastor should pursue. There are abuses here, however, which we shall, in the first place, separate.

1. The study of frivolous things, or study undertaken with a frivolous end. We should beware of studying from mere curiosity, which only serves to feed our vanity; and avoid the foolish questions of which St. Paul speaks.*

2. Expecting from study what it can not give, the true knowledge of God, the love of God, peace of heart. When knowledge has gone so far as to make our darkness visible, it has, as to some things, rendered us the greatest service we can receive from it. It is a preparatory teacher; it is like the law, and has the same purpose—"a schoolmaster to bring us to Christ;" but it is not the way, the truth, and the life. With much knowledge, we may have no faith; we may believe, and believe truly, without having any knowledge: The law of God, still more the Gospel, gives wisdom to the simple.† There is, says St. John, an unction which teaches us all things, after which we have no need that any one should teach us.—John, ii., 27.

3. Lastly, excess; that is to say, giving too much of our time and strength to a study to which, as it has no other end than to prepare us for the ministry, or to give us proper recreation, the ministry should not be sacrificed. This would be neglecting the end for the sake of the means. The least of our duties should appear to us more important than the most interesting book, and should be able to withdraw us from it.‡

A question, a delicate one, here presents itself; that which relates to *school-teaching ministers.* It was not a delicate question some centuries ago, perhaps it will not be always.

* "Doting about questions and strifes of words."—1 Tim., vi., 4.

† "The meek will he teach his way."—Psalm xxv., 9.

‡ *Le Clitophon*, De la Bruyère, *Les Caractères*, au chapitre *Des Biens de la Fortune.*

It was once thought proper by every one that priests should be teachers; it is otherwise now. Knowledge has been secularized; it has been separated from religion, perhaps, to serve it better. Shall we say, however, that teaching school is incompatible with the ministry? No; this also is a ministry. Still, it is out of place, in the actual relations of life, to consecrate ourselves to the ministry, and afterward be at liberty to choose between the pastorate and the instruction of youth.

These abuses being removed, we think we may recommend to the minister to give a part of his time to study.

1. He has studied with reference to his functions; what he has learned, he has learned that he may apply it in the practice of his duties, not the more general results only, but also the particular notions. Now it is well known that we lose what we do not take care of. Besides, we should not think that we learned at the University all that we can learn, or all that we need to know. On many important points science has renewed itself, perhaps has changed its form, since we left the Academy.

2. There is a disadvantage in occupying the mind with only practical, particular, individual questions: It contracts the mind, and injures practice itself. Knowledge is the remedy. It tends to correct the abuse of practice by theory. Bengel thinks it would be well to make trial of the pastoral work in the country, and then resume our studies for a time.* Thus would life illustrate knowledge, action cast light upon thought, and reciprocally. Harms finds motives for cultivating knowledge equally in a great and in a small number of occupations.

* When a candidate has passed some time among country people, as vicar, in a rural parish, and has learned what is the *gustum plebeium et popularem* (how the people look at religion), it is useful for him to remit the work for a while, to return to his theology, and to pass it in review again with greater application.—BENGEL.

Practice apart, thought is impoverished if we do not study. This has been felt by the most lively and productive minds. We can not of ourselves nourish ourselves; we must receive in order to produce. Study, it is true, is not confined to reading: When we have learned something from books, and from the book par excellence, as well as from others, we must exercise our powers to assimilate it to ourselves, as we do our bodily food. But when, without intercourse with books, or in the absence of facts, we labor alone, what supports our labors besides our own recollections? Whence come our thoughts, if not from facts, or from books, or from social intercourse, another great book which demands our study? We must study, then, to excite and enrich our own mind by means of other men's. Those who do not study find their talents enfeebled, and their minds become decrepit before the time. In respect to preaching, experience demonstrates this most abundantly. Whence comes it that preachers, much admired at their beginning, decline so rapidly, or remain so much below the hopes to which they had given birth? Most frequently it is because they did not continue their studies. A faithful pastor always studies to a certain extent; besides the Bible, he constantly reads the book of human nature, which is always open before him; but this unscientific study does not suffice. Without incessant application, we may make sermons, even good sermons, but they will all more and more resemble each other. A preacher, on the contrary, who pursues a course of solid thinking, who nourishes his mind by various reading, will always be interesting. He who is governed by singleness of purpose, will find in all books, even in those which do not relate directly to the ministry, something which he can use in preaching.

3. The apostles recommend science or knowledge (2 Pet., i., 5, 6); there is no difference: For, in saying that knowledge puffeth up while charity edifieth (1 Cor., viii., 1), they spoke of the danger of knowledge—an inevitable danger, in fact, if

knowledge is not counterpoised by Christian humility. Knowledge may even endanger humility; but it is thus with all the developments of human existence, and unless we would institute an agrarian law, at once of knowledge and of land, we must not think to proscribe the culture of our faculties and the development of the mind. If it be said that the apostles had no reference to science with its actual developments, this was because they had it not before their eyes: They sanctioned it, however, without knowing and without foreseeing it. It did not depend on them, it does not depend on us, to reduce this science to a small number of elements: it is what times, and changes, and the adversaries of religion themselves have made it. Friends and enemies have all contributed their aid; and it is sufficient for the justification of real science that knowledge has been recommended. In knowing, at this time, more than the men of the apostolic age, we have not more science than they had; for our science is nothing more than a response to questions which have multiplied since their day.

Is the study which we recommend only that of theology? But what is theology, unless a point of view (the religious point of view) of science, the study of all things as relating to religion? And if the knowledge of the medium in which a thing moves is essential to the knowledge of the thing itself, what is there that a theologian should be permitted to remain voluntarily ignorant of? What an incomplete, false, narrow view would not the theologian have of man and of human life, if he knew theology only in the restricted sense of this word! The simplest of ministers, the least learned, in order to fulfill his ministry, must necessarily look around him. He has also his kind of science—a kind superior in one respect to the pure science of books; and in another, to that ignorant, legal, artful exegesis, to that literalism which makes no account either of common sense or experience, and which infatuates itself with chimeras. All becomes religion for the

Christian, all becomes theology for the theologian; all is application or proof of the truth. Study has a very direct practical importance. There is no development of the human mind which may not be an aid or an obstacle to religion. Nothing is indifferent; all aids or injures. And the most scientific doctrines, the most abstract systems, at the end of a certain time, descend among the people.

We have seen how quickly the fountains of thought will dry up without study: It is with the mind as with the earth; it is the variety or alternation of culture which maintains its fertility.*

* M. Vinet has added in the margin: "As preaching improves by our various reading." This is the complement of the idea. The last two paragraphs received some amplifications in the same lecture, and we think we ought to reproduce them from the note-books of the students.

"We may think, perhaps, that the minister has quite enough to engage him in theology; and that for him the time for studying the profane sciences is past. Let us, first, remark that *profane* is an opprobrious term improperly transferred to things which are not wrong in themselves. For those with whom religion is not every thing, there are, in fact, two spheres, the religious and the profane; but for the Christian nothing is profane; every thing is subservient to holiness. Still, we accept the word, and apply it to sciences which have no necessary connection with religion. What is the meaning of the word *theology*? Its first signification is special: according to this, theology is distinguished from philosophy, from literature, from art, &c. The distinction, no doubt, is useful; but after carefully defining the province of theology, we must not then maintain that it excludes the other sciences. It embraces an immense amount of profane elements; philosophy, history, chronology, grammar, &c. Separating the scientific elements, nothing remains but the religion of the community of believers. It is important, then, to study all that which, as connected with religion, constitutes theology. We must not set absolute and impassable limits. In a wider sense, we may say that theology attracts all to itself, that it subordinates to itself all the sciences, and receives from them their tribute. And without disputing as to the word *theology*, consider that there is not a development of the human

Positions, likewise, are very diverse, and require or permit more or less. There is certainly some difference between a country and a city pastor. But it would be wrong to think that the former might dispense with study; nay, to him it is all the more necessary, as his life is more isolated. We have spoken generally; we have said what ought to be required of an ecclesiastic in an ordinary and a tranquil position. He ought to apply himself to regular, methodical, specific study; to cultivate science liberally, with candor, with a true spirit of research. A minister, doubtless, need not ordinarily re-examine the foundation of his faith; but he may possibly be obliged to do this, as is proved by the example of Richard Baxter, who, finding himself in doubt about every thing, re-established his historical faith by the strongest studies.

To complete what we have now said on the individual life of the pastor, let us add, that he ought to lay out a plan of life, to draw out for himself certain rules; not to allow himself, without any resistance, to be borne and led away by the flow of hours, and by the flux and reflux of affairs. Certainly, no man, in one sense, is less a master of his life than he; nevertheless, he will gain something for his soul, and also for his ministry, by introducing into his life as much of regu-

---

mind which does not either benefit or injure religion. As it borders on every thing, so every thing borders on it. It must embrace all life, under penalty, if it does not, of being banished from it. This is true now more than ever. Our time, notwithstanding its chaotic aspects, is still a time of organization. Piety only can organize the world; and to be organized, the world must be known. Preaching, accordingly, that of the pulpit and that of books, must undergo some modifications. The minister must know many things, not to be cumbered with them, but to serve himself of them with reference to the one thing needful. The more we sift every thing, the more shall we be able "to bring into captivity every thought to the obedience of Christ."—2 Cor., x., 5. The great awakenings have all been promoted by science. The Reformers were the learned men of their age. Unenlightened men have never succeeded in any thing.—*Edit.*

larity as possible, always prepared, nevertheless, to sacrifice regularity to charity. In doing so, he will spare himself much trouble, and gain much time.*

The economy of time is a secret which no one ought better to understand than the minister, since no one as much as he should reverence time, of which eternity is made. He may lose much time without gaining a proportional amount of rest. We save time by doing nothing superfluous, and by not adding superfluous things to our necessary works, and by combining some works with others. We save it by knowing how to defend it against importunity and indiscretion: It is difficult to do this when looked at in a worldly aspect, but easier when regarded as a religious duty.†

We can not here too earnestly recommend to the minister the habit of early rising. The hour of dawn is the golden hour. Later, there is in the mind a sort of noise of all external and internal ideas. At dawn nothing has preceded our impressions, and nothing embarrasses them. Without considering that the minister can answer less than another for what his day is to be, he ought to appreciate more than any other the advantages of this custom. It was thus with the royal

* Duguet refers to a bishop who dismissed persons who interrupted him in his reserved hours with these words: "Sufficient unto the day is the evil thereof."—*Traité des Devoirs d'un Évêque*, art. ii., § 90.

† An aged American pastor relates that in London, at the beginning of his ministry, he visited the Rev. Matthew Wilks, who received him with cordiality. After some moments, when they had told each other the most important religious news they had heard, the conversation dropped. Mr. Wilks broke the silence by saying, "Have you any thing more to tell me?" "Nothing of special interest." "Do you desire any further information from me?" "None." "Then it is best we should separate: I am engaged in my Master's business; good-by, sir." I thus received, continued the pastor, a lesson on the impropriety of encroaching on another's hours, and on the firmness with which we should defend them.—*Anecdotes on the Christian Ministry:* an English work.

prophet, who says, " In the morning will I direct my prayer unto thee, and will look up."—Ps. v., 4. " My heart said to me on thy part, Seek my face."*—Ps. xxvii., 8. " I prevented the dawning of the day, and cried."—Ps. cxix., 147. Now who should say this with more propriety than a minister ?† Moreover, it is a victory over the senses ; and the minister, whatever may be his situation and his views, should act as if he were preparing himself for a career of privations and fatigues : He should, more than any other, be poor in spirit, and exercise himself every day in dying to himself.

This brings us to *ascétisme.*‡

" Bodily exercise profiteth little," says St. Paul.—1 Tim., iv., 8. He speaks elsewhere of human ordinances, which have, as to truth, an appearance of wisdom in will-worship, and in a certain humility, in that they do not spare the body, and that they have no respect to what may satisfy the flesh. —Col., ii., 23.

Saint Paul is against bodily exercise, apart from piety, to which he opposes it in the same verse of the first epistle to Timothy ; and certainly such an exercise does profit little. He found only an " appearance" in human ordinances, of which the principle was self-righteousness and the merit of works. He there opposes in advance, and for all times, the ever reappearing hydra of self-righteousness. But, on the other hand, he would not have us make our liberty a pretext for living after the flesh.—Gal., v., 13. He says elsewhere : " I keep my body under, and bring it into subjection, lest, after having preached to others, I myself should be cast away." —1 Cor., ix., 27. Again, he says : " Make no provision for the flesh, to satisfy the lusts thereof."—Rom., xiii., 14. Hence I do not think that he has condemned, under the name of *bodily exercise*, any thing besides legal practices, " ordinances,"

* The French version.—*Tr.*

‡ Prayer of Bacon. See *Appendix*, note G.

‡ Not asceticism. The French word is retained.—*Transl.*

as he himself calls it; I think he does not condemn exercise as such—voluntary exercise. I do not find, in truth, a trace of fasting, or any thing parallel, in the history of the apostles; but, on the other side, why should these exercises have been mentioned if they had a place, since the apostles' aim was not to permit abolished servitude to put itself in the place of liberty? If these exercises were practiced, it must have been in secret; for they must have conformed themselves to the recommendation of the Savior: "Thou, when thou fastest, anoint thy head and wash thy face, that thou appear not unto men to fast, but unto thy Father, who is in secret."—Matt., vi., 17, 18. Besides, the life which the apostles led was a continual fast, which they had no need to aggravate; exercise was not wanting as to them. It is, however, remarkable that St. Paul, whose life, certainly, was no less a continual fast than that of the other apostles, should have said, "I keep my body under, and bring it into subjection."*—1 Cor., ix., 27.

I do not think that, in a more happy external condition, it is either forbidden or useless to treat our body with severity, and to impose on ourselves, at least now and then, certain privations which our ordinary condition does not impose on us. Moreover, it is well to break through our habits. Do we know to what we are to be called? As to our liberty to do so, "I see that our Lord fasted."—Luke, iv., 21. I see also, in many places, that he supposed the legitimacy of these exercises, forbidding only publicity and ostentation, as the passage above cited proves (Matt., v., 17, 18); and this other place: "When the bridegroom shall be taken from them, then shall they fast" (Matt., ix., 13); which presents fasting under a

* "I was in fasting and in prayers:" Cornelius the centurion.—Acts, x., 30. "That ye may give yourselves to fasting and prayer." —1 Cor., vii., 5. Fasting is always represented as inseparable from prayer; but voluntary fasting is fully sanctioned by this passage: "This kind (of demons) goeth not forth but by prayer and fasting."—Matt., xvii., 21. Now we have demons to cast out.

new aspect, that of a memorial or symbol. Jesus Christ does not recommend the keeping of the Sabbath any more than fasting; He supposes both. The utility of these exercises would be overbalanced, would be absorbed, by the sentiment of self-righteousness, if it should mingle itself with our exercises: But, can not we separate the use from the abuse which corrupts it? We can oppose scarcely any thing to these practices, except the idea of Christian liberty; but in what respect does liberty suffer by an action entirely free? and if there is, in fasting, an appearance of humility which deceives, may there not be, in the suppression of fasting, a liberty which equally deceives?

We now see these things only through the abuse which has been made of them in the Romish Church; but is it through this medium that we ought to look at them? I admit that Massillon, in his sermon on fasting, presents this practice, and recommends it precisely in the sense in which St. Paul condemns it. We must avoid too special prescriptions, which destroy liberty; but liberty has been given to us in order to better obedience.

If it be admitted *that bodily exercise*, supposing it to be free and gratuitous, is generally useful, and even necessary to Christians, it were superfluous to insist much on its utility to pastors. It is, we may add, unnecessary, in any case, to inflict sufferings on ourselves; but we may refuse ourselves lawful enjoyments—even those simple enjoyments, the habitual privation of which would constitute a real injury, and be incompatible with our health.

We ought to remember, in a general way, that the body weighs us down; that by it we are connected with and belong to inert matter; that it is a weight we must throw overboard in order to save the ship. We must not forget that the body is likewise a slave who would be the master: The Christian should treat it with severity. But it is not an intermittent fast which we need; it is a continual fast, one of every day, of the whole life. True fasting, the true *askèse*,* should be applied to the appetites of the mind as well as of the body. Curiosity, ambition, external activity, the desire of influence, the thirst for power, all these appetites, all these attractions, which would turn us out of our course, that is to say, in reality, make us change our course, are very strong and very difficult to vanquish. It is only love, and a holy enthusiasm for our profession, which can carry us through.

* Elsewhere M. Vinet wrote *ascèse*. See page 99.—*Edit.*

PART SECOND

RELATIVE OR SOCIAL LIFE.

CHAPTER I.

SOCIAL LIFE IN GENERAL.

WE are not now to treat of pastoral life in the direct and actual sense. We are to consider it in its relations to general society, regarded, however, from the stand-point and in the concerns of the ministry: not the *office* now, but only the duties.

In this view, however, it is the beginning, the nearer boundary of the ministry. The pastoral impress should show itself in these general relations. If the conduct of the pastor, in these general relations, does not announce him as pastor, it should at least correspond to this character. If we do not recognize him as a pastor, we should at least have no surprise on learning that he is one. Let this be his rule and measure.

It is important for a minister to keep a watch over himself in these social relations. He is a city set upon a hill. In the eyes of the world, he is the representative of Christian ideas, and the majority judge of Christianity by his example.* This, perhaps, will not excuse them, but it involves him in a high responsibility.

* "The people of this world," says Massillon, "regard our life as the reality and the just abatement to which they must adhere." (A passage already cited, page 69.)

The minister is the official Christian; he is a symbolic man. He is so at all times. Those, then, who are not tempted to judge of Christianity by him, will judge him by the Christianity he preaches. In reality, these two things are not alternatives; they both exist. We shall be judged by Christianity, and Christianity by us. We shall not think ourselves obliged to do better, or to be more useful than the pastor; and, on the other hand, we require him to be as perfect as his doctrine. We expect him to be the same when we see and when we hear him. And every one knows very well what he ought to be, for every one knows what a Christian ought to be. And if every one applied to himself the rule which he applies to the pastor, every one would be a model. Men are apt to frame the most exquisite morality as the measure of what is due from their neighbors, and the most relaxed morality as the measure of what is due from themselves. From these two perils the pastor would be tempted to despair, if he did not seek strength from a higher source than the world and himself. The world does more than judge; it binds the pastor to a certain mode of life. Its claims seem to be contradictory. It would seem to require the pastor to be perfect, and to be, at the same time, like other men.* But we may be certain that it knows what the pastor may and ought to be. It is difficult to the minister, as well as to the Christian, to be agreeable to every one; and we should never forget the Scripture, "Woe to you when all men shall speak well of you!"—Luke, vi., 26. But it is possible for him to render himself approved of every one. He may say to the world with St. Paul, "We are made manifest unto God, and I trust also are made manifest in your consciences."—2 Cor., v., 11. In one sense he must seek this approbation: "A pastor," says St. Paul, "must have a good report of those who are without" (1 Tim., iii., 7); with

* Isaiah, xxx., 10; Matt., xi., 27. "We have piped unto you, and you have not danced; we have mourned, and you have not lamented."

stronger reason, doubtless, of those who are in the Church. Thus the approbation of the world, as to all that of which the world can judge, is a thing which the minister must seek, and which he may obtain.

It is at once useful and encouraging to a minister to bear this in mind, while prescribing it to himself as an end and as a supreme rule, "to render himself approved of God" (2 Tim., ii., 15), and while he is preparing himself to say to the world, when it condemns him for what it does not understand, "With me it is a very small thing to be judged of you, or of man's judgment of man" (1 Cor., iv., 3); "If I seek to please men, I shall not be the servant of Christ."—Gal., i., 10. If severe consistency is honored even in evil, much more will it be in good. The condemnation of the world for our acts of fidelity never hurts us, never exposes us to contempt. There is a glory in this reproach, while all worldly complaisance or concession weakens, in every sense, our ministry, and draws reproach upon us.

Let us now see what are the principal traits under which the minister ought to exhibit himself in the general relations of society.

§ 1. *Gravity.*

This quality makes a part of the *relative* life. "A bishop must be grave."—1 Tim., iii., 2. This, as St. Paul says, is one of the first things; it is the first, as the world says.

Our translators employ the words *grave* and *gravity* to render,

Κόσμιος (1 Tim., iii., 2), translated by Luther, *sittig;* by De Wette, *anstændig;* and by the English, *of good behavior.*

Σεμνός (1 Tim., iii., 11, in speaking of the pastor's wife), translated by Luther and De Wette, *ehrbar;* and by the English, *grave.*

Σεμνότης (Tit., xi., 7), translated by Luther, *ehrbarkeit;* by De Wette, *würde;* and by the English, *gravity.*

Gravity, from the word *gravis*, is the weight, more or less considerable, which an interest, an evil, &c., possesses. In external life and in manners it is whatever announces that a man bears the weight of a great thought or a great responsibility. The minister is the depositary of so great a thought, so great a responsibility, that gravity is but decency in his profession. It may be defined, the impress of the respect we bear for the object of our mission.

It is evident that external gravity is true and commendable only in so far as it answers to an internal gravity, which is the feeling of the weight of the responsibility with which we are charged. Gravity is not " a bodily mysteriousness, whose end is to hide the weakness of the mind."*

Nothing is more contrary to gravity than the affectation of gravity. "A too studied gravity," says La Bruyère, "becomes ludicrous: extremities meet; the mean between them is dignity. That is not being grave, but acting gravity: He who tries to be grave never will be. Either there is no gravity, or it is natural; and it is less difficult to descend from it than to arise to it."† But much less must we affect the contrary. There have been ecclesiastics who, wishing too much to avoid alarming, have ended by compromising. This is seen particularly among the Catholics, because the quality of the priest—his habits, his dress—distinguish him from the world; and the frivolity by which he would remove the distinction makes it more apparent. "Could we not make persons of a certain character, and of a serious profession—to describe them no further—understand that they need not have it said of them that they play, they sing, they joke, like other men; and that, to see them so pleasant and so agreeable, one would not think they were also so regular and so strict? Would one even dare to insinuate to them, that, by such manners, they remove themselves from that politeness on which they

* La Rochefoucauld, *Réflexions Morales*, cclvii.

† La Bruyère, *Les Caractères*; in the chapter *Des Jugemens*

pique themselves; that, on the contrary, politeness suits and conforms externals to conditions; that it avoids contrast, and the exhibition of the same man under different figures, which make him a fantastic and grotesque compound?"*

Gravity shows itself in *manners* in general, and *discourse* in particular.

Under the general idea of manners, I class *society*, *recreations*, *occupations*, and *costume*.

As to society—we should not, certainly, restrict ourselves to seeing only one kind of persons, for fear of accrediting the false idea that the minister is not a man; but we should still more carefully avoid being seen every where. The pastor is a social man—not a man of society, still less a man of the world. He should make himself scarce, unless prohibited by charity, which alone is allowed to make him common. A man who is seen every where can not inspire respect. The judgment we form of a pastor who goes much into society is not very favorable. We suspect him of not being sensible of his duties, and of the need of solitude. Society multiplies the occasions for doing good, but much more the temptations to do evil. Then there are men whom the pastor should see neither at home nor elsewhere. St. Paul charges Timothy to avoid certain persons: Men whose lives are bad, and, above all, those who have the form of godliness, but deny its power. —2 Tim., iii., 5.

More than another, the minister should be select as to his associates. Others will be critical for him, and consequently severe, if he is not so for himself. This is important in order not only to preserve an exterior, to regard conventionalities, but to shun a real danger. To ministers, as well as others, this maxim applies: "Be not deceived: evil communications corrupt good manners."—1 Cor., xv., 33. "Strangers have devoured his strength, and he knoweth it not; yea, gray hairs are here and there upon him, yet he knoweth not."—

* La Bruyère, *Les Caractères;* in the chapter *Des Jugemens.*

Hosea, vii., 9. And this, too: "He who loves danger will perish in danger." How can he seek bad society, when good is so necessary to him, and when he can not be too much surrounded, too much sustained by those who fear God?

Massillon would have a priest see priests only. "Permit me here," he says, "to repeat what St. Paul formerly upbraided his disciples with, who, instead of addressing themselves to their brethren, to settle their disputes, had recourse to gentile judges: *Sic non est inter vos sapiens quisquam?* What! can you not find among your brethren wise and amiable ministers to relax yourselves with from the seriousness of your occupations? *Sic non est inter vos sapiens quisquam?* Is it possible that, amid so many ecclesiastics of agreeable manners, edifying, and creditable to you, you need to call the world to your aid, and seek recreations where you should only be attending to your functions and your labors?"* It would, however, be an exaggeration to hold one's self rigorously to such a rule. We must give no countenance to the melancholy idea that the minister is not a man, nor deprive him of what society may give, may teach him.

Moreover, the pastor has a family, a domestic interior, which may, if need be, take the place of a more various society. Old relationships, contracted under unhappy auspices, are often very embarrassing. We must not disregard the past, and break these relationships: All is providential: God may serve himself of one to bless another. If it be impossible to preserve them, let them be dissolved, but without violence. As to our domestic relationships, we must neither break nor dissolve, but sanctify them. The family is the pastor's first parish.

Recreations or *Relaxations.*—It is difficult, on this subject, to give very precise rules. When I say that the minister has need of recreations as well as another man; when I say

* MASSILLON: *Discours sur la Manière dont les Ecclésiastiques doivent converser avec les Personnes du Monde.—Première Reflexion.*

that, on the other hand, there are recreations which, in a simple believer, give no scandal, but which, on the part of a minister, may scandalize the weak; that all which is lawful is not edifying, and that the minister of Jesus Christ should always edify; in short, that, to a certain extent, conventionalities vary with places, I say the whole: good sense must supply the rest. Only let me remind young candidates of the apostle's remark: "Let no man despise thy youth."—1 Tim., iv., 12. Notwithstanding the form, this is truly a command. And, again, the apostle was careful to say to Timothy, "Flee youthful lusts."—2 Tim., ii., 22. This was the only means of securing his youth against contempt; and we may suppose that these restrictions were more seasonable in youth than afterward. We must take care of indulgence on the side to which we are already propense. There are amusements which we must renounce: The chase, gaming, the theatre; under a certain form, music, and, in general, a passionate taste for any art. None of these things are seemly in a minister; the effect upon him will not be good, and it will expose him to censure.

He must avoid, also, being seen, without necessity, in places even the most respectable, where the public come to divert themselves. One can not answer for the company which he may find there, nor for what may take place there. The minister, truly, may adopt this maxim: "It is better to go to the house of mourning than to the house of feasting; for that is the end of all men, and the living will lay it to his heart."—Eccl., vii., 2.

We do not mean that all these abstinences render him who imposes them on himself holy. He who does not impose them on himself, even though he does wrong therein, is perhaps holier than one who spares himself none of them. We may "strain at a gnat and swallow a camel."—Matt., xxiii., 24.

As to *occupations*, we do not yet say that the minister, according to the apostolic precept (1 Tim., iv., 15), should occupy himself in these things (that is to say, the things of his ministry), and be always occupied in them. We shall return to this subject. But in respect of gravity, and supposing that the pastor has more leisure than generally belongs to him, we say that every occupation does not accord with the gravity of the ministry. I do not like agricultural, industrial feats: If a minister has property, let him take care of it; but let him proceed in this kind of work no further than is necessary. In things of this kind, the mere reputation of aptitude will injure him.

Costume, or rather *dress* (for we do not speak of the official costume, or of the insignia of the pastor, in public functions)—costume has the double object of impressing him who wears it and others.

The importance of this badge varies with time. Our time, having little liking for metaphors in social life, or, perhaps, seeking other symbols here, seems disposed to abolish gradually a solemn costume. But no one, as to this, should be in haste to give an example. It is in this almost as with neologisms in language, for costume is a language: It must, in all cases, be freely accepted. It will always be expected that the dress of a minister, if it be not one worn only by ministers, should have a uniform and invariable character; while a man of any other profession may vary his apparel.

It would be better, even, not to wear costume, than in a manner to disavow it by negligence or impropriety.*

Gravity in Discourse.—To speak little is the first rule: To joke little is the second:† To discuss moderately, to

* Propriety, a half virtue, which may unite to itself a true and whole virtue.

† Ephesians, v., 4. (Εὐτραπελία, scurrilitas).—Nugæ in aliis sunt nugæ, in sacerdotibus blasphemiæ.

St. Bernard: *Traité de la Considération*, liv. iii., chap. xiii.

Bien loin aussi le rire intempérant:
Du rire amer il est peu différant;

abridge discussions, is the third: Not to have a loud voice and high-sounding speech is the fourth. "He shall not cry, nor lift up his voice."—Isaiah, xlii., 2. Calmness is imposing. Peace is a silent thunder-bolt. "The God of peace shall bruise Satan under your feet."—Rom., xvi., 20. I add, care to speak of things rather than of persons. I mean, not only care to avoid evil speaking, which need not be said, but every thing which savors of curiosity, and resembles gossiping. I do not like, however, an affected reserve.

Besides, we must remember that the Christian, and with greater reason the pastor, should speak according to the oracles of God (which does not mean only announcing the oracles of God), that the word of Christ should dwell in him richly with all wisdom (Col., iii., 16); that his words should be seasoned with salt, and communicate grace to those who hear; and that, if every one will be required to give account of the idle words which he shall speak, this account will be yet more severe for the pastor. It may, perhaps, be well to remark, that while prescribing to themselves a kind of restraint when in the world, ministers are sometimes tempted to be too free among themselves: ecclesiastical gossiping has, in certain countries, passed into a proverb.*

I have but little hope from the official gravity of one (and but little respect for it) who, in private, violates the decorum which should never be dispensed with in the most intimate relationships, though I would by no means deprive ministers of the sweets of familiar intercourse.

Folle gaîté dégénère en satire;
Tel, qui, d'abord, ne riait que pour rire,
Lance en riant un trait (dard) envenimé,
Et se dérobe à lui-même, ô délire!
En le perçant, un cœur qui l'eût aimé.

* "In no profession are there so many story-tellers (*Anecdochen Kræmer*) as in the clerical, as there is none that furnishes so many anecdotes as this."—Harms. Whence this second circumstance? I well know that it is so.

It is not necessary to be always prescribing rules for the exercise of gravity; on the contrary, this should never be done; for gravity, when it is natural, comes from within.

§ 2. *Simplicity, Modesty.*

Simplicity is opposed to affected dignity and reserve (I should say, *emphasis*, if this word could be applied to manners as it is to language); faults which proceed not from an excessive gravity, but from an undue sense of our own importance and authority. We may, perhaps, look to the severe strictures of the world to correct this vanity. The official character of the pastor is every day becoming less and less imposing; though every one who is not exceedingly ill bred will be disposed to accord to the pastor a certain measure of respect, simply on account of his profession and his position in the civil community. The external character, the dress, are things of small importance, if they have nothing within to sustain them. We gain little, on the contrary we lose, by claiming a blind respect, and taking a rank in society which is not yielded to us. Clerical reserve and stateliness impose on but a small number, and I should not recommend them even with this small number. It is unworthy of a minister to use such means—not to depend simply upon the truth, of which he is the organ, but to seem to think that a mysterious virtue attaches to him. Catholic sermons demand respect for the priests, a thing which can be better understood, since here the priest personifies religion. All this, moreover, may be said without prejudice to authority. The minister has not to ask pardon for the truth.

§ 3. *Pacific Spirit.*

Is he not a man of peace, who is called to "make peace" (Matt., v., 9)? who is a minister of that wisdom "which is first pure, then peaceable" (James, iii., 17); who is a disciple and representative of Him who "did not cry, nor contend, nor lift up his voice in the streets?"—Isaiah, xlii., 2. Moreover, knows he not, from the Bible and from experience, "that the fruit of righteousness is sown in peace?"—James, iii., 18. "If it be possible, as much as lieth in you, live peaceably with all men."—Rom., xiii., 18.

It is precisely because his ministry is a warfare that this recommendation is important. It must not be forgotten that, as a minister, he stretches out hands "all the day long to a rebellious and gainsaying people" (Rom., x., 21); that he is called to rebuke sinners, and even in certain cases to rebuke them publicly (1 Tim., v., 20); that, as a minister and a Christian, he appears upon a stage furrowed with controversies; that there is not a truth whose remembrance is not interlaced with that of an error; that theology is hardly less a discussion than an exposition; that, if his convictions are serious, he has borne them away as rich spoils of victory, dipped in his own blood; and, in short, that he will have, on more than one occasion, to defend the rights of his ministry.

St. Paul might very properly have thought of all this when he said, "That a bishop must not be self-willed (Titus, i., 7); and "that the servant of the Lord must not love strife."—2 Tim., ii., 24. And this not only includes litigation, but disputes, useless or endless discussions, an impracticable punctilious spirit, the love of trifles.*

We can not say that ministers are exempt from this spirit: The habit of living always in the same circle of ideas, occupations, and persons, that of speaking without being contradicted, so that the first and smallest contradiction surprises them, may contribute to it. The world exaggerates, I would fain think, when it says that, in general, they are not distinguished by the facility of their intercourse, and that they are thorny men, with whom one fears to have to do; but to

* Assemblies consuming their time in discussing small concerns.

silence the world on this point, it is necessary to be of a very peaceable spirit. It must be understood that I speak here of ordinary occasions of dispute, arising from the ordinary relations of society, and not of controversies, properly so called, nor of the *odium theologicum,* the best name, it is thought, for hatred par excellence ; and with reason, too, for when one hates in the name of God, he does not hate by halves.

It is, surely, enough for a pastor to find contention in the precincts of his office, and not to be able to avoid it on that stage: He can not restrict himself, like other believers, "to replying with gentleness and respect to those who ask a reason of his hope."—1 Peter, iii., 15. He must, perhaps, engage in discussion, if there is every security for seriousness, order, and decorum : But, on the one hand, he ought not to "cast pearls before swine ;" on the other, he is more frequently called to expound than to discuss, and he should not too easily give up the first of these positions. There is a way of retaining it ; a peaceful spirit is not a stupid one.

§ 4. *Gentleness.*

"Let your moderation be known unto all men."—Phil., iv., 5. There is something particularly imposing in gentleness, since we can not but be struck with it at the first view. We shall speak more at large of the charity of the pastor when we are to examine his office ; it is there that it fully displays itself. Here we have only to look at his gentleness, that is to say, his exhibition of obliging, affable, prepossessing, amiable qualities in the ordinary relations of society. He is the man of the good God : He is the representative of mercy : He ought not to repel, but to attract : But all must come naturally, without affectation ; there should be no studied part ; for a studied part in this matter is never well acted His goodness is not soft and effeminate, but manly. Better a little rudeness than that benign and paternal air which some adopt in despite of their nature. Charity has sometimes rudeness for its true form; gentleness is sometimes treachery; we may exercise charity in vehemence and indignation. But a rude, magisterial air, a short, reprimanding tone, or one of impatience, of humor, of haughtiness, or a want of politeness, or even an air of indifference and ennui (all things not entirely inconsistent with charity), how much will they not injure the minister and the ministry!

§ 5. *Loyalty, Integrity, Candor.*

It was to ministers that it was said, "Be wise as serpents, and harmless as doves."—Matt., x., 16. These two precepts are presented in the text as having their ground in the same fact; namely, that the apostles, in the midst of the world, would find themselves as sheep in the midst of wolves. Jesus Christ hence inferred the double necessity of being harmless and wise. Perhaps, also, it must be understood that he recommends them to be wise, consistently with integrity and candor. The first interpretation is more literal, the second more natural. We may admit them both. Candor is necessary, because wisdom is so. The minister knows better than any other what consequences a single word may involve, and consequences, as to him, are eternal and terrible. Wisdom is so strongly recommended to a minister, that we think he can not have too much of it. Even in the most favorable circumstances, the difficulty of his position tempts him to be prudent to excess. What dangers! Mere inadvertences, inconsideration, vivacity, even accidentally neglecting to avoid the appearances of evil, proceedings which repel and alarm, indiscretion in words, precipitancy in judgments, ill-placed confidence; the possibility of being engaged and drawn away by what does not pertain to him, and is inconsistent with his character; the thought that there are so many who, without seeming to do so, without saying any thing, have an eye upon him, spy out his first weakness, take note of it in order to justify their opposing him, or, rather, make him their authority for hardening themselves after his example to do evil, or who seek to put him in contradiction with himself, and give him a bad standing with the world, with the civil authority, with those of whom he has the confidence:—how many things are there to render him not only wise, but mistrustful, reserved, and suspicious! If he do not consider all this, he risks much; if he consider it too much, he loses that simplicity of the dove which is his duty, his character, his first interest, since public confidence is his first want; in short, which on almost every occasion is better than all calculations. Nothing, in fact, disconcerts artful people like simplicity; they do not comprehend it; they can not anticipate it. It is impossible to estimate the influence of these transparent characters. Finesse, on the contrary, so inspires distrust, that even the reputation of shrewdness injures more than it helps us: We can command the confidence of the world only by a consistent exhibition of the greatest candor.

St. Paul deeply felt these truths. He testifies more than once that his conduct was without artifice.—2 Cor., iv., 2. It rejoices him to say, that in him there was no yea and nay. —2 Cor., i., 18. He ventures to rebuke an apostle who did not walk uprightly.—Gal., ii., 14.

This condemns falsehood, inaccurate statements, dissimulation, breaking one's word, or a facility in forgetting one's engagements, artifices and evasions, an extreme reserve, censures or complaints in the way of insinuation, cowardly allusions, groundless mistrust, excessive precautions, diplomacy, which some consider an honor to ministers, etc.

Nothing is more opposed to candor than party spirit, which believes only itself, never really discusses, hears only for form's sake, neither allows that we are wrong, or that we are ignorant; colors, palliates, explains without end, distinguishes without ceasing, and thinks it is to be strong and to manifest power, never to make a concession.

§ 6. *Disinterestedness.**

Disinterestedness, certainly, is but one form of a general virtue, the abnegation of self. It is necessary, however, to say something of self-denial in this particular—detachment from worldly gain. Absolute disinterestedness is complete indifference of heart for temporal goods. This degree of perfection is certainly too little sought by the majority ; and we know, also, that it is realized by no one : But, nevertheless, it is an object for which we should strive ; and to strive for it, a pastor, besides general reasons which we shall not mention, has particular ones of which we must speak.

1. The spirit of the ministry is a spirit of consecration. The minister has already renounced his life : He has sacrificed the greater, how can he retain the less ? For him were written the words, " He who putteth his hand to the plow, and looketh back, is not fit for the kingdom of God." —Luke, ix., 62. " Every man that striveth is temperate in all things."—1 Cor., ix., 25. Consecration is incompatible with the love of riches. " The hireling seeth the wolf coming ; he forsaketh the sheep, and fleeth."—John, x., 12.

2. Our mission, our avowed undertaking, is to detach from the earth those to whom we preach. We endeavor to make them covet the happiness of the poor in spirit (or of voluntary poverty). How can we do this with freedom, with force, with success, if we ourselves are attached to those goods from which we would detach them ? How, in proportion as we preach detachment, do we increase our condemnation if we remain ourselves enchained to the goods of the present life ? The more we preach to others, though it be with success, shall we not be the more sure of being cast away ?—1 Cor., ix., 27.

* Fr., *Désintéressement.* There is no English word of precisely the same meaning with this. Disinterestedness is used to avoid circumlocution. The exact meaning of it here will not be mistaken by the reader.—*Tr.*

3. We are representatives of Jesus Christ, who made himself poor.—2 Cor., viii., 9. Was it without meaning that he made himself poor? Was it not enough to become man? He had not what the birds had, a nest; nor the foxes, a hole: he had not where to lay his head. A single passage in the Gospel speaks of a place where, at a certain time, Jesus Christ dwelt; and nothing leads us to think that it was more than a temporary abode.—John, i., 38, 39.

4. We are representatives of Christianity, the spirit of which is not to depend on the visible, but on the invisible, and which seeks security where others think to find danger, I mean in a precarious situation.* Can we have a spirit different from it, and yet represent it faithfully, seeking not security only, which even is perhaps too much, but comfort, superfluity, and wealth?

5. The minister is the great almoner of the Church. Distributor of the wealth of others, he ought also to do as much as possible from his own means; even when it would seem that he might be a receiver, it will be expected of him to give. Now the love of worldly good excludes charity and alms-giving.

6. It was said directly to ministers, "The love of money is the root of all evil; which, while some coveted after, they have erred from the faith; but thou, O man of God, flee these things."—1 Tim., vi., 10, 11. We may well say, surely, *Have erred from the faith*, since Judas for silver betrayed

* Jesus Christ desired ministers who would of choice and from love fulfill the office of embassadors: But how do the prospects of fortune, and even too much security for the future, tend to obscure the evidence of their vocation? Precariousness is the soul of every thing pertaining to Christianity, and works of faith prosper only by the principle which has given them existence. It was to consecrate this principle that Jesus Christ made himself poor in every sense, that his disciples did so after him, and that St. Paul lived from the work of his hands; "*wearying* himself even by working with his own hands."—1 Cor., iv., 12.

his master. This avarice is the principle of unfaithfulness and prevarication. It is very remarkable that the fear of prison and of death has made fewer apostates than the love of money. But without speaking of formal apostasy, we may say that no vice is so destructive of virtue, or more incompatible with all elevation of soul and spirit.* It is, perhaps, the most absorbing passion: "Greediness of gain takes away the soul of those who are addicted to it."—Prov., i., 19.

7. Again, nothing more estranges the heart and destroys confidence than avarice; I say not scandalous avarice, but the first appearance of it, or even the mere thought that disinterestedness is wanting. The mercenary pastor draws around him only mercenary souls like himself. "The sheep will not follow a stranger."—John, x., 5. The living will seek for the living, the dead will stay with the dead. While, on the contrary, disinterestedness convinces before examination, implies sincerity, and presupposes truth. Charity, in the eyes of the world, covers a multitude of sins.

8. Frankness readily deserts him who is held in the ignoble bonds of interest, not only because interest weakens in us the principle of this virtue, but because it is not always possible to be frank when we are not independent. A secret, dishonorable instinct impels us to management even when it is useless.

9. Even the appearance of this vice is to be dreaded, because it is the first thing which infidels suspect or espy in those who believe. This is natural: Religion is so powerful that it engages us to make all sacrifices in favor of eternity; and these sacrifices are made with ease, and they are often made to the profit of those who represent the interest or the idea of eternity.

In all *human* religions, it has been seen that the superstitious terrors of the human heart have been made to subserve

* "Nihil est tam angusti, tamque parvi quam amare divitias."—Cicero: *De Officiis*, lib. i.

the cupidity of certain individuals. St. Paul readily recognized that there were, and always would be, persons who make piety a means of wealth, and he exhorts Timothy to separate himself from them, more, unquestionably, by a life different from theirs, than by care to shun their company.—1 Tim., vi., 5. He stigmatizes, no doubt, sordid and hypocritical ministers in 2 Tim., iii., 6, 7: "Of this number are those who creep into houses, and lead captive silly women, laden with sins, possessed with divers lusts; ever learning, and never able to come to the knowledge of the truth." After, as well as before the time of Jesus Christ, there were those "who devoured widows' houses, and for a pretense made long prayers."—Matt., xxiii., 14. We do not see these scandals about us, but yet they are possible, and they sometimes appear in another form. A pastor may take advantage of his influence over his charge to indulge in pleasures which should be repressed. This makes the world suspicious: they are very apt to think that ministers are covetous; whether it be that this is the vice which oftenest appears, or that it is the one, in fact, to which we are most liable, it is that of which the world most frequently accuses us. The minister, by watchfulness, may readily avoid certain deviations, but avarice glides easily into the heart; and there are many ministers who expose themselves to this reproach, if no other. Wrongly or rightly, it is often ascribed to them.*

We must not be surprised that St. Paul directed himself

* "This vice, it would seem, is a curse attached to the priesthood." —Massillon, neuvième discours synodal: *De l'Avarice des Prêtres.* "The world regards almost all of us as infected, soiled by this hideous leprosy. A priest and a covetous man it regards as identical."—Massillon, troizième discours synodal: *De la Compassion des Pauvres.*

"Episcopi plurimi, quos et ornamento esse oportet cæteris et exemplo, divina procuratione contempta, procuratores rerum sæcularium fieri; derilectâ cathedrâ, plebe desertâ, per alienas provincias oberrantes, negotiationis, quæsturæ nundinas ancupari."—Cyprian, *De Lapsis.*

particularly to this point. He saw the danger ministers were in of falling into avarice, and the danger of their being accused of it. He anticipated this double evil. He was not content with saying, "That a bishop must not be given to filthy lucre."—Tit., i., 7. He contends more forcibly, by indirect means, but especially by his example, which, humble as he is, he ventures to set forth and remark upon: "We have wrought with labor and travail, night and day, that we might not be chargeable to any of you," etc.—2 Thess., iii., 8, 9. See, also, 1 Cor., iv., 12. In the ninth chapter of the first epistle to the Corinthians, the apostle recognizes, as he does elsewhere (1 Tim., v., 17, 18), the duty of believers to assist their pastors; but he renounces for himself all advantage from this right. In verses 14–19, of the twelfth chapter of the second epistle which he addresses to them, he abandons every sort of right; he gives without any hope or any claim of requital.

In taking leave, at Miletus, of the pastors of Ephesus, Paul reminds them of his conduct in this respect, and thence deduces for them this lesson: "I have coveted no man's silver or gold, or apparel; yea, ye yourselves know that these hands have ministered unto my necessities, and to them who were with me. I have showed you all things, how that so laboring ye ought to support the weak, and to remember the words of the Lord Jesus, how he said, It is more blessed to give than to receive."—Acts, xx., 33–35. And this truly was the spirit of pastors in the primitive Church, and of bishops long afterward, who gave away all their goods.

All Scripture brands avarice as a vice the most fatal to the ministry. It makes "hireling" a name for a bad minister.*

* Numerous passages of Holy Scripture against avaricious or mercenary pastors: Isaiah, lvi., 11; Jer., vi., 13; Ezek., xxxiv., 1, 3; Micah, iii., 11; Matt., xv., 5, 6; xxiii., 14.—*Passages collected by* BRIDGES.

After showing the importance of avoiding avarice, let us say that it is a vice by which we are incessantly beset. Not without reason did our Savior say: "Take heed, and beware of covetousness" (Luke, xii., 15); and desired his apostles to take no purse with them. Judas, nevertheless, carried the bag; there was then a steward, but this does not impair our rule.

1. This vice may glide into our heart under favorable appearances the best fitted to deceive us, by pretexts the best fitted to seduce us, and by the most insensible gradations. We may be prodigal, and at the same time avaricious, and the first of these vices may deceive us as to the second. We may be decidedly, and for a long time avaricious, without suspecting it. Of all sophisms, none does more evil than that we owe all our wealth to our children; we forget that, before all, we owe it to God. With many people, avarice is a mental mistake, joined, it is true, to a malady of the heart. Francis de Sales says that, in the whole course of his practice as a confessor, he heard no one blame himself with avarice.

2. It is a vice which inherits from all others, and in which is concentrated every unlawful desire of the heart. It grows with years; we may be avaricious when we are no longer able to indulge other passions.

3. It is the vice most compatible with the outward forms of Christianity, with decency, and a certain gravity of manners, although there is a point at which it becomes scandalous. Paul doubtless considered it as having reached this point when he said, "If one called a brother is avaricious, do not eat with such a man."—1 Cor., v., 11. Avarice then might more easily become scandalous than now, by its contrast with that disinterestedness which led the brethren to have all things in common. This is not the case with us, and now it is more difficult to detect this vice.

4. It is the vice to which we are most exposed by our position, which peremptorily cuts us off from all other vices,

and permits us this one ; it seems in some way to breathe itself into us, by means of those petty calculations to which it forces us.

5. Finally, it is the vice most difficult to eradicate. Once give it footing, reason, ridicule, self-love, modesty, can not prevail against it.*

What the duty of disinterestedness includes :

1. Not to embrace the ministry from motives of interest: "Taking the oversight of the flock of God, not for unlawful gain (filthy lucre), but of a ready mind."—1 Peter, v., 2. The *unlawful gain* of which St. Peter speaks is gain coveted. This *unlawful gain* is well commented on in these words: "Freely ye have received ; freely give."—Matt., x., 8. The supplies of believers, then, though due to them, are not a salary, but a subsidy—a succor. "Those who serve the altar are partakers with the altar."—1 Cor., ix., 13. The idea of gratuity then remains, and we have seen how St. Paul labored to consecrate it by his example. The hireling is likened to a thief.—John, x. Micah, after having said, in order to show the iniquity of Jerusalem, "The heads thereof judge for rewards," adds, "the priests thereof teach for hire, and the prophets thereof divine for money."—Mic., iii., 11. Our institutions, in this respect, offer advantages. One may, indeed, become a minister for the sake of the prebend ; but no bait is offered to cupidity ; he is made to wait long for the ease which is promised him.† We may then readily apply to the minister these words of the Savior : "Ye seek me not because ye saw the miracles, but because ye did eat of the loaves and were filled."—John, vi., 26.

2. Not to take advantage of our position for the sake of

* Imagination has to do with this vice. See Advices of Madame Guizot, *Education Domestique*, Letter xxxi.

† *Tandem respicit inertem sera tamen.* "Ease is seen at length, but late, by him who does nothing to acquire it." Allusion to the 27th verse of the first Eclogue of Virgil.—*Ed.*

gain. This sort of selfish calculation is not always possible. Nevertheless, the independence of the ministry may be easily compromised by those cajoleries, those presents, which can not always be refused.* Affection, even delicacy, may sometimes require that they be accepted; but one "should guard himself well, lest he be penetrated with the love of gain."

3. Not to seek, in foreign occupations which are not suitable to us, the means of improving our position.

4. To be, in money matters, as free and liberal as our position will admit.

As to the means of being disinterested: There is an economy which preserves us from avarice or its paroxysms; for prodigality and disorder often make us avaricious. It is with money as with time: he who manages it the best has the most to give to others. In the same way, also, a man of economy is in the best condition to be liberal on appropriate occasions. To be disinterested, we must have no expensive fancies, and not be too much taken up with the things of sense, of the flesh, or vanity. Certain habits procure so little pleasure to many of those who give themselves up to them, that one might say that they are sought as a means of trying new modes of existence, or of multiplying, not their enjoyments, but their sensations.

This means supposes another, which is the chief and the only efficacious one: This is charity. We may correct a vice by a virtue. It is necessary to *displace* avarice, according to a beautiful thought of Quesnel, who says that "the passion of always gaining more souls to God is the only avarice permitted to a pastor."

The maxims of the Catholic Church on this subject are remarkable. "The good pastor," says St. Cyran, "loves the poor, and bestows upon them the whole of his goods."†

* These are but casual; nevertheless, private religious instruction; in some places, funeral services, marriages, &c.

† SAINT CYRAN: *Pensées sur le Sacerdoce.*

The Catholic Church reproaches the priests who have property.* Many have even maintained that, according to the example of the bishops of the early age, the priest should once for all deprive himself of every thing. Duguet represses this idea, but with caution and deference.† It is evident that the unmarried pastor is more free in this respect than the pastor who is married. The latter ought not to deprive himself of his goods, but to use them, and to administer them himself according to the will of God who has given them to him. Jesus Christ said to his Father, "I pray not that thou shouldst take them out of the world, but that thou shouldst keep them from the evil."—John, xvii., 15.

§ 7. *The Minister in Relation to the general Interests of Society.*

We have shown under what characteristics the pastor should appear, and how he should announce himself. It is every one's duty to preach by example. It remains to ask what, apart from his pastoral functions, should he be in his relations to general society. Does he belong only to his parish? does he belong only to religion? Should he remain a stranger to the high interests of society?

It appears at first that, as religion adopts the whole of human life in order to elevate it, the pastor, who is the most perfect representative of religion, ought, in the same degree, to be a representative of human life.

There are striking instances of priests and monks, who were distinguished as instruments of civilization, promoters of science,‡ etc.

* See, on this point, MASSILLON, in many passages, and, for example, in his synodal discourse, *Sur la Compassion des Pauvres*.

† *Lettres sur différents Sujets de Morale et de Piété*, t. ii., p. 6 et 22.

‡ See MALTE-BRUN: *Mélanges Scientifiques et Littéraires*, tome i., page 324 (*On the Norwegian Clergy*).

The nature of his studies and the exercise of his functions develop faculties in the minister which, in the different spheres of human life, find an abundant application.

Talleyrand has said that nothing so prepares one for diplomacy as theology.* In fact, the studies of the ministry are more comprehensive than all others; the study of theology is more *humanizing* than any other, even than that which has social interest and social affairs for its object.

We agree to all this, and we acknowledge that duties may vary with times; but we must make the following reservations:

1. Religion is a speciality. It embraces every thing, it penetrates every thing, but it is not every thing; it is itself. To connect itself usefully with the things of life, it must separate itself from them. Christianity has been in no haste to mix itself with the life of the people, or, where it has done so, it has been dynamically, as a spirit. It should be the same with each individual. He must be well rooted at the centre, to spread his shade over the circumference. Let the minister be first of all occupied with his own affairs; let him be solely a Christian and a minister: As a consequence, his branches will spread out, and his beneficent shade extend itself over all the affairs of society.

2. There is, in the direct and immediate purpose of the ministry, so much good to be done, that one need not run after indirect good. The minister should seek to give a point of rest to the human family, and this resting-point is religious truth: When humanity shall have found it, then it will march directly to its destination. The minister may honor his mission by conferring external advantages; still, when there are others to do this, let him confine himself to his calling. He may employ himself in agriculture, when it is necessary, also in schools, and in religious music; but, before every thing, he should be about his ministry. Nevertheless, when

* *Eloge du Comte de Reinhard.*

it is his duty to act, as did Oberlin and Felix Neff, by all means let him do it without hesitation!

3. Is it not an advantage for the minister to be compromised in nothing, and to be able to come in as an arbiter in every thing, being, as he will be in that case, personally aloof from every thing? If, on the contrary, he interferes too readily in the things that do not concern his ministry, he will often find himself a judge and a party, and will no longer be able to pronounce so impartially.

4. The danger to religion is great when a minister, as a minister, mixes himself with temporal interests, and gives to religion a kind of authority and competency which is inconsistent with it. What stains will it receive!

Let us touch upon a particular point—politics. Let us distinguish it from patriotism, which, if not a Christian virtue, is at least an affection which Christianity adopts and sanctifies, and a duty to which, as to all others, it lends the force of its teachings: Jesus Christ experienced this affection; Jesus Christ has recognized this sentiment; and St. Paul in like manner.* Participation in political affairs is neither the only nor the best mark which a citizen can give of his patriotism; it is one among other specialities that we do not think forbidden to Christians, but it is by no means imposed upon them.

It has seemed desirable to some persons that ministers should engage in politics.† I do not think it the part of a pastor; as for one who has no longer the care of souls, and who has become a politician, he changes his career, that is

* Romans, ix., 1–5.

† "Nothing in the interests of humanity," says M. Naville, "appears to be a greater mistake than to wish to banish from assemblies, from theatres, from debates, and the periodical press, from the spheres where thoughts and sentiments are agitated, the very men whose presence and influence are required to give them a salutary result." —*Mémoire sur l'Amour de la Patrie Suisse*, p. 98, 99: *Genève*, 1839. See, also, the work of Dr. Brown, *The Law of Christ respecting civil Obedience*, p. 228.

all. It is not for us to judge him ; and, in general, we would not condemn him ; we must suppose that he has renounced the ministry proper, for which these occupations are far from preparing him. But how can a pastor intermeddle with politics without destroying his success, and even his respectability as a minister ?

I do not speak precisely of the presence of pastors in assemblies representing the nation : That does not constitute a political career ; but, in general, they are, when there, hardly in their place.* It would not, perhaps, be just to exclude them ; but they would do well voluntarily to exclude themselves. There is too great a distance between the political and the pastoral life : Pastors do not acquire, from the exercise of their functions, the kind of spirit which these assemblies demand, nor reciprocally : We should expect to see them preaching there : As to religious questions, which should never be discussed there, there is no need of the presence of ministers in order that they may be well treated : The stains of political discussion are too easily seen on the pastoral robe—ministers can not avoid hearing things there which their profession at the same time urges and forbids them to answer.

There is another way, and there are other channels, through which religion may infuse itself into politics.

Politics, in promoting religion, has forced religion to promote politics ; but both, in this course, have been corrupted, and the second more than the first. Burnet, who knew how to speak on this subject, has some remarks on the injury which religion does itself by mixing itself with politics (a thing inevitable, I affirm, in the union of Church and State), which I will cite here : "Politics and parties eat out among us not only study and learning, but the only thing which is still more valuable than study and learning; I mean, religious sentiment, and a sincere zeal to obtain results for which the Son

* It is not even seen that the deliberations of ecclesiastical bodies are profitable to them.

of God was willing to live and die, and to which those who are engaged in his service have promised to consecrate their lives and their labors." In short, let us not condemn beforehand all extension of the ministry, nor undertake to define its limit; we think that, at the exigency of the times, it is susceptible of an indefinite extension; but these times have their signs, which it is necessary to attend to and to understand.*

* Is the ministry, as it is now understood and practiced, restricted within the limits of the primitive ministry?

CHAPTER II.

DOMESTIC LIFE OF THE MINISTER.

§ 1. *General Reflections—Marriage and Celibacy—The Pastor's Wife.*

THE Gospel is not silent on this subject: "A bishop must be blameless, the husband of one wife, sober, prudent, grave, hospitable, apt to teach; one that ruleth well his own house, having his children in subjection with all decorum; for if a man know not how to rule his own house, how shall he take care of the Church of God? Even so must their wives be grave, not slanderers, sober, faithful in all things."—1 Tim., iii., 2, 4, 5, 11. "For this cause left I thee, that thou shouldst ordain pastors; if any be blameless, the husband of one wife, having faithful children, not accused of riot, or unruly. For a bishop must be blameless, as the steward of God; not self-willed, not soon angry, not given to wine, no striker, not given to dishonest gain; but a lover of hospitality, a lover of good men, wise, just, holy, temperate."—Tit., i., 5–8.

These passages suppose the minister to be married, and to be a father of a family; but they do not strictly prescribe marriage to a pastor. If it be said that this is necessary to his being in all things "an example of the believers,"* we reply that it is not necessary to be in this particular state in order to be an example to those who are in it. This supposition would be absurd, and contrary to the spirit of the Gospel, which does not confine us within these literal rules;

* "Be thou an example of the believers, in word, in conversation, in charity, in spirit, in faith, in purity."—1 Tim., iv., 12. "In all things showing thyself a pattern of good works."—Tit., ii., 7.

of which we have a proof, for example, in the forms under which the four evangelists relate the same fact. We every where meet in the Gospel with the same large and liberal character. Our Lord is none the less a model to us in all things, although he sustained only the general relations of humanity. In short, St. Paul, the author of all the passages which we have now cited, was himself an unmarried man.

St. Paul, who has claimed the right of marriage for all, has no less honored celibacy, recommending it not merely as convenient in times when the Church was in peril, but as a means of more perfect devotion to God.—1 Cor., vii., 32, 35. He does but reproduce the thought of Christ himself.—Matt., xix., 10–12. In giving these counsels of perfection, the universal realization of which would be incompatible with the existence of society, he falls into no contradiction with himself, since, if this should be so realized, the society of earth would simply become the society of heaven. Celibacy, in the spirit in which Jesus Christ practiced it, would not injure the world; and this is the only point about which there is a question; the words of Jesus Christ give us well enough to understand that such a celibacy would never be more than a rare exception.

St. Paul, and his Master before him, in the passages we have now cited, had in view no particular class in the Church; but still a counsel of perfection to the Church must have special regard to pastors.

When a minister shall find himself disposed to celibacy by a special impulse of the spirit, let him not fear to be, on that account, less useful to the Church; for marriage might not render him more useful, perhaps it would less, than a pure and devoted celibacy. And perhaps it is to be regretted, if not that there are so few unmarried ministers, at least that there are not more who feel in themselves a disposition for this state. There are times and situations in which an unmarried minister could render to the Church services which a married one could not render so well. Men who have accomplished very great things out of the religious sphere have lived in celibacy, or in a state of marriage but little different from celibacy. Voluntary celibacy, moreover, does not put a minister into an estate of hostility to society.

But the celibacy of the pastor is good only as a positive and special call, under the general call of a pastor. If it be not a thirst for purity and for devotion which has counseled or imposed it, it is, even with the greatest decorum of manners, rather evil than good. I should fear that it would induce habits little regular and little consistent with the dignity of the pastor.* I should fear its purity would be suspected, for in such a state a very high degree of sanctity is necessary to exclude every unfavorable idea. It is very true that there is, in the idea of a strictly honorable celibacy, something pure and angelic, but it is indispensable that our celibacy should have this reputation.

As a general rule, when celibacy is not a sacrifice to the kingdom of God, marriage is preferable. It is certain that if the ministry do not gain from the celibacy of the pastor, it loses. For in this case there is no more of devotion, and it may render less useful that which one has. Taking men as they are, the married pastor is more useful, all other things being equal, than the unmarried. In a well-chosen marriage, in a family life, there is first the advantage of a model presented to the parish and to the world; and then the pastor may have useful co-operation, if his wife be truly what she ought to be.†

* The ennui of an absolute solitude will naturally lead a pastor to seek diversions and relaxations abroad, when he can not find them at home. Long and frequent visits, loungings, &c.

† Harms goes too far, not in making marriage the rule and celibacy the exception, for we do the same, but in making marriage a matter of absolute necessity and obligation in respect to the pastor, so that the pastor is not completely a pastor if he be not married (111, 182).

This leads us to speak of what the wife of a pastor should be. This point is so important, that we think celibacy much preferable to a marriage, otherwise well chosen and happy, but badly chosen and unhappy in this, that the woman has espoused the man, and not the pastor; or, if you please, to a marriage in which a minister has had in view himself rather than his ministry.

The first ministry of a pastor is that of a good example, and St. Paul associates the wife in this ministry when he desires that the wives should be "grave, not slanderous; that they should be sober and faithful in all things."—1 Tim., iii., 11. This was thought to be of so much importance in certain Churches, those of Hungary, that the minister was made absolutely responsible for the conduct of his wife.* He is every where morally so, and this responsibility is a grave one; the minister may, on this account, seriously suffer. How much may the irregularities and vices of the wife (her evil speaking, avarice, negligence, display, &c.) compromise the respectability of the pastor! And inversely: Julian the apostate, observing that one of the causes of the success of the Gospel was the pure morals of its followers, and particularly of its ministers, sought to produce a concurrence with Christianity by requiring the pagan priests to maintain their wives, children, and domestics in the same purity of manners.†

If the pastor, in his choice, should have respect to but one thing, would it not be the education of his children, which for the greater part, sometimes almost wholly, and especially in the most direct and most continuous manner, depends upon mothers? The pastor can not at the same time train up his children and his parish; so far from this, with the best intentions, he can not do for his children all that he would,

* He is punished on her account if she dances, if she plays cards, &c. See Bridges, *The Christian Ministry*.

† Bridges: *The Christian Ministry*, page 197.

and that another could do for them; he must be able, in this matter, to depend upon his wife. Besides, how shall his family, under the influence of a mother who is not a Christian, present the aspect of a Christian family? It is very hurtful to the authority of a pastor, when his wife is not seen to be his first proselyte, and, I add, his principal aid.

In fact, the wife must take part in her husband's vocation, and in order to that, she must first partake of his convictions and his sentiments. Without this (however good a wife she may be), she will be to him as an obstacle and as a scandal. And the more zealous he shall be, the more will the impossibility of finding aid, or, at least, interest in his wife, wound his heart and discourage him.

But if she share his sentiments, he has an inexhaustible and ever-present consolation, a double power, and ordinarily an excellent counselor. It is impossible that a pious wife should not become to a pastor, in respect, especially, to his ministry, a "helpmeet for him." He will find in her a livelier and more exquisite penetration, a surer, more prompt, and delicate tact, milder firmness, a more tranquil perseverance.*

She may render him valuable services among the poor, the sick, the schools, etc. She is the natural confessor of women. She is a counselor more readily heard than any other in certain cases. She may aid her husband by information which she may furnish him.

Here let us call to mind the memory of Aquila and Priscilla,† a married couple (of the laboring class), who wrought with St. Paul for Jesus Christ, and to whom all the gentile Churches were debtors (Rom., xvi., 3, 4); who took with

* "He must find in her a monitor, in the best sense of the word—a co-worker, an inciter to good; and if she is not so, she must become so, and this by his pains."—HARMS, iii., 187.

† See the discourse, entitled *Aquilas et Priscille*, in the *Méditations Evangéliques* of M. Vinet.—*Edit.*

them Apollos, the eloquent disciple of John, and taught him more perfectly the way of God (Acts, xviii., 2, 3, 26); and whose two names are never separated by St. Paul.—2 Tim., iv., 19; 1 Cor., xvi., 19.

The wife of a minister is necessarily an obstacle or an aid: There is no medium. Hence it is a law that he should have the ministry in his view in the choice of a wife. This, perhaps, is too rarely done. We engage ourselves before we are quite serious; and if it be otherwise, passion carries us away, and we see what does not exist.

As to the time of marriage—it is, perhaps, too much to wed at the same time a parish and a wife. Would it not be better not to bring too closely together these two acts, which, though not opposed to each other, are different?*

§ 2. *Government of the Family.*

"A bishop must be one that ruleth well his own house, having his children in subjection with all gravity; for if a man know not how to rule his own house, how shall he take care of the Church of God?"—1 Tim., iii., 4, 5.

It is scarcely natural that a minister should be devoted to his parish (jealous for it, with the jealousy of God), and be neglectful of his family; and seldom will this happen. How can one be a bad father and a good pastor, the pastorate being but a more extended paternity? How can the principle of charity, which makes a good pastor, coexist with the absence of the principle of affection, which makes a good father? How can that charity which concerns itself for strangers care nothing for those of its own household? How shall not the pastor be first the pastor of his own family? How can we imagine a zealous pastor who is an indifferent father, when

* On the manner of entering into the state of marriage, see *l'Histoire de Lavater*, by GESSNER, tome i., p. 303–305. The history of young Tobias is not more beautiful.

it is said that "he who cares not for his own is worse than an infidel?"—1 Tim., v., 8.

We must nevertheless admit, strange as it may be, that one may have a kind of zeal for his parish, and not a proportional solicitude for his family; may suffer himself to be absorbed by the details of his office; may, perhaps, like better this external activity than to take care of his household. There are many badly bred children in priestly families, and the fathers of these children are not always (far from it) bad pastors.

It is a grave error to think that the parish should precede the family. The family is the first interest in respect to the pastor, as it is to every other man. If a pastor will not admit this, he would be wiser not to marry. What the family gains by our cares is profitable also to the parish; first, because "the family," as Quesnel says, "is a little diocese where he makes trials of episcopal and ecclesiastical zeal, piety, and prudence;" next, because the parish gains from these domestic cares by the edifying example which hence results, and by the pastoral spirit spread over all the members of the family.

It loses, in the same proportion, by our domestic negligence, even though for the sake of it we should sacrifice our children: first, because it is not natural that a true blessing should rest upon the cares of a pastor, who, having no care for his household, is worse than an infidel; next, on account of scandal. Witness the example of the children of Eli.—1 Samuel, ii. In spite of Eli's wise and grave representations to his children (ii., 23, 25), we see, by the reproaches which they brought upon him (ii., 29), that, by his weakness, he was the cause of their deportment; and already, in chapter first, we perceive that he was not a *spiritual* man.*

We should guard against that united influence of the political spirit of the times and of certain ideas of reform, on

* *Spiritual*, it is to be presumed, is not to be understood here so as to imply that Eli was not, on the whole, a man of true piety.—*Tr.*

account of which children are apt to be brought up in a different spirit from the submissive one of which the apostle speaks.

§ 3. *House and Household Economy of the Pastor.*

A minister, in marrying, should know according to what general principles his house ought to be governed, and the wife whom he has married (the aid he has taken to himself) should learn them from him, if she has yet to learn them.

Without disparaging an honorable liberty, it is necessary that the order of his house, and the habits of the external life of his family, should be subordinated to the interests of his ministry. This is not a yoke which he imposes upon his wife, but principles that she should voluntarily adopt in virtue of an interest which she shares with him.

If there be not this concert, or if principles are observed only at the expense of the liberty of one of the parties, every thing will go wrong.

This being assumed, we believe that the internal affairs (the affairs of the domestic establishment) ought to satisfy propriety in two ways: by order and neatness, if the pastor be poor; by simplicity, if he be rich; which, certainly, does not mean that order may be wanting in a rich house, or simplicity in a poor one; still less, that one will have order simply because he is rich, or simplicity merely because he is poor, without seeking it by other means.

Order is the ornament, the attire, the luxury of poverty. Nothing is so sad as the appearance of riches, and pretensions to elegance in a poor house. But, on the contrary, order in poverty shows a firm soul, a serious character, a peaceful heart. Order and neatness among the poor are almost virtues, inspiring involuntary respect; and their absence greatly injures the influence of a poor pastor.

Simplicity is the only ornament which may properly attach itself to wealth ; it is always in good taste, especially in a parsonage. The contrary presents too great a contrast with the functions of the pastor. But more than this : The parsonage is a second poor-house in the parish. None is so much visited by the unfortunate. It requires but very little to offend their notice. What a rich man, or even one in easy circumstances, scarcely honors with the name of comfort, is for them luxury and show. If, at the house of a wealthy pastor, opulence may show itself, it must be only under a grave form, and there must be no appearance of fancy, of finery, or of sensuality. There is a luxury which addresses the senses, and another which addresses the mind and the imagination, and where matter is made subservient to thought.*

Entering much into society (I mean what are called assemblies, soirées, dinner parties, etc.) offends poverty, by the leisure which it wastes and by the expenditure which it incurs, or at least which it implies. The family of a pastor may have friends, whom they may see familiarly and frequently, but it is not proper that they should *see the world.* The personal austerity of a pastor will not correct the impression which one will receive from worldliness in his wife and children. We do not recommend the government of a cloister. Whatever abuse may be made of the proverb, "Youth must have its way," it is not without truth. But without wishing to force nature, and while authorizing a proper liberty, it is still necessary that the pastor should have a well-governed house, and *dissipated life in* his family would be a real scandal.

We have elsewhere said that one of the prerogatives of a pastor is to belong to no particular class of society.† His wife and children must not deprive him of this prerogative, by courting the society of the gay world.

* Contention between the seriousness of a husband and the vanity of his wife, in the *Vicar of Wakefield.* † Page 70.

More care should be taken in the choice of Domestics than in any other House.—They should be persons who not only may suit in respect of the services we exact from them, but persons of good character, and disposed to enter into the spirit of our house.

Decency, dignity of manners in the interior, in language, in all respects, should be maintained. The way is to have self-respect.

Peace.—The house of a pastor is a house of peace, not of contention and noise.

Simplicity of the Table, Sobriety.—Let no suspicion of intemperance or sensuality attach itself to pastors. The world instinctively discerns in them the first appearances of those vices which are opposed to the virtues that should characterize them.

Hospitality.—This is put by St. Paul (Titus, i., 8; 1 Tim., iii., 2) in the number of the virtues of a bishop. Hospitality had then an importance which it has not now. In addition to her general well-known circumstances of need, Christianity was a wayfarer; zeal, persecution, agitated the Church; and, moreover, the condition of a wayfarer, though rich, was not agreeable; that of the poor was wretched. Christians are commended for having exercised hospitality, widows for having washed the saints' feet.—1 Tim., v., 10. We may cite many examples of the performance of this duty in the primitive Church; Aquila and Priscilla took Apollos into their house.—Acts, xviii., 2–13.

If this precept be now of any general application, it is particularly applicable to pastors. The more hospitality is neglected or avoided, the more should a pastor give an example of it, without, however, conniving in the least degree at that useless and pernicious abuse which is sometimes attempted to be made of it in the name of Christianity. For, decidedly, the form of it at least has changed. I should like to see a pastor exercise it toward the honorable poor of his parish with discretion and prudence. Beyond this, I see no more than a general duty, of which he should give an example to his flock as of other virtues, but not more than of other virtues.

Family Worship.—It is useless to prove that the house of the pastor should be the example and model of this. It is not ordinarily to be enlarged in a manner which gives it the appearance of an *extra-domestic* worship. It should be distinguished from meetings for edification which one may hold with his neighbors and parishioners under the roof of the parsonage. The worship of the family should always preserve its own character. Family worship, properly conducted, may react with advantage upon public worship.

The government of the temporal interests of the parsonage (household economy) is one of the things which shows the pastor the importance of choosing a proper person for his wife. For she has in this department the greatest influence; and it is important that the pastoral mansion should be well governed; that the order and the exactness which reign there should edify every one—should have a Christian character, and this in small as well as in great things. Exactness, punctuality, if they be not virtues, may become so by the principle in which they are exercised; and, in all cases, they are the condition of more than one virtue, and the absence of them compromises many. In evil, as well as in good, the exterior reacts upon the interior. Negligence induces impatience, irritations, lawsuits, falsehood, injustice; and further, by tempting others to deceive us, brings them into sin. It is not necessary, in order to appear good, that we should pass for dupes. Voluntary, free, intelligent goodness is the true goodness; and it is this, especially, which causes us to be loved. Why should we covet any other? It is needless to say that this exactness is consistent with liberality, that it has nothing in common with *finesse.* For the mistress of a parsonage, we should desire the reputation of an orderly woman, but not celebrity for industry and management. To be overwise does not suit her, and I would that her ideal should be composed of the image of the wise woman of the Proverbs (xxxi., 10–31), and of that of the Christian widows of whom St. Paul speaks to Timothy, or of the character of Martha tempered by that of Mary. She should also know, and her husband, in choosing her, should have been well assured that she did know, that there is not only more of happiness (Acts, xx., 35), but more of dignity and more of prudence, in giving than in receiving.

PART THIRD.

PASTORAL LIFE.

Preliminary Reflections on the Choice of a Parish, and on Changes.

A PASTOR'S functions, in his relation to his parish as a whole, are those which pertain to *public worship and instruction;* in his relation to families and individuals, they are embraced *in the care of souls.* He sustains relations, also, to the universal Church, but chiefly as a Christian; nothing, so far as these are concerned, being specially proper to a pastor.

Before examining separately each of these branches of his work, let us consider the work as a whole, and regard the minister at the moment when he is about to put himself at the head of a parish. I do not at present distinguish the work of the suffragan from that of the pastor: I shall speak of the suffragan hereafter.

As there is a call to the ministry in general, there is one also to this or that particular ministry. We will endeavor to give some rules. The first rule is not to have solely or chiefly in view, in this determination, our own convenience or personal advantages; but the measure of our strength, the nature of our talent, the circumstances of the parish, the need it has of us rather than of some other, or of some other rather than of us. After settling this question, but not till then, we may consult also our own convenience, our own particular interest. I will not say that the difficulties and dangers which one may foresee will be decisive as to the question of his call; but that at least, when there is doubt on this point, this consideration will, in very many cases, remove it, and that, in general, we ought less to shrink from a post which promises us difficulties than one which exempts us from them.

The second rule, after dismissing interest, is also to dismiss all those considerations which are not drawn from the nature of things, the interest of the kingdom of God, and the direct or indirect teachings of the Divine word. In this matter, as in many others, superstition, indolence of mind and of conscience, arbitrary maxims, have played a large part. We prefer consulting these advisers rather than God. conscience, and reason.

Many have thought it best, and have counseled others, to remain passive. That we may not decide wrong, say they, let us not decide at all; let us take what is offered to us. It is not strange that a man, especially a Christian, should, in such a matter, fear to decide for himself. There is not one of his steps which is not invisibly connected with a long series of consequences impossible to be foreseen, and often as serious in themselves as their cause is inconsiderable. The Christian knows better than any other how apt he is to deceive himself. He knows that "the way of man is not in himself."—Jer., x., 23. Bengel, on this subject. says, "The less of himself an instrument puts into an action, and the more he leaves God himself to act, the purer and more complete is the action."* It is, indeed, useful to set one's self aside; it is dangerous to have to make use of one's own will when considerations of interest are complicated with those of duty: But we must take care that we do not sacrifice to mental indolence while we think to sacrifice to humility. It is also true that when we are important enough to engage

* Bengel's *Leben von Burk*. p. 145.

attention, and when institutions allow men to anticipate movement on our part, it is a great privilege to be called without having first presented ourselves; and in every case it is better not to move than to act without full conviction; conviction which, in questions of this kind, it is not easy to obtain. In ecclesiastical constitutions passivity is not possible. Even where it is possible, I do not think that, except in very particular cases, we should remain passive. Passivity in the Christian life is the exception, and not the rule.

Jesus Christ would raise Christian obedience to the highest degree of spontaneity, and would invest with the greatest power the element of individuality, which, in the old economy, was compressed. It is only when the exercise of liberty is impossible that we are permitted to wait; and even in this voluntary submission the Christian has liberty. This principle, which, until the sixteenth century, lay in oblivion, makes Protestantism a very serious matter; and if we should rejoice in this restoration of the Gospel, and with it that of personal liberty and responsibility, we should do so with trembling. But if the impossibility of foreseeing and calculating the consequences of each action should restrain us from action, it is evident that we should never act.

That, then, which is required is not passivity, but to purify our motive by prayer; not to act without full conviction (Rom., xiv., 23); not to substitute our will for that of others, or of God, by forcibly turning aside the natural course of things; finally, not to employ intrigue and simony in order to obtain a desirable post. There are here very subtile points, as to which, however, an upright conscience will not be misled. It is seldom necessary, and it is not possible, to indicate their different forms.* With us, the former law shut every avenue to simony in making promotion depend upon age; the new law has not much opened the door. There is

* Bengel held the purity of vocation in such high regard that he excludes all those who are influenced by the wishes of near relations.

in this a compensation for the inconvenience of our not being able to make capacity the standard of employment, or the need of each parish the determining consideration in providing for it.

But, after all this reservation, we may adopt the formula of Harms: "When, in my own judgment, and in the judgment of competent persons, I have the qualifications requisite for a place, and when I feel myself able, with God's assistance, to fulfill its duties, I may then openly offer my services, and, in order to obtain the place, make use of all legitimate and honest means.*

The principle of passivity seems to have prevailed in the first ages of the Church. Not only do we there find forced ordinations, but also calls to such or such a post accepted without saying a word; it was even a virtue not to make inquiry. This is intelligible enough; the contrary would not have been once thought of. The circumstances are no longer the same. Remark, nevertheless, that on a change of circumstances the principle may reappear; it has reappeared, although with restrictions, in the work of missions, so like that of the first propagation of Christianity. In every work where heroism is necessary, obedience is necessary also; the first thing to be broken down is the will, at every point in which there is the most of sensibility and delicacy.

The question may be asked: When there is a direct call on the part of our natural superiors, without our having in any way contributed to it, should we always obey? No; even in this case we may refuse, though not without strong reasons. Here the just presumption is in favor of acceptance; we must, then, seriously examine, and not refuse, except under full evidence that we are bound to do so. We can not, however, admit the opinion expressed by Dr. Schleussner: "My dear Professor Polycarp Leyser strongly recommended me," says he, "to refuse no regular call; for, said he, God punishes

* *Pastoraltheologie*, iii., 217.

those who allow themselves to do so, either by withdrawing them from this world before the end of the year, or causing them to lose their gifts, or permitting them to fall into some snare."*

The third rule is to be certain of the disposition of the parish in this matter, and not to impose ourselves on it against its will. A conscientious and delicate minister, on his own account, would secure to the parish a participation in the choice of a pastor. If he is not precisely desired, he must at least be welcome. This is said in general, and not without exception. For if we think that if we are excluded, the parish will be ill provided for, and if there is reason for believing that our presence will easily and promptly dissipate prejudices which may have spread abroad concerning us, it is, perhaps, our duty to proceed.

The fourth rule is not to exchange lightly one place for another. When one is doing well, when he is blessed in the position which he occupies, when he is sufficient for it, a great point is gained. We must not too easily yield to the thought that we might more profitably use all our faculties and do more good somewhere else. We must not too easily abandon a place to which we are suited. The reason should be a very strong one which forces us from it: The necessity, the danger of another parish: "Come over to Macedonia and help us!"—Acts, xvi., 9. We must have heard this cry before venturing to remove.

Sometimes, also, after having passed a certain time in a place where we have done and are yet doing good, we may remember that where Paul had planted it was necessary that Apollos should water; we may be less suited to the work in the sequel than we were at its beginning. Our part, so to speak, may have been performed; we may no longer increase; the work, in order to advance, must pass into other hands. Still, I think that a true Christian develops himself with

* BURK, *Pastoraltheologie in Beispielen*, tome i., p. 98.

his work and by his work; and that to the new demands to which he has given rise, he answers by new developments of his interior life: If it be thus, there can be nothing better for the parish than that the pastor should remain; as Thomas Adam did at Wintringham, which was his first and his last parish, and where he passed fifty years. In the Wesleyan Church, a pastor remains only three years at the head of the same parish, so as to prevent his peculiar tendencies from becoming deeply rooted in their too affectionate hearts.

These great phases of our life ought to be solemnized: such a day as that in which we take the charge of a parish ought not to pass as ordinary days. It is a sort of vigil kept previous to commencing knighthood, in which we solicit on our knees the *panoply*—the complete armor—of a servant of Jesus Christ; in which we put on the whole armor of God, as St. Paul recommends in the epistle to the Ephesians (vi., 11–17).

We should also, from respect for the parish, be careful as to our first appearance after entrance. Our first sermon should be carefully studied; it should embrace our whole mind, and, if possible, our whole personality, announcing us with modesty and frankness. Nevertheless, we must not speak of ourselves more than is necessary.

We ought, together with this, to take distinct note of the pastoral dispositions, and to make trial of them as one does of a garment which he is to clothe himself with, and no more to lay aside. What are these?

1. *The spirit of humility*, which does not consist in disparaging what we have, but in wishing to be nothing in ourselves; in esteeming others better than ourselves; in knowing how to accept injustice, and suffering ourselves to be counted as nothing. The more a pastor reduces himself for the sake of magnifying God, the more has he of authority. The more we are emptied of ourselves, the more shall

we perceive, in this emptiness, the grandeur of our ministry.*

2. *The spirit of modesty and of moderation.* He must prepare himself in an extraordinary manner, and still choose ordinary paths; not project great things outwardly; not despise the day of small things; walk with the humble; avoid the spirit of an innovator; place his feet as much as possible in paths already made, according to this word of Moses: "Ask now of the days which are past, which are before thee" (Deut., ii., 32); and that of Jeremiah: "Stand ye in the ways and see, and ask for the old paths" (vi., 16). This does not mean, Confine yourselves to the past; perfect nothing, correct nothing, begin nothing; it only imports, Do not lightly reject traditions; forsake not, without reason, that which is established; let there be a legitimate presumption in favor of that which is; make constancy the rule, and change the exception.

3. *The spirit of war, and the spirit of peace.* The spirit of war is essential to the ministry and to the profession of Christianity. Like Christ, we come to kindle a fire, and we should even restrain ourselves until it be kindled; we bring a sword, and not peace; we throw into the mass a burning leaven. The exterior may deceive us; but the exterior ought not to determine our judgment or our stand-point. Even as to that peace, and those guarantees which are incorporated in the civil institution and rooted in the soil, we should act as if there were nothing of these; for all these may be nothing; all these, perhaps, will be no more to-morrow, for us at least. Notwithstanding appearances, Christianity, in its vital and characteristic elements, is always a stranger and an intruder. We must gird up our loins, for this peace is only

* See *Port Royal*, par M. SAINTE-BEUVE, tome i., p. 464, on the remarkable authority of M. Singlin, Director of Consciences in this institution. His humility was the source of this authority; for he cast himself on God alone.

a respite, a truce; we must draw the bow for a mark much further removed than that which seems to be presented to us. "He teacheth my hands to war, and my fingers to fight." —Psalm cxliv., 1. Thus the spirit of strife is necessary, but also the spirit of peace. The pastor should not approach his parishioners as if they were adversaries; he should treat no one as an adversary before he is proved to be such: He should regard his flock as a flock—a family; and in every respect he should proceed upon the principle of benevolence. From the first, let the pastor regard himself as beloved. Nothing more falsifies our position than putting ourselves on the defensive. Those who hate us, or would attack us, will perhaps be disarmed by our confidence, our benevolence, our candor.

4. *The spirit of devotedness to the parish*, for which, in mass and in detail, we should be ready to surrender life, as in certain difficult circumstances, epidemics, war, etc. "It is in our hearts to die and live with you."—2 Cor., vii., 3. It is better to renounce the ministry than to neglect any thing pertaining to it.

Let us pass in review certain general duties of the pastor after entering on his functions. First, that of *residence.*

The law, with us, has in great part provided for this, by requiring the pastor to live in his parish; but this does not forbid frequent and prolonged absences. We must be careful as to these. There are some pastors who prefer to be every where rather than at home. We must avoid even occasions of religious wandering.

2. *Regularity in Functions, and Earnestness in fulfilling them.*—We must avoid the bad taste of those pastors who lament or trifle over the number and the weight of their functions, and stun the ears of the world with them: We must not allow ourselves in delays, which, in certain cases, may have most pernicious consequences. To success and

prosperity in the ministry we may apply these words: "A little more sleep, a little more slumber, a little more folding of the hands to sleep; so shall thy poverty come as one that traveleth, and thy want as an armed man."—Prov., vi., 10, 11.

The minister should be constantly absorbed in his ministry. "Think on these things" (the duties of the ministry), says Paul to Timothy, "and give thyself wholly to them."—1 Tim., iv., 15. It would be deplorable to have a predominant taste apart from the ministry, so that this should occupy only the second place. That minister is in a sad position whose ministry is not his life. If one gives himself entirely to a ministry only when he loves it, he will love it only when he gives himself entirely to it. Nothing so attaches a minister to his flock, and *vice versa*, as the sacrifices which he makes for it.

In order to give himself entirely to the ministry, he must *simplify his life*, avoid whatever would draw him from duty, whatever will not contribute to the success of his work, all the cares of the world,* even the cares which may consist with the ministry, but which are not an essential part of it, and which we may with propriety transfer to others.—Acts, vi., 2.

* "Take no thought, saying, What shall we eat, what shall we drink," etc.—Matt., vi., 31, 32. "Take heed to yourselves, lest your hearts be overcharged with cares of this life."—Luke, xxi., 34.

SECTION FIRST.

WORSHIP.

In a practical and local point of view, we here have little to say; but we should not restrict ourselves to this point of view. Wherever duty and the form of duty are traced, it is useful to ascend to principle, and thus to become penetrated with the true spirit of duty, the spirit which is to be found in principle, and not lower.

Worship is the more immediate expression, the purely religious form of religion. It is the internal or external act of adoration—adoration in act. Now adoration is nothing else than the direct and solemn acknowledgment of the divinity of God, and of our obligations toward him.

Public worship, otherwise called *service*, or *divine office*, comprehends, according to the ordinary idea, whatever is performed during the time in which an assembly remains together in the name of God and for the cause of God.

According to this idea, then, worship includes also exhortation, or instruction, or exposition of the word of God. This, however, is framed into worship, rather than an integrant part of it. It is only when we generalize the idea of worship, and make it to include whatever has God for its object, whatever our intention refers to God, that we may call preaching, or instruction in religious truths, worship. It is so neither more nor less than any other good work. "Adoration," according to Klopstock, as cited by Harms, "is the essence of public worship. Instruction and exhortation* by the

* *Die unterrichtende Ermahnung.*

preacher, notwithstanding their great utility, are not equally essential elements." We add to this, that in a religious system where there is no longer a priest, where one man is not a symbolic mediator between God and mankind, the *minister** is rather the director of worship than exclusively the agent of it: The people, regarding worship in our point of view, may be active in it, and in a certain degree, perhaps, ought to be.† It is remarkable that in our worship passivity predominates, while activity distinguishes the Catholic!

Worship consists in *words*, or in *silent rites;* more frequently, however, in their combination.

We can not well represent to ourselves a silent worship. Again, we can hardly conceive of a worship entirely inward without rites, without symbols. It is important to give a body to the fundamental sentiments and ideas of religion. Life can not dispense with symbols any more than language with metaphors. *Rite* is a metaphor in action. Worship is an action, so the Germans call it. Action is nearer to life, more resembles life, than word. "*Segnius irritant animos demissa per aurem*," etc.‡ Worship, certainly, may be an action without a rite, and even without words; but when we would move others, and be moved ourselves, we need sometimes more than this internal silence.

Comparing the word with the rite, how is the former to be characterized?

The word is successive: The act of worship presents simultaneously many ideas or many relations. The word

* "Ourselves your servants for Jesus' sake."—2 Cor., iv., 5.

† "Else when thou shalt bless with the spirit, how shall he that occupieth the room of the unlearned, say Amen at thy giving of thanks? seeing he understandeth not what thou sayest."—1 Cor., xiv., 16.

‡ "What is addressed to the ear affects less readily the soul."—HORACE: *Art of Poetry*, v. 180.—*Edit.*

analyzes, it divides; the silent rite concentrates. The whole Gospel has been concentrated in the memorial of the Lord's Supper, as in a focus. A rite expresses only what is essential, but it does this with a force which the word has not.

Worship consisting of rites and words is more distinct than contemplation, less than discourse. Contemplation is a synthesis, discourse an analysis; worship which partakes of contemplation and the word, unites synthesis and analysis, and can not, without mutilation, exclude either of these. As a whole, it aspires to elevate harmoniously all the faculties of our being to the sphere of truth (which truth is not a formula, but the substance of one). There is something of music in it; it has the character of song, which also is essential to it; for adoration is a state of the soul which only song can express. Worship is the assemblage of all the elements of our being in an act of pure religion. I do not exclude words from worship; but I would have them symbolic, sacramental, like the rest of it. Words at the same time human and stereotyped do not seem to me to realize the ideal of a Liturgy. If human words must intermingle with it, I would rather have them free and individual. In some Reformed Churches, the prayer which immediately precedes the discourse is made by the pastor, and remains his own, whether he uses always the same one, or varies it with circumstances.

The Romish worship has erred in giving too much to rite, and, through rite, too much to traditions; but its Liturgy, at least, does not dogmatize; it has the spirit of song, and therein it is good; and then the form of worship, with all the rest, is with them an affair of faith and of dogma.

As for us, our worship is too much a confession of faith—a discourse; every thing is articulate, every thing is precise, every thing explains itself. The effect of this tendency has gone so far as to determine the idea we have formed of temples. We regard temples as places for hearing. We go to them to hear some one speak. But is it only because of the doctrine of *the real presence* that the Catholic temples should be regarded as true temples ?* Would the character of the Catholic worship be destroyed if the theurgic element should be separated from it ? Can not worship have its proper effect unless it be regarded as a miracle ? What is the remedy of our defect ? As an excess can hardly be corrected except by another excess, we say that our Liturgy is wanting in what would be a fault except in a Liturgy ; that is, more of vagueness, a flowing of religious ideas into one another ; which might take place without, on that account, making the ideas less fit to express Christian faith and life. Preaching is an addition to worship, but is not worship. Harms,† with reason, recommends houses of worship without preaching. This would not tend to lower preaching, but to elevate worship.

As far as I can judge of the worship of the primitive Church, it must have held a medium between these two extremes. We see in it nothing of the anxious precision of a confession of faith, nothing of the profusion of rites of the Romish Church.

Jesus Christ and his apostles seem to have been less concerned in establishing a new worship than in abolishing the old, or, at least, in destroying the error relating to the intrinsic value of that "bodily exercise which profiteth little."—1 Tim., iv., 8. They directly abolished—they only indirectly and silently instituted. Things were rather born than established. Doctrine only was established ; and that, also, after the same manner : *it* is born in the soul.

See John, iv., 23, 24 (worship in spirit and in truth), and the whole epistle to the Hebrews, which seems to identify religion and worship ; and Col., ii., 16 : "Let no man judge you in meat or in drink, or in respect of a holy day, or of the new moon, or of the Sabbath day ;" and Rom., xiv., 17 : "The

* *Temples*, from *to contemplate.*

† Tome ii., page 123.

kingdom of God is not in meat and drink, but in righteousness, and peace, and joy in the Holy Ghost."

Preaching has its place under the Gospel, but it does not suffocate worship. Our word is a prism which decomposes the light; but this decomposition should only be a transition.

Here, moreover, are all the ritual elements of the New Testament:

The Lord's Day.—The primitive Church had a sacred day, that of the Savior's resurrection. The Sabbath is abolished,* but Sunday is sacred. It was not added to Christianity, it was born of it. God blessed the seventh day, and sanctified it: That was to bless his work, to crown it. Sunday is a summary of Christianity, gives it a moment in time, as a temple gives it a place in space. Internal necessity is the true law, the best authority for Sunday; it speaks more strongly within us than a written ordinance. This necessity determines the mode of observing Sunday. Nothing binds as much as Christian liberty and conscience: this has consecrated a day, it ought then to be holy.

Assemblies.—Hebrews, x., 25: "Neglect not the assembling of yourselves together, as the manner of some is."

1 Cor., xiv., 26: "What is it then, my brethren? when ye come together, every one hath a psalm, hath a doctrine, hath a revelation, hath an interpretation. Let all things be done to edification."

Verse 40: "Let all things be done decently and in order."

James, ii., 1–3 (Poor and rich).

1 Cor., xi., 4, 5: "Every man who prays or prophesies, having his head covered, dishonors his head; but every woman who prays or prophesies with her head uncovered, dishonors her head; for that is the same as if she were shorn."

1 Cor., xi., passim (on the way of employing time in these assemblies).

* Has the Sabbath been abolished? See *Appendix*, note H, by the Translator.

Passover.—Matt., xxvi.; Luke, xxii.

1 Cor., v., 7, 8: "Christ our passover is sacrificed for us. Therefore let us keep the feast, not with the old leaven of malice and of wickedness, but with the unleavened bread of sincerity and truth."

1 Cor., xi., 23–29 (rules for the celebration of the Lord's Supper).

Singing.—Mark, xiv., 26: "When they had sung an hymn, they went out to the Mount of Olives."

Eph., v., 19: "Speaking to one another in psalms, and hymns, and spiritual songs, singing and making melody in your heart to the Lord."

Rites which do not appear to have made a part of ordinary Worship.

Baptism.—John, iii., 22: "Jesus went then with his disciples into the land of Judea; and there he tarried with them, and baptized."

Acts, viii., 36–38 (Eunuch of Queen Candace).

Acts, ii., 44: "Those who received the word joyfully were baptized."

Acts, x., 47, 48: Peter said, "Can any man forbid water, that these should not be baptized, who have received the Holy Ghost as well as we? And he commanded them to be baptized in the name of the Lord."

Acts, xvi., 33: "The (jailor) washed their stripes (of Paul and Silas) and was baptized, he and his household."

Unction.—James, v., 14: "Is any sick among you? let him call for the pastors of the Church, and let them pray for him, anointing them with oil, in the name of the Lord." Compare Mark, vi., 13.

Imposition of Hands.—Acts, xiv., 23: "And when they had ordained them elders in every Church (by imposition of hands), and had prayed with fasting, they commended them to the Lord."

2 Cor., viii., 19 : "He (Titus) was chosen (with imposition of hands) of the Churches to travel with us."

2 Tim., i., 6 : "Stir up the gift of God which is in thee, and which you have received by the putting on of my hands."

1 Tim., iv., 14 : "Neglect not the gift which is in thee, which was given to thee by prophecy, with the laying on of the hands of the Presbytery."

The imposition of hands was then more than a symbol : it was an act to which a supernatural efficacy was attached.

It is in all this to be remarked that we see more a community than its head : We do not see in these assemblies that one man was all, and did all.

Laying aside now all discussion and all parallels, and placing ourselves on the Protestant stand-point, let us characterize appropriately the worship which is in spirit and in truth. A Liturgy should,

1. Express religion, the whole of religion ; give a summary, not an abridgment of it. An abridgment divides, a summary combines and incorporates the different elements of an idea or a fact. In one sense, religion has no parts, can not be divided. Every hour of worship should present an entire Christ to the soul of the believer.

2. Express it in a form the most suitable to all, in symbols and words. Every thing should be quickly comprehended and vividly seized. In respect to symbols, Christ has given us a model, in the simplicity of baptism and the Lord's Supper. To attain this end, we need, more than all things, a biblical worship.

3. Have a character the most appropriate to awaken and elevate the soul, not to distract and amuse it : little ceremony, but significant and simple. Our Liturgy would be improved if it had certain characteristics which belong to the worship of other Churches. The Litany, for example, may seem ridiculous ; but, in truth, there is something in it which represents the normal state of a soul which recollects itself in the Divine

presence. The Christian should be a child, and consequently should speak the language of a child. The simpler, the more child-like the means, the better are they. The Litany is something child-like: This is its excellence, its truth. Every Liturgy should be somewhat lyrical.

4. Be adapted, as to its extent, to the capacity of the greatest number, be adjusted to the nature of worship in general, which is admiration, and raising the soul above itself to an unaccustomed height. As soon as this just measure is transcended, fatigue begins.

The element of antiquity, which gives gravity even to a Liturgy composed of sacred elements, does this yet more to a Liturgy essentially of human composition. It should not, therefore, be retouched by the Church, except at long intervals and with great care; and these intervals should be prolonged the more if the Liturgy was conceived as a true Liturgy, and not as a dogmatic treatise. It ought certainly to express the faith of the Church, but, if I may so say, in a contemplative state. Much more should a preacher abstain, except from real necessity (such as public events, calamities, &c.), from making changes on his own authority. A minister is bound to the Liturgy, which is not his own, which, indeed, is the voice of the flock, and to which he does but lend his individual voice.*

We should not desire, we should fear, to see the people confined to forms which have lost their sense; still, it is useful that there should remain in worship something fixed and immutable. The people, to a certain extent, should be *kirchlich*,† that is to say, attached to the forms of their worship: There seems to be no necessity that this should lead to formalism.‡

Costume.—Harms gives a singular explanation of cos-

* See *Appendix*, note I, *On Liturgies*, by the Translator.

† A German adjective, formed from the word *Kirche*, *église*, to which the derivation *ecclésiastique*, according to French usage, does not correspond.—*Edit.*

‡ "Wine congealed on the lees."

tume, as being, according to his idea, intended to conceal either the too great advantages or the too great imperfections of the person. Our idea of costume is, that it is to efface (to cover) the individual and the man of the times. In proportion as the spirituality of the flock increases, costume becomes less necessary; it may even become disagreeable. In this matter, I think we ought to follow the rules of the Church to which we prefer to belong, and to follow them freely.

Celebration of Rites.—The minister should be on his guard against performing certain rites, such as baptism and marriage, in a too perfunctory and familiar manner. That which to us is a daily occurrence, is often a solemn one to another. All this is more impressive in other Liturgies than in ours, which, in this particular, is poor. The more defective are the text and the form of the Liturgy, the more of his own spirit must the minister put into them, to give accent and rhythm to all things, to animate all rites by an internal life corresponding to them.* Bengel† recommends in these cases great *exactness*, as the hearers readily reason from variableness in these external acts to variableness in doctrines. This care is not inconsistent with liberty and familiarity. Some, from aversion to an affected or formal gravity, have on their part affected an indecent familiarity. They would not have God harangued as an earthly king, and so they undertake to talk with him. Prayer is the medium. It should be *presented.*

> "Avec la liberté d'un fils devant son père,
> Et le saint tremblement d'un pécheur devant Dieu."‡

Reception of Catechumens.—The statutes allow of receiving them privately, provided it be done in the presence of the pastor's colleagues, if he have any, and of the assessors of the consistory.

* "Enliven these solemnities," says Bossuet.

† BENGEL'S *Leben*, by Burk. Stuttgard, 1831, p. 112, § 30.

‡ *Cantique de* A. M. ADOLPHE MONOD, No. 102, *des Chants Chrétiens.*

The Lord's Supper.—I take our Church as it is, one with the state, except as each one's individual will may distinguish him. Discipline here reduces itself, even in respect to scandalous sinners, to a general admonition given from the pulpit, and to a private admonition to be administered to those who are known to him, and whom he expects to see at the table.

The new law says nothing as to form. The former ordinances require the pastors, on presenting the bread and wine, to use "the words of our Lord"—the words, doubtless, used at the institution of the supper. The *ordinances* add that all the communicants, without distinction, shall receive the bread and the wine "after the same manner," that is to say, I suppose, with the same words. Our actual usage is not conformed to this rule, which appears to us a very good one. It is more inconvenient to address a separate passage to each person. The repetition of the sacramental word is serious, imposing, and this word does not lose its force.

It is allowable, and perfectly regular, to give the supper to the sick in their own houses; but this should be done with solemnity, and so that it may be a communion, that is to say, not only should there be assistants, but persons who partake of the supper with the sick.

As to *baptism*, without maintaining that we should absolutely refuse to administer it in the house of the parents, I think we should countenance this as little as possible, were it only to preserve the flock from an error too prevalent on the subject of baptism.*

The pastor should see that every thing in the church be decent, that every thing proceed in proper order, from the entrance to the departure, and during the exercises. He would do well to prevent the plate from being handed round. The sound is not suitable, and may oblige some to give, which is wrong, and contrary to liberty. It would be better to place a box at each door. It matters not if the col-

* See *Acts of the Synod of Berne*, c. xxi., p. 40 and 43.

lection be smaller, as probably it will be, "provided there be a willing mind."—2 Cor., viii., 12. Moreover, St. Paul says, "that your bounty may be ready, as a matter of bounty (a free gift), and not as of covetousness."—2 Cor., ix., 5. "God loves a cheerful giver."—2 Cor., ix., 7.

Singing is more essential to worship than is commonly supposed. It is a language which God has given to man to express thoughts which ordinary language can not express. Besides what we have said of it (in affirming that worship, as a whole, should have the character of music), it is an exercise in which the community unite, which gives believers an active part in worship, and in which their liberty is more complete.

The matter of singing, in general, is prescribed to us; but we ought to use the liberty which the law gives us in the choice of a song.

We may sing too much or too little; we should sing little and more often, three times, perhaps. It would be well to introduce singing immediately after the discourse rather than after the prayer which follows it. This gives repose to the pastor and the hearers, and aids self-possession.

Funerals are the only part of worship which has place out of the confines of the temple, as the supper and baptism, with exceptions, are celebrated only within them. It is not to be admitted that religion should be visibly absent at funerals; this would be to be less pious than pagans. Now it is the pastor who renders religion visible; and, seeing the progress which mind has made, if the pastor be here wanting, some one will take his place, and make his absence more manifest, to the great disadvantage of his character. I would have the minister never absent, either from the house of death or from the cemetery. In many houses the pastor offers a prayer before going out; but this will not suffice; he ought to attend the burial, and there should be another service either at the open tomb or in the church. Some words from the Bible, and a prayer besides, are in all cases sufficient.

SECTION SECOND.

INSTRUCTION.

CHAPTER I.

PREACHING.

§ 1. *Importance of Preaching among the Functions of the Ministry.*

What is preaching? It is the explication of the word of God, the exposition of Christian truths, and the application of those truths to our flock; all this, in the presence of our assembled flock—I might say, in public; since the Church, in the view of the multitude or mass, is regarded as a great school, open to every comer.

We have first spoken of worship, and then of preaching as included in worship, and to be considered as making a part of worship, although worship speaks to God, and preaching speaks of him; but it is only in elevating his soul to God that one speaks worthily of him; preaching which is not of the nature of worship is not true preaching. Things which, in a lower region, are separated, in a higher one are reunited and blended.*

But let us leave this, and see what place God himself has given to preaching in Christianity. It is a place greater than preaching has in any other religion, greater than it had even in the Jewish religion. Christianity is a religion made

* On the relative importance of preaching in the pastoral office, see Harms.

for thought, and, consequently, for speech; it represents itself, it substantively manifests itself by speech, it propagates itself by speech. The Gospel is a word. Christ himself is the *Word*, or the Reason. The term is of no importance; for the word is reason expressed, and the reason is the interior word. The Church itself is truth thought in common, spoken in common. In insisting, a while ago, on synthesis in worship, we did not condemn speech; religion, it is true, appears in a complex state in worship, in the soul and in the life; but there is no just sentiment, no strong affection, which does not connect itself with a distinct idea, of which the reason can not give account, or which is not founded on a relation, the terms of which are well known and well appreciated; and this characteristic should, above all, belong to the true religion, nay, to this religion alone. This alone can say, I know in whom I have believed. In a word, it is a religion of faith or of persuasion, consequently a religion which employs speech.

Hence arises the importance of preaching. Our preaching, it is true, is second hand, a preaching on a preaching, a word on a word; but this matters not, preaching is necessary; for this are we sent; worship, simply, might be celebrated by any Christian whatever; for this no call is necessary; it is sufficient if the person has no reason to doubt the conformity of his faith with this act. If we should interrogate ourselves as to a call, if it is necessary we should be called, it is as stewards of the mysteries of God, as heralds or messengers of justice, as preachers.

To speak the truth, the whole ministry is preaching. Instead of saying that preaching makes a part of worship, we might say that worship makes a part of preaching, that rite is a form of instruction. What we here present, then, as a species, is, in a certain sense, a genus; but still we may so present it, since the word *preaching*, in common language, means a part, and not the whole, of the exercise of the ministry.

Not only should pastors preach, but we think, with Fenelon, under our own explanation, that it belongs to them only to preach.* True political eloquence belongs only to the statesman; true sacred eloquence, only to the statesman in religion or religious affairs, that is to say, the pastor; who alternately passes from generalities to details, and from details to generalities; from theory to practice, and from practice to theory; who has been in contact with individuals, and is familiar with their ways. If certain men without a parish are successful in preaching, it is because they are pastors after another manner and at large.

It is true that the primitive Church divided ministerial functions. They had *κυβερνῆταί*† and *διδάσκαλοι*.‡ "Are all apostles? are all teachers?"—1 Cor., xii., 29. But without saying that gifts are here referred to, and without speaking of what the necessity of the times might require, we may hold that the office of some was absolutely foreign to others. At a period when each Christian was a minister—when an Aquila and a Priscilla, simple artisans, became instructors of an Apollos, how can we suppose that the teacher was not a pastor? We may well think that there were elders (*πρεσβύτεροι*) who did not preach, but not preachers who were strangers to every other pastoral duty except preaching. Paul preached and governed: Timothy preached and governed.

The pastorate, then, is necessary to preaching; but it is yet more evident that preaching is essential to the pastorate,

* "We must commonly leave preaching to pastors. Thus shall we give to the pulpit the simplicity and authority which belong to it. For pastors, who to experience in the work and in the conduct of souls unite the knowledge of the Scriptures, can speak in the manner best suited to the wants of their hearers; whereas preachers, who are merely speculative, enter less into the difficulties, and can scarcely adapt themselves to the minds of their hearers, and speak in a more vague manner."—FENELON, *Dialogues sur l'Eloquence* (Dialogue III.).

† Governors or directors.—*Edit.*

‡ Teachers.

and that we can not conceive of a pastor who does not preach; we would say, who does not preach in public (for, as respects preaching out of season, who can doubt this?); since, apart from preaching, to the minister there remains nothing of the *feeder* and of the *pastor*. But public preaching is essential to the pastorate, which, without this, can not reach all souls, and can not present truth under the most regular and most general form. It is the glory of our Reformation that it restored public preaching to the Church, I say even to the Catholic Church. How noble was it to advance the priest from the mere celebration of rites (which had become a species of magic) to science, to thought, to the word, to conflict?

§ 2. *Principles or Maxims which should be maintained as to Preaching.*

On the subject of preaching, we must adopt certain principles, or acknowledge certain commanding truths.

The first is, that preaching is an action, a real word, not the imitation of a word, and that eloquence is a virtue. Abstracting art, preaching is a work of love, a good work, a good office, a part of the service of God. But this is only the first step: here is the second.

Preaching is a *mystery*. A mystery, I mean, as to its action and its effects, a mystery of reprobation and salvation;* for the word of God (which we assume to be in the preacher's mouth) does not return to him without some effect; something of truth, whether for gain or for loss, always connects itself, and remains with him who has heard it. It is truly mysterious that on the voice of one man the soul and the eternity of another should depend. Mysterious truly! a mode of action so peculiar, so inexplicable, the effect of which so far outreaches our calculations, and so often disappoints

* St. Cyran calls it an almost sacrament, and more awful than that of the altar. (See in the *Appendix*, note B.)

our foresight: How often do we see the greatest effects connected with the smallest causes, as the smallest also with the greatest; power becoming feeble, and impotence powerful; one succeeding by another's shipwreck, and *vice versa*: Laws there are, no doubt, but no constancy; and all rules are subordinated to the liberty of the Spirit, which "bloweth as it listeth."

All this is awful, overwhelming, but suited to empty us of ourselves. It is evident that we carry this treasure in earthen vessels, and that all which depends on us (if any thing does depend on us) is that the vessel has no leak through which the living water may escape, and no impurity by which it may be corrupted. The rest belongs not to us; and so much the less does it belong to us, the more we imagine that it does. In respect to preaching, then, as well as in respect to the whole work of the ministry, we have cause to rejoice with trembling.

The sovereignty of God in this matter (the first point to be recognized) does not exclude human responsibility. Preaching is an action, but an action of the soul, and its effects are connected with the preacher's spiritual state. It is not so much by what he says as by what he is that the preacher may flatter himself that he does not beat the air. Before every thing, he is concerned to "hold the mystery of the faith in a pure conscience."—1 Tim., iii., 9. This pure conscience (that is to say, uprightness of intention) is the true force of preaching. A discourse is powerful from the motive of him who pronounces it, whatever may be the mode in which that motive expresses itself. A discourse is so much the better, the more it resembles an act of contrition, of submission, of prayer, of martyrdom. The preacher should regard himself as "a channel for what ought to be conveyed by him into the heart of his hearers."* "The ministry of the word," says Fenelon, "is wholly founded on faith." We must pray,

* *Praktische Bemerkungen*, etc., p. 49.

we must purify our heart, we must expect every thing from heaven, we must arm ourselves with the sword of the word of God, and not count upon any thing in ourselves: this is the essential preparation."* In a word, our lips are naturally defiled; they must be purged, and purged by fire.† In short, preaching, which is a divine mystery, is also a human action, and the best part of this action is inward, spiritual, anterior even to the act of composing the discourse. The discourse finishes the work which prayer should begin.

To this general direction we unite a more particular one, which is expressed by St. Paul in these words: "Let him who has received the gift of prophesying exercise it according to the proportion of faith which he has received" (Rom., xii., 6), which further signifies, according to the proportion of life which he has in him. It is true that he is obliged to preach on a fixed and prescribed day. If he does not always find himself in a frame for *prophesying* (that is to say, for speaking with that fullness of heart, and that force which will carry the hearers along with him), he must confine himself to *teaching;* that is to say, treating a subject regularly without aiming to impress any thing.‡ "Whether we be beside ourselves, it is to God; or whether we be sober, it is for your cause."—2 Cor., v., 13.

The evil consists not in being in one state rather than another, but in not exercising our gift according to the measure of faith and of life with which we ourselves are exercised at a given moment, to wish to force our state—the hand of

* FENELON: *Dialogues sur l'Eloquence* (Dialogue III.).

† "Then, said I, woe is me! for I am undone; because I am a man of unclean lips, and I dwell in the midst of a people of unclean lips; for mine eyes have seen the King, the Lord of hosts. Then flew one of the cherubims unto me, having a live coal in his hand, which he had taken with the tongs from off the altar; and he laid it upon my mouth, and said, Lo, this hath touched thy lips; and thine iniquity is taken away, and thy sin purged."—Isaiah, vi., 5–7.

‡ *Praktische Bemerkungen*, p. 37, 38.

God; to think that a blessing may be connected with a deception; for there is deception when our thought is surpassed by our word. We would always be very eloquent; we must content ourselves sometimes with being sober, humble, and feeble. A discourse cold and feeble, but honest, will often be more blessed than an eloquent discourse, which transcends the inward frame.

There is, moreover, in preaching an action more intellectual, more our own still. Neither the sovereignty of God nor the spiritual nature of the action diminishes its importance or impairs its necessity. God does not intend that a good and a bad instrument should give the same sounds, and indeed they do not. I admit that the power of God honors itself in our weakness, but not in our voluntary weakness, which is but a diminution of the strength He has given us, and a throwing away, so to speak, or a despising a part of His grace. The more we feel the seriousness, the responsibility, the danger of our mission, the more shall we be induced to watch, to exercise forethought, to make provision: Our own little providence enters into the account in the calculations of the providence of God. It was said to men once that they should not concern themselves as to what they should speak, expecting that what they ought to speak would be suggested to them at the time.—Mark, xiii., 11. But this has not been said to us, at least not in an absolute manner. We must, then, bestow pains upon preaching; we must preach well. Homiletics have no other object than to initiate us. They will be the most careful in preparation who best know that they can do nothing, and that they are nothing.

But an objection here occurs: May we both preach much and preach well? They who make this objection assume as evident, or at least take for granted, that we ought to preach much. All are not of this opinion; we must, then, in the first place, clear this point.

As it is evident that we are not at liberty to multiply

the hours of worship which the law has numbered and prescribed to us, the assertion that we should preach much signifies either that the law ought to multiply the occasions of worship, or that, apart from the places and days which it has consecrated, the minister ought to teach, to explain, to exhort. I suppose that, in one way or another, the pastor is at liberty to give his flock the bread of the word often, and if he may, why, I ask, should he not? In all cases, there are, doubtless, metes and bounds; but surely it is proper that there should be an abundance of what is good and useful; and it would be a calamity, in order to make preaching more solemn, or more perfect in a literary respect, to make more scarce a word which can not too much abound, and which seldom reaches the human heart, except at the price of a frequent repetition. There are various opinions on this subject. Some recommend frequent preaching,* as I have done; others think the obligation to preach often oppressive, especially to young ecclesiastics.†

We should distinguish, I think, between parochial, official preaching (which is not frequent, and, of course, leaves the objection without force), and preaching "out of season." But supposing that official preaching were more frequent, and the objection consequently in force, what is the answer?

We must not reply by making a distinction between places; for good preaching is as necessary, as difficult, in the country as in the city. In this respect a prejudice is still prevalent. Harms,‡ on this subject, relates a passage in the life of Andreas, who, after having preached without preparation to a country congregation, said to his son, "Did you not observe my distress and my hesitation? They were such that I was upon the point of leaving the pulpit. Never have I been as near losing all presence of mind as before these poor peasants. The grace of God almost wholly forsook me, because I

* De Baudry: *Guide du Prédicateur*, p. 114.

† Harms: *Pastoraltheologie*, tome i., p. 39. ‡ Tome i., p. 49

despised this poor people as not deserving the trouble of a careful preparation. Let my experience make you wiser, my son."

We make no distinction, then, but say that there should be a general preparation for preaching; a thorough and continual study of the flock, of human life, of ourselves, and of the Bible; a habit of disciplining our mind and arranging our ideas, which will never leave us at a loss in a simple address or a familiar exposition of the Bible. I would not have this done without special preparation; but a very short one may suffice.*

It is this general preparation, and not natural talent only, which explains the never fruitless abundance of Calvin, who in ten years preached four thousand and twenty-four sermons—that is to say, four a week; and of Whitefield, who in thirty-four years preached eighteen thousand sermons, or ten a week. The parochial preacher is to be distinguished

* "But you have naturally, you say, a memory which unfits you for speaking in public; but is not your heart as faithless and as rebellious as your memory? The solemn, the holy ministry of pastoral instruction is not a dry and puerile exercise of memory; it is the heart, it is the inmost soul, that must now speak. Ah! my dear brethren, if we contemplate the truths of religion in the holy books—if we love them—if we nourish ourselves by them—if we make them our common and most delightful study, we shall not be so greatly troubled when duty requires us to present them to our people. We soon learn to speak what we love; the heart supplies us much better than the memory, and has also a language which the memory does not know. A holy pastor, moved by God, and by regard to the salvation of the souls which are confided to him, finds, in the liveliness of his zeal, and the fullness of his heart, expressions having the impress of the Holy Spirit, the spirit of love and of light, a thousand times more powerful to move, to reclaim sinners, than all those which are furnished by labor and the vain artifice of human eloquence. Do not, then, say that you have no talent. The talent of an orator is not what is required: it is the talent of a father; and what other talent does a father need in speaking to his children but affection for them, and a desire for their welfare."—MASSILLON: *Dix-septième Discours Synodal; de l'Observance des Statuts et des Ordonnances du Diocèse.*

from the Reformer and the missionary; but why should he not, in a small measure, be both? He is, in effect, nothing if he does not combine these two characters; for, excepting some souls that belong to him, or, rather, to God, all the rest are to be conquered. We often have a false image of a parish, and it is well that Christian zeal has promoted acolyths to regular pastors.

We repeat that it is not proper to distinguish between places (country and city); we may, however, distinguish between sermons—some more after the manner of a treatise, others of a familiar exposition or address. Our time should be chiefly given to the first. We add, thirdly, that we should have more time if, on the one hand, we would learn to substitute force for time, the *intensive* for the extensive;* on the other, if we would addict ourselves to recollection, to solitude, to making thorough work with every subject that engages us, to using every moment to advantage.†

We must not delay preparation. Reinhard relates that, being often engaged in occupations which absorbed the greater part of his time, and being subject, at certain seasons, to sudden indispositions which incapacitated him for application, he formed the resolution never to delay to the last moment the composition of his sermons; and that he also made it a rule never to preach one sermon without having prepared that which was to follow it. He felicitated himself that he had formed this habit, as it saved him from the embarrassment of having to preach without sufficient preparation, or after a hasty preparation; and as it enabled him to work over his sermons when it happened that, in composing them, he did not succeed altogether as he wished.‡

* Intensity for length.—*Edit.*

† M. Durand meditated in the streets, and he was sometimes seen going into alleys to take notes.

‡ *Lettres de Reinhard sur les Etudes et sa Carrière de Prédicateur, traduite de l'Allemand, par* J. Monod. Paris, 1816, p. 77, 78.

The question of preaching extempore naturally presents itself here. Opinions on this point are various. "While there are so many pressing necessities in Christianity," says Fenelon; "while the priest, who ought to be a man of God, prepared to every good work, should hasten to eradicate ignorance and scandals from the field of the Church, I think it is very unworthy of him to be passing his life in his closet in rounding periods, in retouching descriptions, and in inventing divisions; for, when one gets into the way of this kind of preaching, he has time to do nothing else; he can pursue no other study, no other labor; nay, more, to relieve himself he is often obliged to repeat continually the same sermons. What eloquence is that of a man whose hearer knows beforehand all his expressions and all his moving appeals? A likely way, indeed, to surprise, to astonish, to soften, to convince, and to persuade men! a strange method of concealing art and letting nature speak. For my part, I say frankly that all this offends me. What! shall a steward of the mysteries of God be an idle declaimer, jealous of his reputation, and ambitious of vain pomp? Shall he not venture to speak of God to his people without having arranged all his words, and learned, like a school-boy, his lesson by heart?"*

We elsewhere read: "Although it is the custom in some countries to read sermons, or, at least, to write and repeat them, which is necessary in certain places, where the preacher may be obliged to produce his discourse as written after having delivered it; still, generally speaking, such a way of preaching does not seem to produce as much impression on the hearers as free discourse, which induces me to prefer this last method."†

Harms, on the contrary, would have the sermon wholly

* FENELON: *Dialogues sur l'Eloquence* (Dialogue III.). See also Dialogue II.

† *Praktische Bemerkungen die Führung des evangelischen Predigtamtes betreffend.*—HERNHUTT, p. 47.

written out: "If the majority of your hearers do not remark a badly-managed transition, a blank, a vulgar or obscure word, an equivocal or unintelligible proposition; if they do not perceive that your preaching is without profound thought, or that you never cite any other than the most familiar passages of the Bible, or that your expressions are too studied, yet be sure that, in the number of those who hear you, there will be some who will not fail to see all this, and who will think ill of you for not being better prepared."*

Spener made it a rule, up to 1675, to write and to commit his sermons to memory. Afterward, yielding to the counsels of friends, he preached for a certain time from minute notes; but he soon returned to his first method, and never afterward forsook it. He recommends in all things a serious meditation on the substantive subject-matter, rather than on the form to be given to the sermon, a meditation to be accompanied by fervent prayer; and he advises preachers, particularly those who, having a facility of speaking without preparation, may be more disposed to yield themselves to indolence, to reserve a fixed time for this exercise.†

If we were required to give a general rule, we should say that a preacher should, as far as possible, be carefully prepared. The preparation may be made in different methods. Some say they can not prepare without writing, and can not preach without reciting what they have written; others maintain that they can not prepare in this way, because they are not able to fix in their memory a written sermon. We must discard these two impossibilities: the minister should be able to speak without having written, and every minister should have it in his power to learn a sermon which he has composed. Some, it is true, though a very small number, have so treacherous a memory that we can not oblige them to learn and recite. These have no liberty of choice, and the

* *Pastoraltheologie*, tome i., p. 48, 49.

† See Burk, *Pastoraltheologie*, tome i., p. 164.

mode of their preparations is prescribed to them by necessity; but then they are exceptions, which are very rare. Now, all that we can recommend, in general, is preparation. If we do not recite a sermon written and learned beforehand, even this preparation, in order to be complete and sufficient, will require more care and labor, a more intense and vigorous effort. Extemporizing can not be authorized, unless when it be such as can hardly take this name. The sermon ought to be well and solidly prepared. Without this, we run the risk of becoming always more careless, and of contenting ourselves with what costs us little. In general, the young preacher should write and recite. Let him take care, however, and seek to acquire the memory of ideas with and before that of words. He will thus prepare himself for a freer way of preaching. As to extemporaneous preaching, properly so called, we absolutely reject this method. Great orators, Bossuet, Fenelon, etc., have fallen by it, not only below themselves, but below ordinary preachers. We may, however, extemporize if it be unavoidable; an occasion may occur, and even frequently, when the preacher may either find himself, after having entered the pulpit, induced to make changes in a sermon which he has written, or be in unforeseen circumstances, which require him to speak without preparation.

Spiritual meditation before preaching is of great importance. "He must," says St. Cyran, "labor long at mortification of spirit, seeing that we ought to be more afraid of offending God in the pulpit than elsewhere."*

"The best preparation for preaching," it is said in the practical observations of Hernhutt, "is daily communion with Christ, watching our own heart, and constant reading of the word of God. Thus is secured that precious simplicity which has always been the chief characteristic of all the distinguished witnesses of the grace of Christ."

* St. Cyran: *Lettres à M. Le Rebours.* Lettre XXXI.

§ 3. *Object of Preaching.*

The object of preaching (of every sermon, I mean) should be "Jesus Christ crucified, who of God is made unto us wisdom, righteousness, sanctification, and redemption."—1 Cor., i., 30. In every sermon we must either start from Christ or come to him. The whole of Christianity should be in every sermon, in this sense that sanctification never appear in it independent of faith, nor faith separate from sanctification. Where this combination does not appear of itself, where these two elements are not so incorporated and consubstantial, the one with the other, that it is morally and rationally impossible to speak of one without speaking of the other, there no true Gospel is present, and that which is preached is not the Gospel.

It is according to this sense that we must understand the words of St. Paul: "I determined not to know any thing among you, save Jesus Christ, and him crucified."—1 Cor., ii., 2. These words signify, first, that St. Paul did not seek and did not publish salvation in any other than Jesus Christ; but they also signify that in whatever he taught he returned to this, came back to this, that this was every where present in his preaching, actually or virtually, as substance or as savor. But these same words do not signify absolutely that St. Paul knew nothing else. On the contrary, he knew, and the true pastor, after his example, should know, a great deal else. It is true, very often, that a preacher who literally knows nothing but Christ crucified, who puts nothing but this in his sermons, may produce excellent effects; so great is the value and the expansive force of the Christian doctrine. But this does not form the rule: The rule rather is to show, to enforce the relation of religion to whatever pertains to man and to human life. So far from having us ignorant of every thing, the rule much rather would have us know, or at least understand, every thing; not in order to declare, not in order to display in the pulpit an encyclopedia of knowledge, but that nothing may be said which may meet a contradiction, or that will not find confirmation in facts; and also that every thing which we speak may be more direct, more striking, more true. There are a thousand things which we should never speak of in the pulpit, of which, nevertheless, we should not be ignorant; and an experienced hearer will discern in a sermon which speaks only of Jesus Christ and of religion the imprint or the reflection of diversified knowledge, which the orator does not outwardly produce, but which turns within him *in succum et sanguinem*. Besides, we can not in all cases say beforehand what a Christian orator should or should not speak. Necessarily, he is to speak of human life; and, to be instructive, he must enter into details: Who may say where is the limit. What would be superfluous in certain times or in certain places, in others would be no more than necessary.

In theology, it is very necessary to distinguish between doctrine and morality; but a nice distinction between sermons on doctrine and sermons on morality is of small importance to a Christian preacher. Doctrine and morality, which are interfused, identified in the Christian heart, should be so in Christian preaching. I would have no other rule than this: let doctrine abound in moral preaching, and morality abound in doctrinal preaching. But, without doubt, a preacher should oblige himself to give to his parishioners instruction, both moral and doctrinal, as complete as possible.

§ 4. *Unity of Preaching.*

What we have now said leads us to observe, that preaching in a parish should be regarded as a whole, and not be made up of detached discourses, of each of which chance alone has furnished the subject. It is one continuous action; it is only one and the same sermon formed of many consecutive sermons.

This may be so, it should be so, even when we pursue neither a systematic order of subjects, nor preach on a book or books of the Bible. Both these methods have their utility. The one relieves us of the trouble of choosing a text, the other that of choosing a subject. There is a consecutiveness —a progress in them also, which interests and which attracts.

But even without following either of these courses, the true pastor will have one marked out to him by his own observation and experience.

In order to this, it is necessary that we should regard the parish as a whole—a unit, as it is to every intelligent observer. It has a life, the phases of which are successive: it receives from our ministry a development which authorizes and urges us to modify our preaching. There is, there ought to be, between the pastor and his flock a common life, a reciprocal sensation, which conforms the auditory to the preacher and the preacher to the auditory. When the preacher has not received from his life as a pastor the *word of command* as to his successive preachings, we may doubt whether his ministry is well understood and well discharged.

In a congregation where there are two pastors, who preach by turns to the same auditory, it is very desirable that there should be so much union, and so much mutual confidence and agreement between them, as to enable them to suit their sermons to one another, so that they form, in a certain sense, but one instance of preaching, only one whole, in which repetition is avoided no less than contradiction.

§ 5. *Different Classes combined in the same Auditory.*

The unity of the parish is consistent with classes, and classes very distinct.

In a religious view, there are the converted and the unconverted; or, if we will, those who have not yet received the Gospel—whether they admit or reject revelation, or whether they are in doubt on this subject, or whether it is vague and confused in their apprehension, all, however, in this respect equal, that the cross of Jesus is yet to them a stumbling-block or foolishness—and those who, consenting to seek their salvation in Jesus Christ, need henceforth to be more and more confirmed in their hope, and to walk with more steadfast step in the way in which Christ himself walked. Shall we preach alternately to these two classes? or, should we not rather introduce into each discourse something suited to both? I think it essential to speak in such a way that no one may deceive himself as to the unchangeable condition of salvation, and, what comes to the same thing, of sanctification. This secured, explicit and formal classifications do not seem to me generally necessary; and I think they are subject to more than one inconvenience, especially when they assume, as they commonly do with certain preachers, a direct and allocutive form. As occasion may require, describe the situation of each of these classes, but do not give them *form;* do not *design* them; do not teach your auditory to divide themselves into envious and hostile groups.* The auditory, no doubt, includes many sorts of men; nay, more, it includes so many shades of character, that your word can not suffice for all. We speak of sermons of appeal and sermons of sanctification: let us make both; or, let the same discourse exhibit both elements successively; but let us bear well in mind that the word of appeal applies to those who have already responded to the appeal, and the word of sanctification to those who have not responded to it. In one sense all, even the most advanced, have need to be called

* "To separate your hearers into two classes, and to apostrophize them, one after another, in these terms: Ye sinners who have been graciously accepted; ye awakened sinners, and ye unrepentant sinners, tends only to irritation. Hold up to all the clear mirror of the Gospel, and each one, beholding himself in it, will see in what class he ought to place himself."—*Praktische Bemerkungen*, p. 33.

anew; and the most alienated and the greatest strangers may be *called* by a sermon of sanctification. Of this there are a thousand examples. Conversion is but a moment in sanctification, and sanctification is but conversion repeated (continued) and prolonged.

The auditory is susceptible of further divisions. The only distinction of importance is that between the wise and the ignorant. St. Paul declares that he was debtor to both. I would not that the wants of the wise should be neglected; but, certain cases excepted, which may be easily represented, and of which the reckoning is soon made, we have before us an auditory, mixed, of the wise and the ignorant, and in which the ignorant make the majority. Now what for the second is necessary is not unsuitable to the first; but what is proper to the first is not suitable to the second. A man who understands his subject and his work can speak to the ignorant in a manner interesting and instructive to the wise. Depth and simplicity meet at the same point. Have you an audience composed of forty-nine wise and one ignorant? speak for that ignorant one. It is more necessary to efface than to render prominent the differences which exist among the different classes of an audience. The accidental, individual man should disappear, and give place to the universal man. In this consists the force of the ministry, the greatness and power of eloquence. Study your discourse with reference to all your hearers indiscriminately; but give no particular class occasion to think that you design to flatter their ears and obtain their favor. In Germany they make sermons *für Gebildete.** What are these? Great eloquence is popular: great orators have been popular ones. Bourdaloue himself was such, with all his knowledge of composition.

* For educated people.—*Edit.*

§ 6. *Popularity, Familiarity, Unction.*

Popularity and familiarity are two similar though distinct qualities. The first respects, in the auditory, only the people—man; familiarity regards the relations not only of religion to man, but of the pastor to the parish, which is as his family. Familiarity is not vulgarity; it consists with nobleness; and, well conceived, it is the noblest language. In this familiarity of the pastor with his parish there is something of the grasping of a naked hand by another naked hand. The warmth of life is reciprocally felt when the hands are ungloved, that there may be nothing intervening between man and man.

Authority, in the objective sense, is the right or privilege of being obeyed or believed; subjectively, it is the consciousness of this right. A preacher speaks with authority when we perceive in his language a sense of this right, and that this sense is what it should be.

In the second sense, we may say that authority is generally essential to eloquence, essential especially to preaching, and that it comes well from all. But it has its conditions, its means, its obstacles.

In general, to speak with authority, we must be convinced of the truth of what we say, have confidence in the intrinsic power of truth, and be penetrated with the interest we defend. We must also have a certain confidence in ourselves. I do not mean self-importance. These qualities affect the hearers immediately and mediately; immediately by their own influence: we believe willingly in one who himself is a believer; mediately, by the calmness, the serenity, which they impart. More is revealed than is spoken.

As to the preacher in particular, his authority comes from his speaking not in his own name, but in the name of God, and from his depending not on the power of his word, but on the power of the word and Spirit of God; finally, from his expecting his approval from God. Hence authority in him should be regarded as a duty.

What he adds to this from his own fund, experience of the truth,* and the conformity of his life to his doctrine,† pertains to causes before mentioned; it is not the source, it is derived from the source. Even with convinced, established, and pious men, authority is diminished by excess of reasoning and by vehemence.

The preacher certainly ought to *demonstrate*, that others may share his own conviction; but it often suffices to *show*, as most splendidly did Jesus Christ. In fact, Christian truth is perceived by intuition. Free exposition doubtless does much; but we greatly obstruct our path‡ by the language of asseveration, and at the same time we diminish our authority. It is not, however, implied that we should so demean ourselves as to say, Believe because I believe. In one way or another, the force of demonstration must be in what we utter.

Vehemence lessens authority. It is in place on certain occasions, but the ordinary tone of preaching is a tranquil force. Serenity is more impressive. Bourdaloue had a sorrowful calmness, Bossuet a luminous serenity.

Has the Protestant preacher an authority equal to that of the Catholic? The Catholic is supported by an imposing human, and of course factitious, authority. In him the religion, so to speak, gives her authority to her minister. The Protestant is the representative of free investigation; he has no support but from himself; he speaks as an individual; has he not, however, enough of authority if he be a Christian? In the Protestant Church, one may have a certain

* "That which was from the beginning, which we have heard, which we have seen with our eyes, and which our hands have handled of the word of life."—1 John, i., 1.

† "Nil conscire sibi."—HORAT.: *Epist.*, lib. i., v. 61.

‡ French, *On croise le fer.*

catholicism which lends to the minister as much authority as catholicism, in the proper sense, does to the priest. As the law makes the whole community a Church, there is a compact mass (a unit), which gives authority to the minister. The march of thought, on this point, has put men very much at their ease. In our times, the majority is dissolved, or, rather, the true majority is discovered: The state of things is not worse; on the contrary, it is but better known. The number of believers and faith itself have not suffered from it. The position of the pastor toward his flock has, without doubt, changed; but the preacher has always his flock—his sheep. Few wish to remain or enter within the pale of the Church. We have to be missionaries. But if this new position is difficult, it is noble. It neither destroys nor weakens authority; it purifies it, and reduces it to its true elements. Authority has become, truly, the authority of conviction. The priest is "a plaintive king."* Is the sentiment of authority, in these days, stronger, or more rare and feeble? I dare not answer. It appears to me, however, that the preacher does not assume the authority he might have.

The *modesty* or *humility* which restrains us from speaking or acting with authority is a poor apology. We are to be neither modest nor humble at God's injury, or at the expense of truth. To a man who, in personal respects, is our superior, we have superiority from our commission. An embassador, a plenipotentiary, regards not what he is, but the powers with which he is clothed; and, however modest he may be, with these he may become peremptory.

Between him and us there is doubtless a difference, which leads us into error and blame by the inferences we draw from the analogy. We know that we ought not only to represent, but that we ought to *be*, and that what we are confirms or enfeebles our word. But if, because we can never rise in character to the height of our mission, we may abstain from

* St. Beuve: *Port Royal*, tome i., p. 469.

fulfilling it, no one would ever fulfill it. Whatever we are, we carry this treasure in earthen vessels, which never will be golden ones; but God himself has appointed these vessels to bear and to distribute this treasure. If we feel humbled by the unavoidable comparison of the vessel with the treasure which it contains, this humiliation is beneficial; it does not divest us of all proper authority; it casts us altogether on that of God.

There is a state of mind, doubtless, which hinders us from taking the statutes of God in our mouth; it is the state we are in when we hate correction.—Ps. l., 16. But if the humiliation which we experience as feeble Christians, and which increases in proportion as we advance in the Christian life, should restrain us from reproving, it should restrain us also from teaching; for teaching is equally above us, and all teaching reproves. So far is humility from injuring authority, that it is in humility that authority should temper and purify itself. It is useful for us to say to ourselves, "Homines sumus, nec aliud quam fragiles homines, etiamsi angeli à multis æstimamur et dicimur."*

St. Paul (Tit., ii., 15) would have us "reprove with full authority."† Reproof, an element of preaching, is a principal part of the pastoral office. And, moreover, how can we refrain from it? Have we a right to be merciful if we have not first been severe? Will the hearers accept pardon if they have not felt condemned? I do not speak here of individual or private reproof, but of that which has place in the pulpit. Easier than the first, because that reaches every one, and less afflicts individuals; this still is difficult, on account of its publicity, its solemnity, and the narrowness of

* "We are men, frail men, and nothing more, though many regard us as angels of God."—*Imitation de Jesus Christ.*

† "He shall reprove with equity; he shall smite the earth with the rod of his mouth, and with the breath of his lips shall he slay the wicked."—Isaiah, xi., 4.

its range.* Being collective, it is more general, less cutting, less penetrating. It is, however, to be understood that I speak of the censure of the flock as a special individuality, not simply as some portion of humanity. We must put our finger on the particular blemish in the flock we are addressing. This special censure is necessary if the flock is a reality: It makes it more serious, it gives it a sentiment apprizing it of its existence as a flock, and of its relations to the pastor. It is a great force when it is used as it ought to be.

Times and places, unquestionably, do not allow the same thing to all. We have not the same liberty with a promiscuous auditory as we have with a particular and chosen Church. A young man may not do what an old one may. Still, I see not why a minister may not do whatever a private person, who exalts himself to be a censor of morals, may do, pen in hand. Only he must, 1. Avoid all appearance of personality, and to this end, he must not give portraits; his object is never to nourish malignity; 2. Prefer direct censure to oblique allusion; 3. Not forget that the wrath of man worketh not the righteousness of God, and that, in general, the fruit of righteousness is sown in peace. If it be truth that offends, this is not our concern; but if it is we that offend, then are we responsible. A satirical spirit never does good. Young preachers should keep themselves most seriously on their guard, lest, without thinking of it, they yield to a temptation no less natural than subtile, that of using the pulpit simply as an instrument of sharp censure. Vehemence, a holy indignation, may sometimes be allowed, invective never. If indignation impresses, anger inflames and rebels. This distinction is just; for we may hate evil without loving good.

From our usages as to preaching, eulogium seldom has place in the pulpit. St. Paul, however, gives us examples of it, in addressing certain Churches. We may not, then, pro-

* Public reproof can extend to but few points, comparatively.—*Tr.*

scribe praise or approbation: When, however, we consider what the primitive Churches were, we may learn that what was done then can not be as commonly done now.

Unction.—This word, taken in its etymology, and in its primitive acceptation, denotes no special quality of preaching, but rather the grace and the efficacy which are connected with it by the Spirit of God; a kind of seal and sanction which consists less in outward signs than in an impression received by the soul. But as, in ascending to the cause of this effect, we distinguish particularly certain characters, it is to the reunion of these characters that we have given the name of unction. Unction seems to me to be the total character of the Gospel; to be recognized, doubtless, in each of its parts, but especially apprehensible in their assemblage. It is the general savor of Christianity; it is a gravity accompanied by tenderness, a severity tempered with sweetness, a majesty associated with intimacy; the true contemperature of the Christian dispensation, in which, according to the Psalmist's expression, "Mercy and truth have met together, righteousness and peace have kissed each other."—Ps. lxxxv., 10. It is so proper a thing to Christianity and to Christian matters, that we scarcely can think of transferring the term to other spheres, and when we meet with it applied to other things than Christian discourse, or Christian actions, we are astonished, and can only regard it as an analogy or a metaphor.

From the fact that the whole modern world has been wholly imbued with Christianity, many modern works, which are neither Christian nor even religious, can not be otherwise marked than by the word *unction;* while there is no work of antiquity that awakens this idea.

The idea that Maury* gives of unction is no other than that of Christian pathos. The definition of Blair is more dis-

* MAURY: *Essai sur l'Eloquence de la Chaire* (chap. lxxxiii.), *de l'Onction.*

tinctly identical with ours. "Gravity and warmth united," according to this author, "form that character of preaching which the French call unction; the affecting, penetrating, interesting manner, flowing from a strong sensibility of heart in the preacher to the importance of those truths which he delivers, and an earnest desire that they may make a full impression on the hearts of his hearers."*

M. Dutoit Membrini thinks that, in order to define unction, an intimate and mysterious quality, we must guard against formal definition and analysis. It is by the effects of unction and by analogies that he would explain it, or, to speak better, give us a taste of it:

"Unction is a mild warmth which causes itself to be felt in the powers of the soul. It produces in the spiritual sphere the same effects as the sun in the physical: it enlightens and it warms. It puts light in the soul; it puts warmth in the heart. It causes us to know and to love; it fills us with emotion."

I willingly admit that it is a light which warms and a warmth which enlightens; and I would recall on this subject the words of St. John: "The anointing which you have received from him abideth in you, and this anointing teaches you all things."—1 John, ii., 27.

M. Dutoit Membrini continues thus: "Its only source is a regenerate and gracious spirit. It is a gift which exhausts itself and is lost if we do not renew this sacred fire, which we must always keep burning: that which feeds it is the internal cross, self-denial, prayer, and penitence. Unction, in religious subjects, is what in the poets is called *enthusiasm*. Thus unction is the heart and the power of the soul, nourished, kindled, by the sweet influence of grace. It is a soft, delicious, lively, inward, profound, mellifluous feeling.

"Unction, then, is that mild, soft, nourishing, and, at the same time, luminous heat, which illumines the spirit, pene-

* Blair (Lect. xxix.), *Eloquence of the Pulpit.*

trates the heart, moves it, transports it, and which he who has received it conveys to the souls and the hearts which are prepared to receive it also.

"Unction is felt, is experienced, it can not be analyzed. It makes its impression silently, and without the aid of reflection. It is conveyed in simplicity, and received in the same way by the heart into which the warmth of the preacher passes. Ordinarily, it produces its effect, while as yet the taste of it is not developed in us, without our being able to give a reason to ourselves of what has made the impression. We feel, we experience, we are touched, we can hardly say why.

"We may apply to him who has received it these words of the prophet Isaiah: 'Behold, I will make thee a new sharp threshing instrument having teeth.'—Isaiah, xli., 15. This man makes furrows in hearts."

From all that has been said, we must not conclude that unction, which has much the same principle as piety, is exactly proportioned to piety. Unction may be very unequal in two preachers, equal in piety; but it is too closely related to Christianity to be absolutely wanting to truly Christian preaching. Certain obstacles, some natural, others of error or of habit, may do injury to unction, and obstruct, so to speak, the passage of this soft and holy oil, which should always flow, to lubricate all the articulations of thought, to render all the movements of discourse easy and just, to penetrate, to nourish speech. There is no artificial method of obtaining unction; the oil flows of itself from the olive; the most forcible pressure will not produce a drop from the earth, or from a flint; but there are means, if I may say so, by which we may keep, without unction, even a good basis of piety; or, of dissembling the unction which is in us, and of restraining it from flowing without. There are things incompatible with unction: Such are wit,* analysis too strict, a tone too dicta-

* Nevertheless, St. Bernard and Augustin have wit and unction.

torial, logic too formal, irony, the use of too secular or too abstract language, a form too literary; finally, a style too compact and too close, for unction supposes abundance, overflow, fluidity, pliableness.

It is the absence, rather than the presence of unction, that gives us its idea. It is from its opposite that we obtain its distinct notion, not, however, that it is but a negative quality; on the contrary, it is the most positive; but positive in the sense of an odor, of a color, of a savor.

But let us not contract the idea of unction by reducing it to an effeminate mildness, a wordy abundance, a weeping pathos. We must not think that we can not have unction except on the condition of interdicting strictness and consecutiveness in argument, and that boldness of accent, that holy vehemence which certain subjects demand, and without which, in treating them, we should be in fault.

Massillon has unction, as Maury thinks, in a piece which contains nothing but reproaches.* As an example, we cite Bossuet also, in the conclusion of a sermon on *final impenitence.*

§ 7. *Form of Preaching.*

The true form of a sermon is composed of the double impression of the subject and of the subjectivity of the orator. The form of a sermon acknowledges only these two laws, which, so far from opposing, combine with one another.

As to general forms which we may observe among preachers, as the psychological and logical form, that of continuous discourse, and that of parallel developments, or of discourse ramified, the analytical and the synthetical sermon, they are neither conventional nor artificial; they are less differences

* MAURY: *Eloquence de la Chaire* (chap. lxxii.), *de l'Onction.* See MASSILLON, the conclusion of the first part of the sermon, *Sur l'Aumône.*

of form than of thought, points of view, methods of conceiving the subject of discourse. They exist in the subjects themselves, and in the human mind anterior to all tradition.

There is the same difference between the conventional and the spontaneous form as there is between the two physiological systems, one of which makes the prominences of the skull to depend on the internal developments of the brain, and the other these same developments to depend on the prominences of the skull; one expressing the internal by the external, the other, by the external compressing and determining the internal; one subordinating the external to the internal, the other the internal to the external. We ourselves prefer that the external should spring from the internal, and, in respect to form, we give no rule but this.

But this rule we do give; and, in order to follow it, we must resolve upon doing this with a positive and determined will; for the arbitrary forms will be incessantly besetting us with their importunity; or, rather, being born in the midst of them, we shall have trouble to withdraw ourselves from their dominion. Now let it be observed that the most natural forms constantly tend, by servile and blind imitation, to become conventional types; they are a liquid always on the point of coagulation; so that we must constantly, by warmth and by spontaneity, keep them in a fluid state, or restore them to it, that we may, as far as possible, exclude formalism from our subject, our end, and our mind.*

I understand by the form of preaching not only the frame or the architecture of the discourse, but the tone, the language, and even the topics, for to introduce new topics into it will somewhat change the form of the preaching: these are nothing more than the form of an act, which is more particular or more special only as it is a discourse on divine things. Thus, in making a sermon on the life of a godly man, after the manner of Catholics in preaching on the lives

* See HERDER'S *Briefe das Studium der Theologie betreffend*, tome i.

of their saints, we only change the form, not the object of preaching, since a life may as well serve for the text of a sermon as a passage of Scripture. On this subject a new question respecting form remains to be considered, but it is one of inferior and subordinate importance.

Now, whatever extension may be given to the idea of form, I think we are in a strait, and that we have no excuse for remaining in it.

There is a uniformity, or a too constant return of the same form—of one discourse after another, and one preacher after another.*

In the structure of our sermons, taken separately, there is something stiff and scholastic : While all things are in the process of renovation, and when, as the result of a general revision, we have effaced whatever separates unduly the means from the end, the sermon retains a costume somewhat superannuated.

Language itself has taken a costume. We are far from not liking and recommending biblical language. Religion has a language, terms which it has introduced for the expression of new or renovated things, for Christianity "makes all things new," and there must, of course, be a change in words. But we should not think ourselves obliged to express things in no other terms than those which the Bible has consecrated. That we may better reproduce the spirit of the sacred authors, we must less imitate than be inspired by them. They used a liberty which we refuse them. We need not debar ourselves from spheres which they appear not to have permitted themselves to occupy, merely because they had no occasion to enter them. According to the old scrupulosity of the pulpit in the use of language, Paul was not justifiable in citing Aratus and Epimenides. Most certainly

* On individuality in the form of the sermon, which is very rare, see THEREMIN, *Die Beredsamkeit eine Tugend*, deuxième edition. Berlin, 1837, p. xxiif., de l'Introduction.

we ought not to make the temple a rendezvous for all those worldly recollections which our hearers should leave at the door; but it may be very useful to call certain things by the names which are given to them in common parlance.*

The rule is a good one of preaching from a text; I like it, provided place be left for exceptions. We ought to be allowed to preach without a text, or from two texts united.

So far as respect for our ministry and our flock will permit, we must avail ourselves of all our advantages. "All things are ours."—1 Cor., iii., 21. But let us beware of the spirit of innovation, which changes for the pleasure of changing, or for the sake of appearing independent.

The homily, a species of preaching deserving great attention, has this among other advantages, that it almost necessarily breaks certain traditional forms of the sermon—those at least which respect the structure of the discourse.

As to *delivery*, which is the eloquence of the body, the most important rules are negative ones.† Let us remember how much the multitude is influenced by what is external, and endeavor, if possible, not to *preach*, but *speak*. Bad habits, bad traditions, perpetuate themselves; the good becomes bad by an unintelligent imitation. Let us avoid a theatrical, very familiar, excessively free manner.

§ 8. *Festival and occasional Sermons.*

We have said that the fundamental ideas of Christianity, and the chief conclusions from them, should reappear, and be felt in every sermon: How much more should they be amplified in the entire course of preaching. But it does not hence follow that sermons on festivals, and the Sundays preceding them (weeks of Advent and Lent), should not have a distinct character of their own. These observances are rep-

* See Reflections of Burk on the *Simplicitas Catechetica*.

† For the details, see *l'Homilétique*.

utable and useful, and, if the evangelic year is of the same tenor, still it may have more emphatic moments. These seasons are good and acceptable to all, and the sad but too evident fact is to be taken into consideration, that these with us are the only occasions which bring certain members of the flock into the Church. We may be serious and solemn on every subject, even of Christian morality, as was M. Manuel, who preached on a communion day on the fifth commandment; but, in general, the festival itself must be our theme.

I would not distinguish a fast-day only by more vivid and more accumulated censures, but would be popular and natural in my manner; the people now, as a people, come to humble themselves before God.

Sermons, preparatory to the Lord's Supper, present a delicate point. There should be much of tact in them, and of sound and precise instruction on the nature and the duty of communion.

We are scarcely required to preach on particular circumstances, but circumstances, by judicious use, may become excellent texts for our sermons. In every case we have a double task, to make the eternal actual, and the actual, so to speak, eternal. If it is unfortunate to regard a circumstance only as a theme for oratorical display, it will be unhappy also not to take advantage of it largely and freely, for the purpose of edification. The best of all guides, on these occasions, is the simplicity of a Christian heart, and the true point of view is secured by prayer. Every one has not the secret of making exquisite allusions and delicate turns; but every one finds in the seriousness of the Gospel a true measure, true concord, and just caution.

§ 9. *Several Questions relative to Preaching.*

Length of the Sermon.—Length and brevity are relative qualities. A sermon which bears one along seems shorter, while a sermon in which the development of the idea does not advance always appears long. We must not, then, dwell much on details, but give the discourse a progressive movement.*

But the question may be taken absolutely.

"Believe me, I speak from experience, and long experience: The more you say, the less will be retained. The less you say, the more the hearers will be profited. By overcharging their memory you destroy it, as we put out lamps by overfilling them with oil, and drown plants by immoderately watering them. When a discourse is too long, the end obliterates the middle and the beginning. Ordinary preachers are acceptable if they be short, and excellent ones weary us when they are too long."†

We must not, in a word, expect too much from the auditory. In a country congregation, especially, close attention can not be sustained for a long time; but even to them a sermon too short is an offense. Men have an impression that matters of great importance ought not to be merely glanced upon.

Repetition of Sermons; that is to say, the habit of reproducing, after a certain time, sermons which have been preached. This is the point of view in which this matter should be placed: In two ways a sermon may be true—when it expresses the truth, and when it expresses the preacher himself. A preacher may have nothing to change or retrench in a sermon; he may admit its power, and yet not be able to put himself into his sermon a second time, or his sermon into himself. I would by no means forbid the repetition of a good sermon, which the preacher may perhaps modify, so as to accommodate it, in spirit, to his own actual state, or the

* Compare here the sermon of BOURDALOUE on *La Passion*, with that of MASSILLON on *Consummatum est.*

† *Guide de ceux qui annoncent la Parole de Dieu, contenant la Doctrine de Saint François de Sales*, etc. Lyon, 1829, p. 8.

actual wants of the flock. We must guard against abuse. We are not slow to give ourselves great license here, and we may proceed to a ridiculous and scandalous excess.

May a Pastor have one to preach for him?—The interest of the flock may sometimes justify the pastor in obtaining an aid in preaching. Why refuse to the flock good nourishment which may be offered it, or the advantage of hearing the same truths from two different men, and under two different forms? Why refuse one's self a repose which is, perhaps, necessary, and the advantage of hearing the word, of being *preached to?* But, on the one hand, the responsibility we are under forbids our having men to preach for us in whom we have not confidence; on the other hand, the course and continuity of instruction may be impaired by too frequent interruptions; and, finally, facility in yielding or offering our pulpit would not fail to injure our standing in our parish. Harms replies to those who say, But when we are sick? "Do not be sick."* I would rather say, do not imagine yourselves to be sick.

What should be done before Preaching.—Before preaching we ought to have an exercise of mortification, remembering, as St. Cyran says, that we should be especially afraid of offending God in the pulpit.† We must possess ourselves of the feeling of our unworthiness and our weakness; like the publican, we should smite upon our breast. If it be robbery to undertake a mission to which we are not called, it is so likewise to be occupied in it with unsuitable feelings. A carnal confidence, a desire to make a show, is of fatal influence on preaching. We must pray, not for ourselves alone, or with anxious feeling on our own account, but especially for the flock. Prayer for ourselves is good and necessary, but we must not in this spend too much time. If we pray too little for others, we shall not pray well for ourselves. We

* *Pastoraltheologie*, tom. i., p. 41.

† ST. CYRAN (Lettre xxxi.), *à M. Le Rebours*.

should travail in birth for souls, till Christ be formed within them.

What should be done after the Sermon.—Not less useful is an appropriate exercise after preaching than the preparation which goes before it. This exercise includes:

An act of gratitude toward God for giving us the honor of preaching the word of life, for our having strength for it, and for our having been kept from error and contempt.

An act of humiliation and of mortification. We ought to confess our unworthiness of so great a function as that which we have been performing, and to humble ourselves on account of it.

Self-examination and contrition, in view of our sins of the tongue and the secret sins of our heart in the pulpit.

Prayer. After having planted and watered, we should ask God to give the increase.

All these may be abiding in the state of the heart; but it is useful to turn feelings into acts, to give these things a form, an utterance.*

The Preacher should know what is thought of his Preaching.—We can not, in this case, apply in every sense the words of St. Paul: "It is a small thing for me to be judged of you, or of man's judgment."—1 Cor., iv., 3.

Theremin thinks that the only absolute test of good preaching is consciousness of having sought the glory of God.† It is not the less important, on this account, to be admonished of any errors which may need to be corrected.

There are indirect or silent admonitions which, if we are

* See, on this subject, the *Guide de ceux qui annoncent la Parole de Dieu*, p. 217.

† He may be satisfied if he has done all he can to please God, and none but him. This is not only a good test of the worth of a sermon, but the only one which we can depend upon, and we can recognize no other. In place of this, we can not accept even the blessing which may be connected with a sermon.—Theremin: *Die Beredsamkeit eine Tugend.*

willing, we shall not fail to receive. There are praises which are criticisms, as there also is a criticism which praises and a silence which speaks. The air of our flock, their silent reflectiveness, shows us what is passing within them, better than visible tokens of emotion. There are many things, however, we never can know, or never know well, because too much frankness is required to give us the knowledge of them, or too much judgment to receive the idea of them. We live, for the most part, in so much seclusion, that we shall be without admonition if we do not desire it.

Faites choix d'un censeur solide et salutaire,
Que la raison conduise et le savoir éclaire,
Et dont le crayon sur aille d'abord chercher
L'endroit que l'on sent faible et qu'on veut se cacher,*
Aimez qu'on vous conseille, et non pas qu'on vous loue.†

We may find such a monitor not only in a brother in the ministry, but in the humblest member of our flock. A simple parishioner, a poor woman, a child even, may be such a one. We should, without doubt, use caution in this matter, and not consult every one who may come in our way; but, with the view of correcting our faults, we must seek to know the truth.

On the immediate Effect, or immediate Impression of the Sermon.—As to this, whether good or evil, we are often disappointed. Many preachers are astonished to see the small effect of discourses from which they expected great success; and *vice versâ*. Many discourses, longly drawn out with anguish of soul, composed with poverty of feeling, have been richly blest, have produced more effect than others prepared with alertness and delight. When alertness, memory, fervor itself, have been wanting, the ray which, in passing through the lens, has left it cold, has been a burning one beyond it.‡

* Boileau: *L'Art Poétique*, chant iv. † *Ibid.*, chant i.

‡ See, on this subject, an anecdote related by Burk, *Pastoraltheologie in Beispielen*, tome i., p. 241.

We are very often only the occasion of the Divine blessing.* These trials are useful, and even necessary; they keep us from appropriating our success to ourselves, and from saying to ourselves, I myself have done this. They efface the *I*, always odious, and especially in this case. But we shall fall into a great error if we draw from these experiences the conclusion that it is indifferent whether we do good or evil. They should only teach us that we should be neither discouraged nor inflated.

On the Fruits of Preaching.—The words "Ye shall know them by their fruits" (Matt., vii., 20), are not, without qualification, applicable to preachers. The fruits, so far, at least, as we can see, are not always exactly proportional to zeal and devotedness.

It is important to remember that the grace of God is sovereign, lest we be not tempted to regard ourselves as the efficient agent of our success. While we see one who has sown less reaping more, apparently, it is useful to accustom ourselves to think that God, in this, hath done as he pleased.

It is also important that we do not prescribe conditions to God, by not being willing to sow, unless we have a security that we shall reap. Even when we are not permitted to reap, we must be content, and give thanks that we have sown. The spirit of the ministry, in this respect and in many others, is admirably epitomized in John, iv., 36, 37. "He that reapeth receiveth wages, and gathereth fruit unto eternal life; that both he that soweth and he that reapeth may rejoice together. And herein is that saying true, One soweth, and another reapeth." For a stronger reason should we patiently wait: It is important that our faith and our spirit of prayer should be exercised by waiting. Unfailing success, a harvest which should always come according to our calculation, would be fatal to us. "Be not discouraged by the unprofitableness of your pains and instructions among

* Burk: *Pastoraltheologie*, tome i., p. 276.

your people: God does not always reward the zeal of his ministers by immediate and visible success. Be always casting in, cultivating, watering the holy seed; he who gives the increase will not fail to make it productive in his own time. We would be recompensed, according to our labors, by a sudden and visible fruit; but God does not permit this, lest we should attribute to ourselves and to our feeble powers a success which can come only from the work of grace."*

Besides, we should have no misunderstanding in respect to fruits. There may be more when to us there appears to be less. We can not estimate them when they are spread over the field, but only when they are stowed in the granary. When we see around us the evidences of a religious revival, the Bible abundantly distributed, the word of God zealously preached, we may say, Here the wind of the Lord has passed. But this is wheat which has but sprung up; the harvest is not yet: The harvest consists in sanctification, charity, the whole course of a lowly and pure life.

A quite superficial impression may produce much noise and agitation. A profound impression may express itself more by a whisper. We must not rely too much on results of the first kind, nor distrust too much the second. Sometimes, after rising in a mist, the sun pierces the clouds, and the day is warm and fine; at other times the morning is bright, and the day cold and damp.

Without forgetting that "few are chosen," or that "the gate is strait, and few enter in thereat," we must make it our aim to gain many souls, and not once for all be content with a small number of adepts. We must reckon among the fruits of good and faithful preaching, not only a decided and remarkable awakening of a small number of souls, but a true reformation of a large number. In the inventory we must include every thing, and overvalue nothing. He who has

* MASSILLON (Neuvième Discours Synodal): *De l'Avarice des Prêtres.*

established order in his family, in his habits, is already prepared to enjoy a higher truth. And why should not a minister be a benefactor of his country, and endeavor to promote order and good neighborhood, and give popularity to virtue and moral honesty?

On the Success of Opinion, or the Popularity of Preaching.—We may honor a mere flower with the name of fruit, and take success of opinion, the prevalence of our views, for real success. Now not only is there a great difference between these, but the first, which is not necessarily the means of the last, is often an insurmountable obstacle in its way.

It is dangerous to be popular;* because gratified self-love, which is so dear to us, terminates by taking the means for the end, and induces us to make concessions, which gradually lead us away from the truth. Here we begin to have two masters; and "no man can serve two masters; for either he will hate the one and love the other, or else he will hold to the one and despise the other."—Matt., vi., 24.

We may deceive ourselves as to our own dispositions and motives. We may easily mistake highly-excited feeling for a reduplication of our zeal.† We may also easily mistake tenderness for unction, and take for charity the glow of benevolence which we give in exchange for what we receive. We may know the just value of this kind of animation and excitement by making an experiment on the individual members of our flock: we shall very probably find that we shall not have it now. If our interest does not abate—if we are as earnest now as we were in the pulpit, we may have confidence in our zeal; but if we do not now feel ourselves at home, we may know that we have been sustained partly by self-love.

It is useful to a popular preacher to see himself for a while deserted, or restored ultimately to his true place: He may then learn what he is, and, if he abide this crisis, he will

* See *Omicron*, *Letters of* J. NEWTON. † See *Omicron*.

have true unction. Either he will be no more than a mere man of office, or his motives will be purified.

Between popularity and permanent unpopularity there is a point below which it is not desirable to sink, but above which it is not necessary to rise. And perhaps it will be found that, with some exceptions, true success has been granted to those who, as regards talent, have received neither poverty nor riches, but whom God has nourished with food convenient for them.

Of unpopularity there are two kinds : That of indifference, or personal dislike, no one covets ; not so as to the other kind, which respects doctrine as its cause : This, from its nature, may be made an object of ambition, and it is, I think, dangerous. I should not so regard it if it were inseparable from faithfulness ; for what is necessary can not be dangerous ; or, if it be, it is not, in this case, to be taken into consideration. But let us first be sure that unpopularity for doctrines' sake is the necessary consequence of faithfulness. Some so think, and, accordingly, they regard unpopularity from this cause as a matter of obligation. If it be unavoidable, we must let it come, not cause it to come ; and in no case should we add to it by our manner of presenting the truth. As far as strict integrity will permit, we should, I think, do every thing to avoid becoming unpopular, whether in the one way or the other, because when once the boundary between popular favor and the want of it is passed, self-seeking is as probable in the second case as in the first. The mere impression, or at least the idea too constantly present, that we shall be unpopular, will prescribe the measure of our fidelity, place us in a false point of view, give acerbity to our discourse, put us in an attitude of hostility,* &c.

Thus as to the question in the abstract : If we consult facts in regard to it, I think many examples prove that faithful and conscientious preaching may procure to the preacher

* See *Omicron*.

the high esteem and even affection of the people.* But, after saying this, I add, without hesitation, that the Gospel would not be the Gospel if it should flow into the minds of men as easily and as pleasantly as the doctrines of natural religion or of moral philosophy; for, until the spirit of God opens the heart to the sublime truths of the Gospel, they are as bitter to the taste as they are afterward sweet to the inner man. In evangelical preaching there is always a germ of unpopularity, an element of acerbity, which may reveal itself even at periods when orthodoxy becomes popular and fashionable: The thing may happen. There are periods, also, when a general repugnance to the Gospel and a mysterious attraction to it vividly discover themselves together, and when every one is already excited in favor of it or exasperated against it. But, in general, the preacher's wisdom in this matter adjusts itself to this thought of the apostle: "It is a light thing with me to be judged of man's judgment" (1 Cor., iv., 3); and this other no less apostolical thought: "The fruit of righteousness is sown in peace."—James, iii., 18. "If it be possible, as much as lieth in you, live peaceably with all men."†—Rom., xii., 18.

* See *Omicron*.

† Chrysostom has represented with much force the danger of permitting ourselves to be preoccupied by the desire of favor or the fear of unpopularity.—*De Sacerdotio*, lib. iii., c. 9, et lib. v., c. 2, 4, 6, et 8.

CHAPTER II.

CATECHISING.

§ 1. *Its Importance and its Object.*

AMONG our functions, this occupies the first rank. Religious instruction, well attended on, renews continually the foundation of the Church, and is the most real and valuable part of that tradition by which Christianity, not only as a doctrine, but also as a life, perpetuates itself from age to age. In this tradition, the importance of the sermon, properly so called, is the greater in proportion as it is addressed to hearers who have been prepared by religious instruction.

Catechising is useful to those who are its immediate objects ; it is useful to the parish, which has need to be, and, with its children, is catechised ; it is useful to the pastor himself, who, by the duty of adapting religion to the apprehension of children, is incessantly carried back to simplicity and the true names of things. On all these accounts, it deserves our earnest attention, which it also demands by its difficulty, not the same for all pastors, but always great. For it is a work which, besides all the requisites to good preaching, includes special requisites of its own. He who catechises well will not preach badly ; though he who preaches excellently may be a bad catechist.

It is true that catechising has repulsions which do not pertain to preaching ; but it has attractions, too, which preaching has not.

It is also true that it encounters a formidable obstacle in the small agreement, or rather in the contrast between the teaching which the children receive from the minister, and that which they receive for the greater part of the time from the world and their own domestic relatives. But as far as this obstacle is not absolutely insurmountable, it presents itself to us less as an obstacle than as a motive to give the greater care to this part of the pastoral office, and as itself a reason for this institution.

The object of religious instruction is not simply to teach children *their* religion (as if they already possessed it, and it was *theirs* before they had learned it), but to lay in them the foundation of a life.*

It is undoubtedly an *instruction*, taking this word in its ordinary sense, and below its etymological meaning; but it is more properly an *initiation* into the sacred mystery of the Christian life. "My little children," says St. Paul, "of whom I travail in birth again, until Christ be formed in you."—Gal., iv., 19.

We must not give the preference to the more intelligent children, to those who answer best, but in more limited minds we shall very often recognize a superiority of heart. Answers from the heart, when they are right, are of more value than the most remarkable ones from the understanding. A dull, vexatious child is perhaps more serious than a bright one whom we are fond of caressing.

§ 2. *General characteristics of Catechising—Source and Method of religious Teaching.*

Instruction, as instruction, should be as solid and thorough as possible; still, we should aim at spontaneity and life; and therefore there should be in this study nothing of haste or of excessive labor (that which too much occupies the mind often leaves the heart indolent); nothing which should give it too much resemblance to an ordinary study; nothing which may leave behind it a disagreeable recollection. Let the preacher do what he can to make the child remember,

* See, for the development of this idea, *the Catechetical Course.*

through life, the instructions he gives him. Let the hours of teaching be hours of edification; let the child have the feeling that the exercise is one in which he is to be active;* let religious teaching have the character of worship:† *Action* and *worship*, these two characteristics, which ought to be interfused into one another, are too often lost sight of.

Where ought a child to find his religion? All that he can find himself, he must find, but that is little; all the rest is in the Bible. It is the Bible that must teach him.‡ Catechising presupposes the Bible, which it does but digest and systematize; and we say in passing, that its use after the Bible has not the same inconveniences with its use before it. It would be a sad error to retrench it, but not so great a one as to retrench the Bible.

It is by their mutually interlacing one another that the ideas of the Bible live, as do the fibres of a living body: To separate them is to destroy their life. Facts may be distinct, and the mind may distinguish them; but in reality, in life, nothing is isolated; and all those individualizations, all those personifications, all those entities which appear in Catechisms, are fictions; all the truths here are but different forms or different applications of the same truth. But there are difficulties connected with the use of the Bible; we must not pursue this path without reflection; a method is to be arranged. It is important to understand how we should read, what we should read, where begin, and then adjust every thing carefully to the measure of time we have at command.

* This feeling is promoted by interrogations which elicit the exposition.

† See, on this subject, a passage from Madame NECKER, in her *Education Progressive.* "Religion is never prescribed in its most sacred aspect to the young, if even the teaching of it is not worship," etc Livre vi., chap. ii. (this and the following paragraphs).

‡ See in the *Semeur*, tome ix., numéro 27 (1 Juillet, 1840), an article on M. MORELL'S *Sacred History;* and in the *Appendix*, note K, the portion of this article relating to the use of the Catechism.—*Edit.*

§ 3. *Advice to the Catechist.*

It would be well for the pastor to begin with the youngest children, and, if he is to have them under his direction for many successive years, to proceed leisurely with their instruction: If he is to have them for a short time, he will, I apprehend, be obliged to use a Catechism. But whether he will be under this necessity (and especially in the case now supposed), or whether the Catechism is to come after the Bible, the use of this manual will require special care. It is difficult to make a Catechism, and there are but few good ones. All things else being equal, I should prefer the most elementary—one which, conceived after a Christian plan, and reducing all things to a small number of principles, presents only the fundamental ideas on each subject, but expressed with vigor and feeling. Of all the Catechisms with which I am acquainted, I still give my preference to that of Luther. By adding to it a collection of passages, we shall have all we need.*

Whatever mode of catechising may be adopted, whether the Bible or some manual be its text, if it be public, it should be adapted to the class for which it is specially intended, I mean for children. It is very desirable that adults should take interest in the exercise, and be attendants on it, but we should not think ourselves obliged to change its character on their account. It would be unfaithfulness in respect to the children, and would be rather a damage than a benefit to the adults. Religion is never more penetrating, nor is instruction really more profound, than when Christianity is put in an infantile point of view. To present it thus, is to make it attractive to adults; the best sermon is not so attractive as a catechetic exercise, well managed.

Whether in public or private, we must prepare ourselves well for it, and not say to ourselves, I have only to speak to

* Make use of good *religious tracts.—Réal, Fabre.*

children ; for in this, as in every thing, *maxima debetur puero reverentia.** It is certainly no easy matter to speak well to children : the talent to do this belongs not to every one. Our manner with children should be such as to give exercise to their intuitive power, incisory, penetrating ; but then the danger is at hand of violating propriety. On this point I have pleasure in citing a remarkable confession of Bernard Overberg : In his journal he says, " I am again in school this morning without sufficient preparation. O God ! help me to reform in this matter. I am deceived by saying to myself, That will do well enough—you know your business ; something else is more necessary than preparation for it ; for every thing which can be postponed is less important at this moment than this duty. The want of preparation involves many inconveniences ; it makes teaching dry, confused, loose, diffuse ; the children are embarrassed, they can not fix their attention, and the lesson becomes uninteresting to them and to myself.†

Preparation for catechising, even public catechising, called *oratory*,‡ does not include a discourse written and learned by heart, much less preparation for private instruction given in the pastor's domicile. It is most valuable when it has the character of a free and familiar conversation, difficult to be retained in a written discourse. But the best preparation for it should always be made. In general, if the elements of preparation, under its two forms, are not the same, we may say they compensate one another.

Gentleness and patience are the first qualifications ; ridicule is unpardonable ; hardly less so is embarrassing a child

* JUVENAL : Sat. xiv., v. 47. "We can not be too respectful to a child."

† *Notice sur Bernard Overberg, instituteur à l'Ecole Normale de Münster*, etc., by J. H. SCHUBERT, *professor at Münich ;* published in French by the Society of Neufchâtel,1840, p. 26.

‡ In German, *Predigtcatechismus*.

in the presence of the others. Gentleness should be paternal, but manly. Love for children is the sure means of an amiable deportment toward them, and will happily replace an affectedly mild and evasive manner. As to familiarity, it should certainly not be wanting, but it should be *serious* : Seldom should smiling, never laughing, have place in religious instruction. We must be interesting, not amusing. We have the way of intermixing anecdotes with our instructions ; but they ought to be interspersed with moderation ; to be serious, and well brought forward.

The physical comfort of children in the time of the catechetical exercise is not to be disregarded.

The exercise should not be continued too long : We should especially guard against going beyond bounds in exposition, and economize time for questioning, which less fatigues children, because they have a part in it. We should not say every thing in the exposition, but leave it to the questioning to complement general ideas by particular ideas. The worse way of conducting the business is to allow of digressions which exclude from view the principal object, and from which neither the children nor the pastor can well return. This is the danger of the Socratic method ; an excellent one, and also too little in use. In the absolutely Socratic mode, the child is too quickly persuaded that it is he who has found out every thing, who has said every thing : This will injure the pastor's authority, and the child himself, by exciting his self-love. And then we can not foresee how far we shall go with our familiar detail in giving a simple answer to the child's question. We should avoid too much circuity.

We can not judge of a child with certainty from the answers he gives in the course of instruction ; we must, toward the end of the course, see and examine him by himself : They are not the best who know the most. We ought to see him also, in order to establish him in the true views of the communion to which he is to be admitted. We must explain the Lord's Supper to the child. In a practical point of view, the Lord's Supper is a subject about which many prejudices prevail. This is, in part, the fault of the human heart. In general, the child has no prejudices, but he is ignorant; he should well understand what he is about to do; and the confirmation of the baptismal vow should be presented to him in its true character. The formula used among us is very defective; it says nothing of the Lord's Supper, nor of that grace of God which it is so necessary to have in thought when so awful a promise is made as is required in the formula. This promise should rather be a declaration. The formula, then, ought at least to be complete.

The age at which this confirmation takes place among us* seems to be suitable, having regard to the idea of confirming the baptismal vow freely, with knowledge of its nature. What, besides, is to be had in view as to the question of admitting or not admitting, is true knowledge of the mystery of piety according to each one's capacity, and especially the intelligence of the heart, the religious appreciation of this mystery. For the first, we have a measure; for the second, we have no sure means of knowing it. In respect to the last point, of course, unless we have decisive evidence that the child has dispositions directly contrary to Christianity, we ought to admit him. We have a right to adjourn, to refuse confirmation; but it is exorbitant to arrogate to ourselves the right of preventing another pastor from granting, if he thinks he can do so, what we have refused. We have discharged our responsibility if we have given our brother warning.

* Sixteen years.

SECTION THIRD.

CARE OF SOULS, OR PASTORAL OVERSIGHT.

CHAPTER I.

OF THE CARE OF SOULS IN GENERAL.

§ 1. *Its Relations to Preaching. Ground of the Duty of the Care of Souls.*

In treating successively of the office of the preacher and that of the pastor, we have not meant to say, most assuredly, that preaching was not a pastoral office, and that it did not itself include the care of souls. No more would we say that the care of souls, properly speaking, is substantially distinct from preaching, since it is through the word that the care of souls is accomplished, and, under one form or another, preaching reappears every where.* We may say, in one sense, that the preacher is to the pastor what a part is to the whole; but, in making of these two offices two parts, which are united to one another in order to make together a whole, we easily perceive differences as well as relations between them. The preacher instructs; the pastor trains up (in German, *erziehet*). The one acts on the mass, the other on individuals. The one receives and nourishes those who come; the other seeks those also who do not come. We may further add, that the first occupies himself with spiritual interests; the second unites with these, more or less, temporal interests. For the pastor, in the full extent of his employment, and as

* See, in the introduction to the *Course on Homiletics,* what we have said of the word in the Christian religion.

conformed to its idea in the example of Christ, is the benefactor of his people.* If the present state of society leaves him less to do, another state may chance to come which will invest him anew with his ancient responsibilities.

But, considering only the moral interests of the parish, he is not completely a pastor, that is to say, a father, if he is only a preacher. What is the pastoral spirit? A spirit of paternity and of solicitude; for this is the spirit of God himself, as the Bible reveals him to us when it shows to men "the Spirit of the Lord all-gently leading them as one leadeth a beast going down into the valley" (Isaiah, lxiii., 14); when it promises them that they shall "be borne upon the sides and dandled upon the knees" (lxvi., 12); and when God himself says, "I will seek that which was lost, and bring again that which was driven away, and will bind up that which was broken, and will strengthen that which was sick."—Ezek., xxxiv., 16. If such a charity is beneath us, shall such condescension appear to be beneath God? And if he displays it, ought we to exempt ourselves from it? And if this is, indeed, the pastoral spirit, can we think that such a spirit would not find preaching alone too narrow a sphere for it? Now this spirit is formally prescribed, in express precepts and recommendations, when God says to his prophet, "I have set thee for a tower and a fortress among my people, that thou mayest know and try their ways" (Jeremiah, vi., 27); and when St. Paul recommends to Timothy, "to be instant in season, out of season."—2 Tim., iv., 2. This spirit is but the spirit of simple believers, when they are believers in truth. Of them we expect that they will be attentive to one another, and warn one another; for the Christian, as St. Cyran says, is but an imperfect priest, or rather a priest commenced, and the priest is a perfect and accomplished Christian.† Besides this, the minister should never

* "In *all* their afflictions he was afflicted."—Isaiah, lxiii., 9.

† SAINT CYRAN: *Lettre à M. Guillebert*, chap. xvi.

forget that preaching alone does not accomplish his object: first, because he is the pastor of more than those who constantly come to church; next, because even these have need of a more individual and more intimate treatment.*

The pastor may not content himself with having been to his flock "as a very lovely song of one that hath a pleasant voice, and can play well on an instrument of music" (Ezek., xxxiii., 32); and, if he does so, he will always have to reproach himself with having "healed the plague of his people slightly."—Jer., vi., 14. It is at last only by the care of souls that he can realize and identify to himself his flock as a flock, and not only as an auditory. "I know my sheep, and am known of mine" (John, x., 14)—he only is *the good* Shepherd who can thus speak. This is the ideal; we must be striving to reach it. There is a constant proportion between diligence in the care of souls and the life of the parish.

So much does all this belong to the essence of Christianity, that wherever there is a revival of it, the care of souls regains its importance.

Let us add that it enhances the beauty and enforces the obligation of these functions, that they offer small inducement to self-love and imagination. Here may be seen in their purity the seriousness, the austerity of the ministry. Public preaching is comparatively agreeable and easy: only then can we be sure of our vocation to the ministry, when we are inwardly drawn and constrained to exercise the care of souls. At the present time, especially, we can not but be aware that this work has become more difficult. It is difficult, because of the extent of the parishes; it is, above all, difficult, because it is not as acceptable as it was once. The flocks know our duties well, but their own they know no more;

* In Harms' view, public preaching is the least important part of the pastoral office, and, in some respects, that which might be spared with the least disadvantage.—*Pastoraltheologie*, tome iii., p. 2. See further on, chapter ii.

and the precept, "Obey them that have the rule over you" (Heb., xiii., 17), is to them without signification; or, to speak more correctly, flocks hardly have an existence any longer.

This state of things has its own disadvantages, which it is superfluous to specify; but in these same disadvantages it finds its advantage. It does not abolish, it rather, in some sort, perfects the duty. It makes more than ever necessary love—moral authority, of which love is the principal element, the indispensable condition—discretion, thoughtfulness.

To exercise and enforce authority without startling the spirit of independence; here is a problem which simplicity and charity alone can solve. Even in their day, the apostles had to protest that they did not desire to domineer over the Lord's heritage, and that they claimed not the government of souls, except as having to give account of them.—Heb., xiii., 17. Distrust of pastoral ascendency is natural, and, to a certain extent, legitimate. It appears to me a matter for congratulation that, in our day, the pastor can come to his flock, not as preceded and introduced by a foreign authority, but under the sole protection of the pastoral name and the holiness of his undertaking: So that the less he is in favor under one title, the more welcome will he be under the other.

§ 2. *Objections against the Exercise of this Function.*

Against the exercise of the care of souls certain objections or excuses arise, which we must pass in review.*

1. *Want of Taste.*—But it is not an affair of taste that we are concerned with; it is an affair of duty: an essential interest, not a detail of abstract perfection. If taste for this part of the ministry is wanting, what kind of taste is there for the other parts? If we have not a call to care for the souls of the flock, one by one, we have not a call to the min-

* HARMS: *Pastoraltheologie*, tome iii., p. 19.

istry. This objection, then, is all-weak or all-powerful—all-powerful because of its very weakness.

2. *Want of Time.*—What are we to understand by this? Does it mean that we are to apply ourselves to this duty only when we have nothing else to do? I confess I would rather hear the care of souls objected against preaching, than preaching against the care of souls: I would rather one should say to me, My sick, my poor, my scattered sheep require me, and forbid me to give my preaching all the attention which is desirable. This objection assumes the point in question as settled, namely, that we know that the care of souls is second in importance; but who has said this, and how can it be proved?

3. *Not acceptable.*—This is possible, but be careful that you say this in good earnest. Do not say it after a first and indolent effort. Why, you expect doors to open themselves to you at your mere approach! We are, in general, too hasty in saying that we are not acceptable. There are many more ways of access than we suppose, because there are more *necessities*, more *accessible sides*, more *occasions* than we think of. Our ministry is not so sure to be repelled when it exhibits itself under the form of Christian affection.

After all, it is natural that we should not be acceptable. The truth, we all know, is not received with cordiality; and the chief Shepherd, certainly, is not better received by us than we are by others; never will they receive us worse than we have received God. And yet he came "to his own."—John, i., 11. The servant is not greater than his Lord. Is not patience our duty? Is it not the proof and the exercise of our faith?

§ 3. *Conditions or Qualities requisite for the Exercise of the Care of Souls.*

The requisites or necessary means are these:

1. *Health.*—The details of the care of souls are neither necessarily nor generally dangerous to health, if the parish is not too large: A measure of physical force and a good constitution are, however, necessary. But, in general, he who can bear the burden of preaching has sufficient physical ability for the care of souls. There may, however, be exceptions, and one should examine himself well as to this point when he is examining his call to the pastorate, which is not divisible in itself.

2. A certain *presence of mind*, which ministers possess in different degrees, but which may be in a greater or less measure acquired, and which very often is no other than *presence of heart*, or what this supplies.

3. *Psychological Knowledge.* — Many put logic in the place of psychology, which is a great evil. Logic is rectilinear; it cuts its way, it traverses moral facts; psychology is sinuous and flexible. The psychology of books is very useful as the basis of research, but it is nothing without experience and without study of one's self. To know one's self well is a means of thus knowing others; although we should be prepared for a strong encounter with moral combinations which we have not anticipated, which might have seemed impossible, on which account we should study facts in the facts themselves, with candor and docility.

4. *Knowledge of the Parish.*—The parish is not an abstraction; it is a concrete fact, it is an individuality, which has no absolute resemblance except to itself. It is very true that the knowledge of it supposes that of man in general, since, if we do not know man in general, we can not know him in a certain place and certain time; it is also true that this general man is to be sought out and evolved in man of

a certain time and certain place. It is true that there are things which, with equal force, interest and engage man, though placed in the most different conditions ; and that there are things which are important above all others. But it is not less true that, if we take no account of what individualizes a flock, we are not only likely to be less useful, less agreeable, or less welcome, but also to counteract, in many particulars, the object we propose to ourselves. As all external circumstances modify the state of the soul, they thereby modify also the agency we should exert upon it. We must, so to speak, ask the individual man to introduce us to mankind, at least we must not let this individual man obstruct our road. St. Paul speaks to all as men ; nevertheless, he was to the Jews a Jew, to the Greeks a Greek ; all things to all men. We must not strike keys to which no chord corresponds, and leave those untouched to which are connected chords of the fullest and richest sound.

The care of souls, then, will not be the same in city and country, in a farming and a manufacturing district, in the bosom of a population of simple manners and with refined and effeminate people. The pastor should take account of all this, as also of geographic, climatic, economic, dietetic, and historic circumstances. He should acquaint himself with customs, interests, wants, prejudices, opinions. He should not limit himself to certain fruitful data developed by certain inductions ; he should prefer studying things in the things themselves. For between two parishes in the same circumstances, both mountainous, both agricultural, both rich, or both poor, he should still distinguish. The pastor should, above all, understand the religious state of the parish which is transferred to him. This, and all the particulars to which we have referred, should be the objects of prolonged and persevering study, dating from the moment of entrance on his duties ; but before his entrance he must have informed himself of every thing of importance, and certain details which appear small are important. Without the knowledge of these, he may wound, may shock, may be misjudged, and may create prejudices, which are very apt to be formed, and are very slowly dissipated. He must know the good and the bad, the strong as well as the weak, in order to know what needs to be developed and what to be repressed. We may hence see how advantageous it may be for the same pastor to remain a long time in the same parish.

5. *Care to maintain Relations of Confidence and Affection with the Parish.*—These he will secure in part by the care of souls ; but, with a view to the care of souls, he should also in every way create and maintain them. The means are *positive* and *negative*. We shall not speak here of the first, intending to present them hereafter in the aspect, and under the name of duties. We shall now speak only of negative means, which may be summed up in this : the avoiding of all useless collision with interest and self-love, the voluntary relinquishment of his right, according to the word of the apostle, "Why do ye not rather suffer yourselves to be defrauded ?"—1 Cor., vi., 7. The pastor, unquestionably, should not encourage evil by weakness on his part, but he should not show himself too fond of his own opinion, and ever ready to make difficulty. Let him also be careful not to enter into obligations too readily, and to keep himself in this respect as independent as possible. It is well here to call to mind an advantage we have from our institutions, according to which the pastor receives nothing from the community, and the chance of dependence can scarcely have existence.

§ 4. *Three-fold Object of pastoral Oversight.*

We will now resolve the pastoral office into its different elements or different acts, regarding it as including not only the religious care of families and individuals, but every thing except public instruction and the celebration of worship.

Pastoral oversight has a three-fold purpose—to promote the material, the moral, and the spiritual interests of the parish.

1. *Solicitude for material Interests.*—If I speak of this first, it is not as being the first, but rather as the least of the interests which the pastor is concerned with, and that I may rise by degrees to the true object of his ministry and to the highest exercise of his activity. There are positions in which he will have few occasions to interfere, in which, indeed, he can not interfere with propriety; there are others from which he can not withhold himself. In every case, we would have him regardful of material interests, and attend to them according to the exigency of circumstances.* We have no reference here to care for the poor, which is always required of the pastor. Let him, in every case, avoid the character of intermeddler and intruder, and the air of a man of business.

2. *Solicitude for Moral Interests.*—I speak not yet of *spiritual* interests. There are unjust or immoral prejudices, errors of education, violations of law and of morality, which have passed into customs, usages indecent and pernicious, etc. All evil may and should be displaced by Christianity; it will not, however, be enough to preach the cross, although this should be done indefatigably, and with reference to the removal of evils, as included in the supreme end which is to be aimed at in preaching: We shall still have to make battle with all these evils—descend upon the stage of natural morality, of good sense, and even of worldly interest. It is very often the only means, the indispensable condition of success with many persons. Nor do we hereby compromise the main object; we prepare the way for religion: it brings us into contact with more persons, and gives us influence over a greater number of wills.

Christianity certainly applies itself to every thing; it sub-

* Wild lands tilled by monks—priests civilizers.

divides and ramifies itself, so as to reach all abuses, all errors. Its great principles may be successfully called into action against the subtilest forms of error and of sin; and we must not say that it is an abuse thus to employ it, and that it is applying Niagara to turn a mill-wheel. No, it is a matter of regret that Christian preaching does not, from time to time, conduct Christians as by the hand, from its loftiest principles even to their last results. But that individuals may thus apply Christianity to their personal conduct, may introduce it entirely into the external and material details of their life, they must first have received it, and society suffers and languishes while it waits for this to be done. Time presses; let us, then, attack evil with all the weapons we have at our disposal; let us apply to society, with Christian charity and in a Christian spirit, means which are within every one's reach, motives which all accept, and which, after all, being legitimate and true, are really a part of the truth. Let us never forget that good is self-evidencing; that evil carries its condemnation in itself; that Christianity has not come to create morality, but to lend it the most irresistible motives, without opposing, without accusing of absolute inefficacy, those which may be drawn from conscience and the nature of things. It is very true that motives of this sort do not produce internal renovation, the moral resurrection of man; they accomplish less, but this less is not valueless; it is worth more, assuredly, than that nothing to which we reduce our influence in the esteem of many persons by not urging these motives.

It may not be suitable, it may scarcely be practicable, to attack directly every evil which may present itself. Besides that it is necessary to give time in order to know evils well, we alarm and repel men by this impatience and this indiscretion. It would be of more avail to begin by training up in the parish supporters and aids, who, when they shall have the same conscience with ourselves as to the nature of evil, will take the initiative with us, or perhaps in our place.* The pastor will pursue an excellent and a Christian policy, not to do every thing himself, but to inspire others with the desire, and to teach them the art of co-operation. Not only has he need of aids in his parish, but he will accomplish the more good by not having to do every thing himself.

3. *Solicitude for Spiritual Interests.*—We so name this only to complete the circle of pastoral solicitudes; for otherwise it controls and covers the others. It ought to be the soul of all our proceedings and of all our activity. Before all, we ought to have in view the spiritual, that is to say, eternal good of the members of our parish; and if it is true that a minister, preoccupied with this order of interests, may, to a certain extent, lose sight of other interests, it is still more evident that a pastor, who is not one in this highest sense of the word, is generally little suited to advance the purely moral, or even the material well-being of the community.

§ 5. *The School.*

We have as yet only considered the parish in general; we are approaching families and individuals; but between the parish in general and families and individuals, there is an institution of which we must speak, namely, *the school.*

We shall in vain attempt to secularize it: It will remain attached to the Church or to religion. I speak of the popular school, of that in which more or less may be taught, but always in so far as the school deserves its name, whatever is necessary to the man and the Christian. The school has need of religion, and religion has need of the school. The Church can not dispense with the school, nor the school with the Church. The pastor, for this cause, should interest himself in whatever pertains essentially to popular instruction;

* HÜFFELL: *Ueber das Wesen und den Beruf des Evangelisch-christlichen Geistlichen*, third edition. Giessen, 1835, tome ii., p. 270.

but should connect, or, rather, intermingle religion with every thing. He is never to forget that he is its minister, nor lay aside his character as a minister in his co-operation in the government of the school. This does not imply that he is to limit himself exclusively to religion ; does not mean that the minister, as much as any other man, may not concern himself with the entire assemblage of interests which are involved in this great work of popular instruction.

I do not mean to intimate that he should take from the regent of the school the province of religious instruction ; but that, without excluding him, he should teach him how to instruct, and aid him in teaching.

As a member or president of the school commissioners, the minister may use what influence he has, but not seek to domineer or do every thing : He should think it more proper and more useful to teach others to do well, and, as the case may be, in his turn to learn from others. If circumstances in which his relative superiority gives him the preponderance, secure to him the ascendency, he should be condescending and deferential : He should not make his colleagues instruments or mere supporters to himself, but as much as possible collaborators.

This counsel is applicable to all institutions, to all works, in which the pastor may be called to take a principal part.

We come to the pastor's relations to families and individuals.

§ 6. *Relations to Families : Pastoral Visits.*

I speak of families, because it is especially through families that the minister reaches individuals, of whom we are to speak hereafter ; and because, again, it is important that he should maintain relations to families as families. The family, the only group which remains in society below the national group—the family, a natural bundle, not compact enough, perhaps, but not dissolved, is a most valuable fact for the minister, who through it reaches without effort many individuals at once, in a manner sufficiently indirect not to alarm their liberty, sufficiently direct to act upon them closely and strongly. I add, with earnestness, that the minister should have to do with families, that he may, as much as he possibly can, verify, consecrate, confirm this divine institution.

Nevertheless, individuals are to be reached, since it is only the individual who is or is not a Christian ; who receives or does not receive the truth. We shall not, therefore, dwell long on families ; but before we pass to individuals, not again to leave them, we will say something concerning an important duty which relates to families and to individuals, and is a powerful means of reaching both. I refer to *pastoral visits.*

These pastoral visits are neither purely social visits, such as well-bred people pay to one another from convenience or taste, nor those official visits, domiciliary visits, so to speak, which have a somewhat inquisitorial character. They ought to be pastoral, and purely pastoral, but familiar and friendly. Those to whom they are made should recognize the pastor, but should recognize in him the friend and the father. We should not be burdensome ; we should leave or put at ease those who receive us ; we should exclude every idea of ceremony and worldly politeness.

Tissot has very well shown what pastoral visits in the country ought to be, and how a true pastor can make them inexpensive to himself, and secure their just result.

"What fatal influences has not effeminacy in the churchman? I fear not to say that on neither his knowledge nor his eloquence does the well-being of the precious deposit which is confided to him depend ; it depends on his vigilance, his activity. It is not by adorning his sermon in his study-retreat that he enlightens the people ; the sermons he delivers in the temple are not his most efficacious sermons. When the people hear the holy truths ; when they see the man commissioned to announce them, only in the sacred place, they do not take them home—they come to make them a ceremonious visit on the following Sunday. It is in the midst of their field, it is when they are repairing their hedges, it is when they are taking repose at the shop-door, it is when the severity of the weather keeps them within doors, or when an event of some importance occurs among them, that you may hope, sacred men, to inculcate the truths that should direct that conduct which is to appear one day as a witness for or against you.

"If you would instruct your parishioner, associate the truth, his duties, your idea, with his daily labors: Let his harvest-field remind him of the conversation you had with him when he was sowing; let the cutting of his second crop recall the ideas you unfolded to him when he was mowing his hay; and, in a word, let him find you every where, and let him every where love to find you. But how may this be if you venture to go nowhere? How attach him to his duties when you seem to be so little concerned to make him love them? How shall he not fear his yoke (and this fear is the pest of virtue), if you fear so much to touch it? How not hate his condition, if those whom he thinks happy so carefully estrange themselves from it?"*

Visits like these have many advantages. They make the pastor well acquainted with the moral and material wants of the families of his parish; they knit and tighten friendly relations; they open the way to action on individuals.

Shall we wait for some particular occasion before we make them? It is well to make them without an occasion, without any immediate motive, that when a special case shall render them particularly necessary, they may not have a strange and alarming character.

It is also well, however, to take advantage of events which impress the soul, and dispose the heart to open itself (*mol-*

* *Essai sur la Vie de Tissot, par* Ch. Eynard. Lausanne, 1839, p. 109.

lessima fandi tempora), without affectation, and without abusing them. Dread procrastination, or the habit of delay—How many pastors, how many Christians, have had cause to deplore that, by their repeated delays, they left destinies to consummate themselves, of which, for a moment at least, they had the power to determine the course.

As far as possible, all the parishioners should be visited by the pastor; all, at least, should be approached—the friends of our ministry, and also its adversaries (as adversaries never should be recognized, unless they have given us flagrant proofs of enmity), the rich and the poor. If the pastor saw only the rich, we might boldly say, without closer examination, that his visits are not pastoral, but social ones: If he should see only the poor, we ought not to say as we have often heard said, that the poor man alone has a pastor; for, indeed, he has not one; he is not a true pastor who concerns himself only with the poor; that is to say, with him whose poverty obliges him, whether he will or no, to accept his pastor's attentions.

CHAPTER II.

OF THE CARE OF SOULS APPLIED TO INDIVIDUALS.

§ 1. *Introduction—Division of the Subject.*

It is only an absolute impossibility that can justify the pastor in not occupying himself immediately with individuals. If he had the leisure to examine thoroughly the situation and the wants of each one, and to be his pastor as assiduously as he is that of the flock, he ought to do it. Even if each individual might be preached to apart, and directed at leisure, still preaching to the whole flock should have place ; of this we have elsewhere given the reasons ;* but it is not the less, on this account, a secondary office for the pastor, and the instruction of individuals remains of the first importance. The pastor, then, as much as possible, must address himself to individuals.

Solicitude for individuals is one of the characteristics of the New Testament and the new ministry. It is very remarkable that the same religion which has founded a Church, and has given to this institution a reality which is almost a personality, has consecrated the individuality of man as a religious being, and put this beyond controversy and beyond attack. This same religion it is, and this alone, that has regard only to individual effects, or makes these the last end of its efforts. The Gospel is addressed, the preacher is sent, not to peoples, to masses, but to all the individuals of which the masses or peoples are composed. If the preachers seek to act on masses, it is with reference to individuals ; not that one individual is of more value than a thousand, which is an absurdity, but more than a people, as far as it is a people,

* See the Introduction to the *Course on Homiletics.*

more than a mass as such. It is, then, with individuals that we have to do, less directly in preaching, more immediately in the care of souls, which is without object, without reason when the individual loses his reality, or even his importance. The minister seeks them in worship or in public, only because he is not sure of finding them elsewhere, or because he has things to say which he can speak only to assembled individuals, or, finally, because the public assembly symbolizes equality, the community of interests, the communion of hearts. But so far as he may hope to find them elsewhere, he is to seek them there. This is the first duty, the first form of pastoral ministration; public preaching is only its complement. A friend who, wishing to enjoy a familiar conversation with his friend, is contented to see him in a great company, and who, having some particular thing to say to him, which concerns no one but him, should fuse what was specially applicable to him into a general discourse, would be a singular friend. Now every one needs instruction suitable to himself only, or, at least, he needs to have us appropriate to his particular use, his particular circumstances, that general instruction which he may have received in common with others, but which very often, for want of such care, is lost to him. One after another he passes through different states, internal or external, for which general preaching does not suffice. The pastor knows this; if he can deal with this soul apart, shall he not do it? How can he avoid reflecting that preaching may have prepared the way for a work in this soul—that preaching may complete it if it be once begun, but that the decisive moment, either of the life or of the particular situation, may call for a more minute and more delicate work. And, lastly, with what eye will the whole parish look on a pastor who is a pastor only in the pulpit, who does not, so to speak, descend from the pulpit, and who, though he may know individuals, wishes only to know the mass? As much as pastoral zeal in the care of souls adds force to preaching, so much does negligence in the pastor enfeeble the preacher.

We have now indicated certain natural, and, so to speak, legal occasions of approaching individuals; there are others which charity induces, and which prudence determines us to improve. They are not wanting to him who desires them. We recommend no offensive importunity: at the same time, it is important that the pastor should assure himself that the solicitude which makes him seek occasion is rarely taken amiss when it is characterized by frankness and simplicity.

We now discriminate between individuals. Individuals are distinguished from one another by their external circumstances and by their internal state. We shall give our attention first to circumstances which pertain to the latter.

§ 2. *Internal State.*

The same tendencies reappear at all periods, and we may affirm that the smallest flock presents all the shades of truth and of error. But the proportion varies, and each period, each place has its character, which results from the predominance of certain elements. Every where there is some excess or some void. Mysticism, antinomianism, legalism, the bondage of the letter, by turns prevail.

However it may be as to this, there are, as concerns the internal state, different classes, which in each flock are more or less numerous.

I. The first is that of *decidedly pious* persons, who are at a more or less advanced stage in the evangelical life. We do not think that these should be left to themselves, or that advice and direction should be refused them, but we insist that they ought not to be withdrawn from the discipline of God's Spirit. It is important that we do not interfere with—we should rather cherish—their sense of their liberty, their responsibility, and their own privileges. The pastor should beware of permitting himself to be erected into a pope, or even into a director of conscience. He should be the aid of liberty, not its substitute.

These individuals, who form the choice ones of the flock, naturally feel a need of more intimate relations with the pastor, and of more thorough and more minute instruction. As they know more, they see they have more to learn. It would be wrong to have no regard to their case; and the pastor, isolated as he is in his parish, has as much need of them as they have of him. But he can not, in this matter, satisfy entirely them and himself. On the one hand, the pastor is pastor of the whole flock, and, according to the precept of St. Paul (Acts, xxii., 28), must care for the whole flock; on the other hand, he ought, for the sake of the peace and unity of his flock, to be willing to deprive himself, and to deprive them also, of some lawful delights. Not without reflection and caution should he appoint an extra-official service for their sakes especially.* The means of intercourse which pastoral visits, in some parishes, offer, should be preferred. We must not, however, let our measures for the welfare of the multitude carry the appearance of timidity or the fear of man, nor should the pastor dissemble his sympathy for those who are most zealous in serving God.†

All pious men are not pious after the same manner: Almost always one element predominates, and some other suffers. There is always a weak side to be strengthened, with

* No small offense was given, in one instance within the translator's knowledge, by a service intended distinctively for a class supposed to be in a higher state of religious feeling than the rest of the flock. It may be allowable to appoint a service of this description, but this instance gave proof that such a service ought not to be appointed "without reflection and caution."—*Transl.*

† See the *Praktische Bemerkungen* of HERNHUTT, p. 103; *Gemeinschaft der Erweckten.*

which we must, in the first place, make ourselves acquainted.

1. To those in whom the principle of *faith* prevails we must recommend *works*, by insisting that, whatever changes may have taken place in our disposition and our state toward God, the law remains law; and that we may renounce by our works (Titus, i., 16) the God whom we profess to know, and whom we may know in truth. We must warn them of the snares which our natural man may find in Christian liberty; we must, without taking this liberty away, teach them how to use it prudently, and especially not to despise Christians less advanced or weak in the faith (Rom., xvi., 2), who dare not use their liberty, but whom we ought not, on that account, hastily to regard as strangers to the covenant of grace.

2. To those who, endeavoring to add to their faith *virtue* (2 Pet., i., 5), are in danger of forgetting in this so necessary industry that the first act of obedience is faith, and the work, par excellence, *the work of God* (John, vi., 29), is, to believe on Him whom He hath sent—we must show, as open at their side, that abyss of self-righteousness in which true righteousness is lost and disappears.

3. To the scrupulous, the timorous—that the kingdom of God does not consist in meat and drink, but in righteousness, in peace and in joy, through the Holy Spirit (Rom., xiv., 17); and that if we must be always proving anew what is acceptable to the Lord (Eph., v., 10), this useful exercise of conscience and of reason represses anxiety, and should unite with itself a feeling of tranquil trust in that God who, having given us the substantial truth, will certainly not permit an upright and sincere intention to err very seriously.

4. To the superstitious, that is to say, to those who, through a weakness of imagination, or a sort of spiritual sloth, prefer, in inquiring for the will of God, to consult some sign exterior to the conscience, which is the internal sign, we must show that the benefit of faith is to be found, not in our renouncing the natural means of knowing and judging, but in causing

us to make a good use of them; and that to proceed otherwise is under a vain appearance of piety, to remit to chance, or rather to passion, which authorizes all chances, the labor of determining our course.

In short, the task of the minister as to those pious souls, whose various errors consist in the exaggeration of some true principle, is to re-establish the equilibrium, by inculcating the particular principle which they have lost sight of, either in practice or in theory. Certain doctrines, certain points of view, to which preaching ordinarily allows but little place, regain their importance in the care of souls; and we may say that in this sphere no article of truly Christian theology ever remains inactive. It is with all individual Christianity as it is with the forms of human government; at first each of them corresponds to the general idea of society, then more particularly to some one of the conditions of social life; in other words, each has a principle from which it borrows its form; but each also tends to exaggerate the principle on which it is founded, as if that principle were the social principle itself. Pure Christianity, which has been in some part defined, while pure society has been in no part, has a principle which can not be exaggerated, because it includes all principles, that is to say, all the weights and counter weights of truth. But with no individual has it this largeness and this perfection; all individual Christianity makes a principle to itself, which it incessantly tends to exaggerate, instead of tempering it with the opposite principle. To this contemperature must we recall the individual, either by presenting Christianity to him as a harmonious whole, or by preaching to him the truth which he has forgotten, or of which he makes no use.

The work of grace in some souls conceals itself from all the world; it is concealed from themselves. These souls whom God has endued with a priceless docility are as mouldable as the water to the form of the vase. They are not born Christians, but they become Christians with so little effort, that they seem to owe to the beneficence of their nature what others obtain only at the expense of painful conflicts or of long reflection: So that these latter may say, "With a great price bought I this freedom;" while the others, at least in one sense, may reply, "but I was free-born."—Acts, xxii., 28. These souls sometimes betray themselves by wondrous signs at the solemn hour of death; but during life no one observed them; and had any one interrogated them, he would have obtained a very imperfect account of their faith. It is even possible that the imperfection of their theory reveals itself in some measure in imperfection of practice, and that they have not said as often and as loudly as others, Lord, Lord! Their faith remains in a state of involution and of synthesis. They have thought little of their religion because it was not in their nature to think much. We can not say that they have laid down their arms; for, to say the truth, they have never resisted. But by slow degrees they have conformed themselves to the Christian spirit, it has entered into their habits of life; they feel all that others think, and that which others, yet more happy, both think and feel; they renounce from the heart all righteousness, they embrace with the heart the mystery of mercy; their conscience has become tender; without method they practice a severe self-discipline; they know nothing, and they know every thing. Seek out these souls; they are more numerous, perhaps, than you suppose. Learn to encourage and cherish them: Turn them not out of the course which their nature prescribes to them: Force not these instruments of music to give forth sounds which they can not give forth; disturb them not with formularies; deprive them not of their *naïveté;* accept their language—accommodate yours to theirs; and do not undertake to correct their expressions unless required by regard to their religious welfare, and only as far as this demands.

II. We pass to the *new converts*. The fervor of their first-love is useful directly by the works it produces: There are important ones among them which are peculiar to this period of the spiritual life. This fervor is also useful as a rebuke to those who have suffered the gift which was in them to be impaired: It is a leaven which God is incessantly casting into the mass of the Church. But this period is not ordinarily that of moderation and balance of mind; and we know that the primitive Church interdicted the ministry to new converts. It is ordinarily the period of bitter zeal, of a controversial spirit, of severe judgments: we forget what we were the evening before, and we forget it the more, it seems, because we have ascended from so great a depth. Though we know that we ourselves have been the objects and the monuments of so great a patience, we are too ready to say impatiently of our neighbor, as the man of the parable, "Cut him down; why cumbereth he the ground!" It is also the time when we abuse Christian liberty; the time of presumption: We would preach to and school all the world, and perhaps the very person from whom we obtained our first light, whence results a danger to this last, also, who may not be always disposed to say with Moses, "Would to God all the Lord's people were prophets."—Numb., xi., 20. Let all this show the pastor that new converts should be treated with indulgence and with severity. He must not depress the spirit which is in them, nor permit a demon to enter through the breach which an angel has made.

III. Another class is that of the *awakened*, although very often he whom we call awakened is a true convert, and the convert, as we term him, is but an awakened person. The awakening of a soul is the emotion of interest or inquietude which, after long unconcern, it feels toward spiritual things, and which differs from emotions of the same kind which it may have before felt, in that it has become an habitual and dominant state. It is a delicate matter to direct such souls.

We must concur with the work without precipitating it; we must assist them in walking, but not carry them; must have respect to their individuality; neither anticipate nor require a series of impressions and of states of mind conformed to a catalogue prepared beforehand; not desire to give a name to each of the states; and especially not to call for the exercise of a principle before the principle has been obtained;* not forget that if there are dispositions and actions which at any moment of the spiritual life are to be recognized as bad, there are others the character of which is revealed gradually, and in proportion as Christian principle becomes more distinct and more manifest; and that in the conduct of souls we have reason to stand in doubt of too easy success, or of complaisant sacrifices performed without any sense of their necessity, and consequently of a merely arbitrary nature.

IV. There are souls not only awakened, but *troubled*, in whom inquietude, which is the ground of all awakening, has the character of anguish and despair. We may even say that with many trouble precedes true awakening; and often such souls in whom a strictly spiritual concern does not yet exist are induced to seek the pastor by a vague but insupportable anguish, and come to him in the simple thought that there are remedies for the soul as physicians have them

* It may be no less important to guard the awakened against supposing that they may have an excuse for not having the principle; or that because they are without the principle, the exercise of it, or the action in which it expresses itself, is not to be required of them. It is often necessary to admonish them that the exercise of the principle is the sum of their duty; that no right action can be performed while they are destitute of the principle; and that to obtain the principle is what concerns them above all, and before all. "Make the tree good and his fruit good."—Matt., xii., 23. "Make you a new heart and a new spirit, for why will ye die?"—Ezek., xviii., 31. "Break up your fallow ground, and sow not among thorns."—Jer., iv., 3.—*Tr.*

for the body, and that they would be better received of no one than of him. The pastor may always assure himself that this trouble arises from reminiscences that disturb the conscience, and from a need of expiation rather felt than distinctly recognized. This trouble may not cease, and the principle of a new life be formed in such souls unless they make a sincere confession.* This we must know how to obtain; but love will obtain every thing. The more this proceeding costs, the greater the reason for it. Often all appears easy after the first effort, and the soul, as if released from a burden which was crushing it, rises up and walks.

We may speak here of a class of persons whose *soul*, in the strict sense, is not troubled, but who are more troubled in *mind* by doubts or scruples. This, with some, is the effect of a natural skepticism; with others, of a self-tormenting disposition about every thing, or, finally, of an indiscrete curiosity. Religious movement has exceedingly multiplied the demand for counsels and solutions, but it has not proportionably increased by its own activity the resources of religious and moral instruction which we have need of, and which the pulpit is expected to afford.

In our Church there could not be a ministry if the secret of confession was not inviolable as it is in the Romish Church: Every one who confesses himself to a pastor should have reason so to regard it; but when the revelation of a secret is the only way of preventing a crime, secrecy on the part of the pastor would involve him in the criminality. But in this case he must give the person no reason to think that he holds himself bound to secrecy, so that he shall have no show of occasion to be surprised when the disclosure is made.

The formal absolution which follows Catholic confession rests upon a purely Christian idea. The Catholic Church is not mistaken in adding absolution to the external act of

* "He that covereth his sins shall not prosper; but whoso confesseth and forsaketh them shall find mercy."—Proverbs, xxviii., 13.

confession, and not to the dispositions and motives indicated in the passage we have referred to, Prov., xxviii., 13. The minister should make this well understood, as also the absence of all merit, and of all intrinsic power of reconciliation in the acts of privation and reparation which perhaps should follow confession, and which in certain cases may be useful and praiseworthy. Among these acts, a confession made to others besides the pastor, especially a confession made to the offended person, if there be one, may be of great importance, and sometimes of real necessity. Sometimes, even, nothing short of a public confession can fully satisfy us; but I doubt whether the pastor should ever suggest this idea; he may, indeed, sometimes dissuade his penitent from taking this course; he assumes a great responsibility in confirming him in his purpose; nevertheless, he may see himself called to do so. The scandal of a whole life may demand, at the moment of death, a reparation of this kind.

V. We have next to speak of the *orthodox*, who pervert the faith, not objectively, but in its character, by erecting it into a work, and disconcerting, defeating, so to speak, the purpose of God, while accepting it with the appearance of perfect submission. They verify the observation contained in these lines:

> "De mal croyant à mécréant
> L'intervalle n'est pas bien grand."*

The cure of this religious disease is one of the greatest difficulty; since here the merit of a most servile strictness may be attached to a belief the most evangelical. Some have the unhappy art of making Christianity a prop to the lowest parts of their nature, and a comfort to them in their licentiousness and their envy. Strictly, what is wanting here is life, and life is to be awakened. The work which seemed to be done, has to be begun again; and it can have no begin-

* "There is not much difference between one who believes in a bad manner and an infidel."—*Transl.*

ning but in repentance. The orthodox man must retravel with his heart and his conscience all the road that he has gone over with his understanding and his imagination, and he must believe in one manner what he has for a long time been believing in another manner. This dead orthodoxy has two shades, which produce their colors under two characters. There are orthodox *formalists,* who must be taught to worship in spirit and in truth (John, iv., 12); and there are orthodox *legalists,* who attach themselves to the letter of the evangelical precepts, and let their spirit escape from them. As to these last, however, we must avoid a hasty judgment, since these are slaves of the law who are nowise pharisees, that is to say, nowise filled with a sense of merit and self-righteousness. We must consider whether, in the servility and anxiety of their obedience, they are not still of the number of those whom the Gospel has at the same time characterized and blessed, in the following declarations: "Then Jesus beholding him, loved him, and said to him, One thing thou lackest: go thy way, sell whatsoever thou hast and give to the poor, and thou shalt have treasure in heaven: And come take up the cross and follow me" (Mark, x., 21); "And the scribe said to him, Well, Master, thou hast said the truth; for there is one God, and there is none other but he. And to love him with all the heart, and with all the understanding, and with all the soul, and with all the strength, and to love his neighbor as himself, is more than all whole burnt offerings and sacrifices. And when Jesus saw that he answered discreetly, he said to him, Thou art not far from the kingdom of God." In persons of the class to which these two belonged, there is the foundation or the germ of a true faith.*

* Was not this foundation or this germ that "one thing" which the first of these two "lacked?" What meant his going away "grieved," verse 22; and the observations which Jesus made to his disciples, after he had gone, verses 23, 25?—*Transl.*

There are souls in a singular state, to which we have given too little thought. They are those which have anticipated, I was going to say taken on credit, the grace of the Gospel; or who have appropriated the promises before having felt all that grief, that disgust, that fear, that species of death which naturally belong to conviction of sin. They believe, they bless, they confess, they profess intelligently and sincerely, all that is essential to Christian character, but may want, I will not say the joy, which is not the habitual disposition of every true Christian, but the peace, the love, and, in a word, the life of the Christian. We must not confound them with those we call orthodox; they have not their security; they are at the same time in a worse and in a better state; they have not fulfilled all righteousness, but they know that they have not. This state, though singular, is no less common; and though it is difficult to disentangle it, since he who is in it can scarcely give any account of it, a minister whose experience and study of his own interior have rendered him searching can readily discern it. To apply the remedy is more difficult. The degrees, the movements of the spiritual life have been inverted. This Christian is one by anticipation, and, so to speak, by hypothesis. He is used to the profession and the outward joy of the Christianity of the intellect or imagination. His mouth has been before his heart in saying, Lord, Lord! He is familiar with the words, with the forms, with the thoughts of Christianity, without having his soul in them, and consequently in a way rather to be without a taste for them than to be in union with them. To have a taste of life, we must first taste death; but if we may ascend naturally from death to life, we can not re-descend also from life to death, and we can not at once pass at will through all the phases of a sorrowful novitiate. This difficulty is one of the greatest we have to encounter in the spiritual career, and it may put to the proof the patience and the prudence of a pastor. One sign by which these persons may be recognized is the want of progress and movement in the spiritual life. When the pastor visits them, he may find them well disposed, ready to confess their sins, their insufficiency, their need of redemption, and the aid of the Holy Spirit; but at each succeeding visit their language will be the same; variety is wanting, because the reality is wanting. If he is called to treat a malady of this kind, he ought, on one hand, to see that the soul, of which we speak, takes account of its own state; and, on the other, to take care that he does not renounce what he has, because of the manner in which he obtained it. He should not refrain from speaking to him of grace, or withhold the promises which he has accepted, and which we do well always to accept. He must not change at all the conditions of the covenant of grace, and withdraw from this soul the privileges which belong to it; but he should guard it against hypocrisy, against the usual evidences which both to itself and others exaggerate the advantage of its state; he must then exhort it to a silent and interior activity, to the severe study and application of the law, and to whatever disciplines and mortifies the soul, as well as to all works which, while they imply charity, develop it without danger of inflating the heart; in a word, silently to imitate Jesus Christ. But the shades of this state are exceedingly various; each of them at once requires and indicates particular measures; the important point is (and it is what he had specially in view) precisely to distinguish and estimate each of them.

VI. We may form another class out of *skeptics* who are neither indifferent nor troubled, neither unbelieving nor believing, but who, through an infirmity or an evil disposition, can be settled in no point. There are minds naturally skeptical which are forever considering, and never come to any conclusion. The pastor can hardly hope to be a reformer of them; but, after trying as much as possible to throw arguments in one of the scales, or, rather, before even trying, he should strongly endeavor to make them much more serious, who, without being of the same class with the indifferent, are perhaps far from giving to religious questions all the interest they deserve. In order to make a man of this character serious and capable of decision, let him be filled with a sense of the infinite. The most wavering skeptic does not doubt that he has a soul; and if we can succeed in giving him a sense of the reality and the great value of his soul, we have put him at the true point of view as to questions of this kind, and we have in some sort turned his face to the east.

There are sincere and unhappy minds who, impressed by the spirit of truth and touched by the Gospel, believe in their state of sin, abjure all self-righteousness, desiring to be clothed only in that of God, which they would be prepared to receive if they believed it were offered to them, and yet find themselves detained from entering at the gate, as by a chain which seems to be stretched before them by their education, their first impressions, too much or too little knowledge, I know not what —a skeptical temperament, which shows itself in them, even in things the most foreign from religion. It is well when we meet with such as these, to remind them that "faith," according to the expression of an enlightened author, "realizes itself in the will; that faith is nothing else than willingness to accept a pardon from God, and to renounce the pursuit of all other means of salvation; that doubts which remain in the mind do not change it; that God has not made our salvation to depend on the vacillations of our feeble understanding; that it is not the understanding which consents to accept of grace; that it is not the imagination which is moved by it; that it is the will, the only faculty always free, though feeble, which receives pardon, turns itself to God, and may even cry, 'Lord, I believe; help thou mine unbelief.'"

VII. The *indifferent* are a numerous class, inferior not only to the orthodox, but to unbelievers themselves, inasmuch as these latter are unbelievers in a positive manner. Their opinions, however, or rather their want of opinions, give them logically an intermediate position.*

These are, in general, worldly persons, dissipated men or men of business, who have not leisure either to be orthodox or to be unbelievers. There are occasions of reaching them in the actual state of things. They are not without relations to the Church, in the bosom of which they are still retained by habit or decency. They meet the pastor in social intercourse at the houses of others, or in civil affairs, or in solemn circumstances. They have affections, domestic pleasures and sorrows; they are men: on the side of humanity they may be reached; all their natural affections have an affinity for religion, without which, also, none of them have *complete exercise.* All these fundamental relations call and invite to a higher one.

When we have obtained the ear of the indifferent, we must destroy their security, and make them see that their position is not indifferent. We must not hesitate to arouse fear in them; in the majority of cases, it is impossible to connect the idea of God, in the mind of an indifferent person, with any other sentiment than fear; but, without neglecting to use this means, if we may give vibration to other chords, we should make them vibrate.

VIII. There are many *unbelievers* that we have full right to approach as such. And doubtless we can scarcely engage with these without a preliminary step, a conversation, which, from the circumstances, will necessarily have the interrogatory form. But infidelity has practical maxims as well as forms of doctrine; and the first, in default of the second, may open for us a door to religious discussion; and then infidelity is sometimes unwilling openly to declare itself; it more frequently appears in oblique forms; allusion or irony contents it. We must not start with the idea that every attack, direct or indirect, should lead to a discussion. Much rather should we avoid discussion in the presence of company, if it

* See a discourse by M. Vinet on *Religious Indifference*, etc.—*Edit.*

be not directly provoked. We must absolutely decline it when the attack is only a sarcasm or an abuse. As far as possible, we must change the discussion into an appeal to conscience and edifying conversation.

It can not be reasonably required of the pastor to engage in formal conflict on the stage of science with professed men of learning who draw their weapons against religion from their special pursuits. A clergy of such a stamp (so M. Vincent* insists) is an impossibility. Men of a particular class should be met by men of a corresponding class. Religion has more than one class of ministers, and more than one kind of proofs.

Infidelity, even with the most ignorant, piques itself on an aggressive character; that is to say, on believing something in opposition to the beliefs which religion proposes. Each has his system, which is often nothing more than a mass of gratuitous and incoherent assertions—a collection of pithy phrases, stolen, without understanding them, from conversations and books. There is no point of doctrine so abstract or subtile that it does not produce itself under some trivial and puerile form in the language of these bold spirits of low degree. Contempt is never seasonable, never useful; but we must not give these ambitious proverbs of ignorant infidelity honor which they do not deserve, and engage in discussions which, though they may have a limit and a result with persons of a cultivated mind, have often neither result nor limit with narrow and ignorant minds. If, nevertheless, it is useful to convince them that they have not so stately a system as they imagine, it is yet more useful, either in the sequel or at the beginning, to transfer them to another stage, namely, that of conscience and experience—to awaken in them the wants which they have proudly put to sleep, and to show them in all their beauty the work and character of God, as revealed by the Gospel, and the privileges of a Christian as attested by a truly Christian life.

* *Mélanges de Religion et de Théologie.*

IX. We have more to do with *rationalism*, which accepts the sacred documents, than with infidelity, which discards them. We refer not only to learned rationalism, with which a simple pastor can not always contend as a formal polemic, but to superficial and second-hand rationalism, which seeks to blunt the edge of that evangelical truth by which it is wounded. We venture little in assuming that this rationalism has for its ordinary source a repugnance of heart, and that it is in the rationalist's conscience that the weapons, in contending with him, are to be sought. Without, therefore, omitting arguments of another kind, furnished by science, and without seeming to shrink from the combat, we must make great use of internal evidence, and call conscience to bear witness.* Let us not forget how strong the Scripture is, and that it is sufficient in itself: The more we use the Scripture in explaining the Scripture, the more shall we be struck with the excellence of this method. We can not too earnestly remind ministers that the word of God should *abound* in them, so that, having learned it by heart and by the heart, the principal passages of the sacred books will recur to them easily and promptly whenever they shall be needed. This knowledge should be not of isolated parts, but of parts combined or forming a whole; and the sense of each verse should be presented as penetrated with the sense and the savor of all the principal passages that relate to the same subject. Such a knowledge of the Bible (*talis et tanta*) can not be too strongly recommended to all ministers of the Gospel (or stewards of the word of God).

X. Out of the pale of Christian belief there are *Stoics*, more or less religious, whose religion is strictly *that of duty*, even when they seemingly and sincerely desire to make God the object of duty. This class of men deserves more atten-

* We may properly refer here to some works more or less popular on the evidences of Christianity: Cellerier, Bogue, Erskine, Whately, Jennings, Paley, and Chalmers.

tion, and should be proposed, if not as a model, at least as an instructive example, to those Christians who have, perhaps, too easily and too quickly received grace before they had well felt all the weight of the law. These Stoics are in a great error, in which they keep themselves by regarding too constantly the abuse which is made of Christian liberty. But if the first service we should render to them is to show them, by our example, that Christian morality is not lax, this service is not the only one. We must explain to them, as we have opportunity, the infinite character of Christian morality, the awful disproportion between the law regarded in the Christian point of view, which is eternal principle, and the capacity of man. We must, finally, give them to taste, in the midst of their hard labor, the solace which is to be found in love, which alone can impart the joy of fulfilling the law, and which is only diffused through the heart by the spirit of Jesus Christ, and by the assurance of having been the object of his love. It is manifest that I do not confound these Stoics, these zealots of duty, with those vulgar moralists who submit themselves not to *the*, but to *their* morality, and who only accept the law when they have brought it to the measure of their carnal and worldly interests.

Two Duties of a Pastor toward the Members of his Flock considered as Sinners, and subject to the Precepts of the Moral Law: Reprehension and Direction.

Reprehension is a duty of the pastor. It is involved in every spontaneous performance of duty in the care of souls: It is, moreover, imposed upon pastors in the Gospel. Reprehension is difficult at all times and with all persons; it is yet more difficult in the actual state of our flocks. To be sensible of this, we need only compare this state with that of the primitive Church, or any other in which its essential characteristics are reproduced. This duty, in a homogeneous and closely united community, approaches to that of paternal correction, and may have respect either to tendencies or to *negative* facts. In almost all associations for worship of the present day, it would be a real inquisition if it should go beyond notorious public facts ; and it would be so, in every case, if it extended beyond *positive* facts.

Absolute non-attendance on public worship is a negative fact : May we call those to account who are to be reproached with it ? How and under what authority may we approach them ? Do we owe them a duty, or do we not ?

A man who is not of our parish, in the sense in which all his acts witness that he is out of the pale of the Church, has no claim on our reprehension, and the discipline of this soul does not properly enter into our pastoral obligations, if we only have respect to our official or conventional position. But if the pastor be also a missionary in spirit, or if, apart from the pastor, there is no missionary, who will dispute his right to show compassion, and even to extend aid, beyond the sphere of his pastoral obligations ? Sin is a misfortune—a crime is a disaster : Would it be less natural to go to the assistance of a man thus grievously afflicted than of one whose house has been destroyed by an incendiary ?

Charity and humility, these two inseparable virtues—inseparable because essential to one another, give to reprehension, appropriateness, proportion, true force.*

St. Paul (1 Tim., v., 1–5) has said, or, at least, intimated every thing essential to reprehension as adapted to different ages and sexes : By analogy we may discern how it should be modified by other distinctions.

Constituted as our churches are, it is very evident that public reprehension can have no place in them ; and it is doubtful whether, even under any form of ecclesiastical government,† it would be expedient or proper.

* "Il ne faut pas casser les vitres,
Mais il faut bien les nettoyer."
—See Bengel, *Pensées*, 27.

† See part iv., chap. i., *Discipline*.

Direction.—If we are called to give a soul judicious advice, or to direct it in its way, without departing from or contradicting the principles of Protestant Christianity:

Let us beware of parceling out morality—always referring particular rules to general principles: Let us preserve the mean between that ultra-methodic spirit which would regulate every thing beforehand, and tends gradually to legal bondage and self-righteous pride, and that vague spirituality which feeds on feeling, and will hear nothing either of caution or means. Let us not repel the idea of an art or method of living well, but let us not make it too minute or prescribe the same method to all. Bossuet has said that "love knows no order, and can not adjust itself to method; that confusion is its order; that distraction can not come from that source." But I see nothing inconsistent with love in the care with which one seeks the best means of showing his love to the Lord (Eph., v., 10), and the best means of cherishing that love. Our weakness obliges us to observe order, and does not allow in us an absolute contempt of method. In our directions, we ought not to restrict ourselves either to the internal life or the external life.

We must have regard to the principle of liberty and responsibility, and avoid taking the place of conscience in any one; for there will not be wanting those who would resign theirs into our hands.

If, to refer to a different matter, men must not be borne on shoulders so as to deprive them of the use of their limbs and their locomotive inclination, no more should we exact too much from them in a short time. To condense these two rules into two words, let us not direct too much, nor urge too much. We must teach men to wait, but, at the same time, to be active; not to make those who are confided to our care impatient or despondent, but rather to be constantly assisting them.

We must not encourage—on the contrary, we must repress

the curiosity, the vain words, the religious talkativeness of those (souls) who are "ever learning, and never able to come to the knowledge of the truth."—2 Tim., iii., 7. Discourse in their case becomes as a vent through which the steam that should move the engine makes its escape.

General Counsels.—We have enumerated the different states, both as to doctrine and conduct, in which the members of our flock may be found; now we will lay aside this distinction, and, taking all the classes we have spoken of together, give summary directions in relation to the care of souls in general.

Maintain always, and with all persons, a frank and direct bearing.

Rely readily, and as far as possible, on the good faith of others.

Regard ideas more than words, and sentiments more than ideas. Sentiment, or affection, is the true moral reality. How many heresies of thought correct themselves in the heart. And, in return, how much orthodoxy is in the heart heresy. Men refuse us the word—they concede to us the thing; or, again, they refuse us the thing in granting us the word.

When you recognize in an adversary a caviling spirit, and perceive that you have to do with a fabricator of difficulties, decline a contest in which there is no seriousness, and "answer not a fool according to his folly."—Prov., xxvi., 4.

Beware of considering yourself as personally offended by opposition, and by what is said, however unjustly, against the truths which you preach.

Appear not to regard as so much blasphemy all rash or inconsiderate assertions, whether relating to doctrine or morals.

Persevere without harassing.

Expect not that arguments will have an identical and absolute influence on all minds. We do not always know why an argument which has no power on one should prove efficacious on another; or why an individual who at one time received no impression from the word, should at another time be deeply impressed by it.* This is God's secret, and, after all our attentions, all our measures, the final result is left in his hands. All our hope is from him ; to him let all be ascribed. Attend more to the dispositions with which you acquit yourselves of your work, than the skill with which you used your talents.

The first of lights, of powers, of preservatives, of defenses, is charity. The spirit of the government of souls and of the whole pastoral office lies in the sentiment which these words of the Master so profoundly express : "Ye will not come to me that ye might have life."

Add to your instructions the weight of your example, well knowing that the true mode of communicating moral truth is contagion ; that it is only from life that life can proceed ; and that, in fact, the decisive arguments for or against Christianity are Christians.

Unite, mix prayer with all your efforts, all your proceedings, either to ask counsel of God, or to commend souls to him, or to keep yourself at the true point of view, and in the true understanding of your work.

In short, such is the solicitude, such the constantly-reappearing cares which the ministry draws in its train, that we must, as did the Jews who rebuilt the Temple, hold a sword in one hand while we build with the other. "Besides those things that are without," said St. Paul, "that which cometh

* "It must be acknowledged," says Leibnitz, in a letter to Madame de Brinon, "that the human heart has many windings, and that persuasions are according to tastes. We ourselves are not always in the same state of mind, and that which strikes us at one time does not touch us at another. These are what I call inexplicable reasons. There is something in them which is beyond our understanding. It often happens that the best proofs in the world do not move us, and that what does move us is properly no proof."—*Œuvres complètes de* Bossuet, Paris et Besançon, 1828, tome xxxv., p. 132, Lettre I., *Sur le Projet de Réunion.*

upon me daily, the care of all the Churches. Who is weak, and I am not weak? who is offended, and I burn not?"—2 Cor., xi., 28, 29. "Wherefore, also, we pray always for you, that our God would count you worthy of this calling, and fulfill all the good pleasure of his goodness, and the work of faith with power."—2 Thess., i., 11.

§ 3. *External State.*

The internal state is always modified by the external, and this by that; and this combination, forming, as it does, the real and total state of the individual, ought to be carefully appreciated; one of its elements separated from another has no complete signification; but these combinations, which are infinitely various, can not be foreseen or provided for; we are obliged to study the external states independently of the internal, and reciprocally.

As to external states, they are naturally of two opposite kinds, happy or unhappy; but pastoral prudence, it is obvious, occupies itself almost exclusively with the second. There are exceptional and sudden felicities which resemble catastrophes, and may be so regarded. Every event which excites in the human heart a lively feeling of joy, may furnish the pastor, while expressing congratulations, with an opportunity for admonition. And when he comes not to sadden a natural joy, but to invite it to seriousness, he has, for the most part, a chance of being well received; there are, however, cases of a kind the opposite of those, which make the most direct appeal to his sympathy.

A pastor should see, as far as possible, the afflicted of every class; but there are many cases in which he can not easily gain access to them. In conspicuous misfortunes, whatever they may be, he may and should be present; fraternal affection, shown by the pastor in cases of this kind, is the chief office of his ministry, and may, if it be accompanied with all the respect which is due to great misfortunes, gain him the confidence of individuals and families. But the most frequent and favorable occasion is that of severe sickness.

1. *The Sick.*—Care for the sick is the most sacred of the pastor's duties, the touchstone of his vocation for himself and others; and we may say that the manner in which this duty is understood and discharged measures the Christian life and the Christian spirit of each religious epoch.

Pastoral visits to the sick are not only useful to them, but to those who are about them, and who by this circumstance are made more accessible to religious instruction. They are useful to the pastor himself, who has no better opportunity of acquainting himself with mankind, with life, and with his own ministry. Sickness places a man in a situation in which we have more hold upon him. A sick man is man in a state the most natural and the most true.*

The success or the zeal only of the pastor, in this part of his ministry, is one of the most appropriate means of his becoming popular. Every one is sensible of the merit of this work, even without appreciating sufficiently its entire object and results.

Were it only from the repulsiveness inspired by the view of sorrow and of death, the pastor doubtless would find it necessary to overcome many distastes and many fears. The world, as much as it can, contrives to forget that we suffer and die. He who seeks to forget this was not made to be a pastor.

As to danger, it is said that "the good Shepherd gives his life for the sheep" (John, x., 11), which teaches us that the ministry is not a profession, but a virtual martyrdom, and that the soldier who voluntarily exposes his life every day on the field of battle for the sake of glory or promotion, differs

* BRIDGES: *The Christian Ministry*, p. 78; and MASSILLON: *Du Soin que les Curés doivent avoir pour leurs Malades.*

from the minister, the true soldier of the Gospel, only in this, that the latter not only exposes his life, but gives it.

The apostles did not understand this matter differently from their Master, and we can not understand it differently from the apostles. With St. Paul, we must be prepared to say, "I will very gladly spend and be spent for you."—2 Cor. xii., 15. "I now rejoice in my sufferings for you."—Col., i. 24. "I count not my life dear unto me, that I may finish my course with joy, and the ministry which I have received of the Lord Jesus."—Acts, xx., 24. He to whom his life is dear is hardly a Christian; how can he be a pastor?

The celibacy of the Catholic ministry, all other things being equal, cuts some of the chords which attach a man to life. But are there none but unmarried men who are called to expose and give their life? And can the marriage of the pastor remove any of the essential conditions of the pastorate?

The danger of attending on the sick in cases of epidemics or contagions is generally in inverse proportion to courage and devotedness. Danger will flee, if you do not.

Must we visit the sick when we know that they are well prepared for death? These also have need of us; probably they desire us, and if they have no need of us, we have need of them.

We must be careful to avoid going too late, and for that end keep ourselves informed whether there are any sick, by means of confidential friends, which every pastor ought to have. Even those sick persons must be visited whose condition gives no cause for serious concern. We shall find a great advantage from having accustomed the people to receive visits from us when they were in good health; the first visit of a pastor, where this has been neglected, may have a somewhat sinister aspect.

Should the pastor go without being sent for? Authors answer differently.*

* See HÜFFELL: *Wesen und Beruf*, &c., t. ii., p. 318, troisième edit.

We should say no, if the members of the flock made it a positive and constant duty to obey the precept of St. James, v., 14. As it is, however, if the pastor should wait to be sent for, he would run the risk of not visiting a single sick person. We must desire to be called, we must in some way contrive to be; but called or not called, desired or not, we must go. There is a way of presenting one's self, and even of insisting on a reception, without suggesting the idea of those doleful men who thrust themselves upon the dying as upon a prey. And, at any rate, whatever prejudice we may have to encounter, how can we forbear insisting, when we know in some measure how important are seasons of sickness to the life of the soul, and that the most active resistance and hardened indifference often conceal the germ of a new life and of salvation, not to be discovered except by the zeal of a pastor, who hopes against hope? The first visit, we should remember, is the most difficult, and often the only difficult one. We should know how to be importunate, yet always with gentleness. We should not force an entrance at once, but return again and again, until our affectionate patience prevails, and the door opens itself to us. Let us not be sustained and animated by a desire to discharge our responsibility, a narrow and fruitless motive truly; love alone has no limits, and is never weary.

The pastor should not neglect to learn from the physician the sick person's bodily condition, and from his relations and friends his moral and religious state.* As to this second point, however, let not the pastor receive every thing as fact, independently of the observations he himself may have occasion to make. We are often ill-informed, and it might be better for us to be without any information.

According to our idea of the case which presents itself, it is well to reflect on the point of view in which we should regard it, and on the course we should follow; but a too mi-

* See BRIDGES: *The Christian Ministry*, p. 410.

nute preparation is likely to be injurious, as in all cases of the same kind that we may meet with.

Faith and hope are the soul of every pastoral work; but those dispositions which have God for their object have nothing in common with the illusion of feeble minds and lively imaginations. Before attempting this difficult and important task, we may think we shall exert great influence, or witness striking things: especially may we count on a singular sincerity on the part of a man who sees himself on the border of eternity—for we may suppose that one can not dissemble who has but a moment to live; but in all this we are mistaken. We also imagine that the tragic solemnity of death-scenes will always so affect us as to sustain us at the height of our function: another mistake. Much sooner than we would think, this function ends in discharging itself with inconceivable tranquillity, and even with a wandering mind. Nothing avails but truth. Let us obtain a complete idea of these difficulties and these dangers; and as we every day put off our armor, let us put it on every day. Endeavor to be alone with the sick. It is very difficult, very uncommon, for a sick person to open himself perfectly in the presence of others, even if they are his most intimate acquaintances.* Always begin with manifestations of affection. Take time and pains to show the design of God in sickness; represent it as an extraordinary *Sabbath;* assert the grace of God to us in preserving to us in sickness the use of our faculties; show this period in life to be of great value and moment. Let the pastor place himself and place the sick man in a true point of view, as regards his mission, and remove from him both the feeling and thought that an intrinsical and a magical virtue attaches to the visit of a pastor: From ourselves, from each one of us, will our soul be required; and no one can either pray, or repent, or be converted, or love God in our place.

* HÜFFELL: *Wesen und Beruf*, &c., t. ii., p. 318, troisième edit.

If, shortly after these preliminaries, the sick person would open himself, a zealous and intelligent man will have no difficulty in preparing the way. But, in beginning, he must not be too urgent. We should first accustom the sick to see us and hear us. With a lively solicitude, which seeks no concealment, let us neither give trouble nor feel troubled. In every sense our strength is "quietly to wait for the salvation of the Lord."—Lam., iii., 26.

If the sick person keeps every thing to himself, or, what comes to the same, if we obtain from him only a complaisant assent, let us endeavor to open his heart by prayer, which, at the bed of the sick, is preaching par excellence, and in which we may say every thing. Nothing can give us a better idea of what prayer is, and what it can do, than the admirable prayers of Pascal* in asking God to enable him to make a good use of sickness.

We may add to prayer the reading of these passages of the Bible, to which nothing has equal power: The song of Hezekiah (Isaiah, xxxviii.); many of the Psalms of supplication and thanksgiving; the recital of some of the cures of Jesus Christ; certain verses of the beautiful fifth chapter of the second epistle to the Corinthians: But we may also cite less special passages: those words which raise our views to the dawn of an endless day, and mark eternity as containing the true good of man and the true end of the soul.

Let the knowledge which we can obtain respecting the sick, from himself and by other means, also direct us in our prayers and in the choice of our readings, and let us persevere in this course. Formal interrogation is scarcely possible, promises little good, shuts the heart rather than opens it.

It may be impossible, however, to pursue this course after a certain period of effort and attention, when we have to do with a man obstinately blind, hardened, or impenitent; or only if we have reason to be greatly pained at the disposi-

* Pascal: *Pensées*, Part II., Article XIX.

tions shown by the sick man. I do not think that his silence should have this effect upon us ; for silence, even the most obstinate, proves nothing. After having used all gentle and insinuating methods, we must sometimes frankly demand a hearing.

The true Christian disposition is a calmness which is born of trouble. There is no legitimate calmness which trouble has not preceded. It is hence ordinarily not simple calmness, but joy, more or less sensible—a sweet resulting from bitterness ; in all cases an humble joy mixed with a profound sense of unworthiness. It is a joy mingled with trembling and love. With persons thus exercised, we have but to employ what may augment compunction in joy, or joy in compunction ; not to abate either the one or the other, but to temper the one with the other : The general state is not to be changed.

There is a Christianity which makes salvation to depend on the mere assurance of salvation ; so that one is saved purely and simply because he believes himself to be. Weigh well our words, as we ourselves have weighed them. They imply no condemnation of the assurance of salvation ; they by no means deny its legitimacy ; they leave to this estate its beauty, its truth, its claim as an object of our desires and our prayers ; much more, they do not forbid our regarding the assurance of salvation as the complement, the coronation, the perfection of faith. But the assurance of salvation, considered in its principle, is the Spirit of God himself " bearing witness with our spirit that we are the children of God."—Rom., viii., 16. No other witness is sufficient and available ; and to replace this by a simple argument, by a syllogism, is to encroach upon its rights. In other terms, this witness is from within ; it is as intimate as irresistible, as the consciousness of life : This perfection of faith is of the same nature with faith, which is the substance itself, or the appropriation of evangelical blessings ; in its commencement as in its consummation, a mysterious grace, of which a purely intellectual faith and a purely logical assurance of salvation is but the vain counterfeit. Conscience, however carefully interrogated, can not make one such assurance the pledge and essence of salvation. We are not saved because we feel sure of being saved, but we feel sure of being saved because we are saved. We must then invert the terms; logic itself and all analogy demand this; there is no sphere in which the reasoning we oppose can be admitted by any person of good sense. Why should reasoning, which is bad every where else, be found good here, and here only?

This doctrine, which is thought to be the only means of giving all to God and giving nothing to man, has, on the contrary, the effect of attaching salvation to a work, and, I may say, a servile work, since, in the rigor of the doctrine which is advanced, no particle of affection, no truly religious element, can enter into this work. This doctrine, which, for the most part, is preached by pious men, finds easy access not only into humble hearts that confound it with the implicit submission of faith, but in souls arid and mercenary, which it does not disturb and does not trouble in their interior habits; and as it forbids man to look to his feelings even less than to his works, in order "to know that he is of the truth, and to assure his heart before God" (1 John, iii., 19), it very soon annuls, without denying, every part of the Gospel which relates to the government of the heart and the reformation of the life. I speak of some souls—not of all; for a good many of those who derive their assurance from the simple and naked acceptance of salvation derive it unknowingly from the witness of the Spirit, who by his presence and agency within them attests to them with irresistible force that Christ abides in them, and that they abide in him. It is painful to have to prepare for death the partisans of this false and dangerous assurance of salvation, who take away not faith precisely, but every thing which forms the true substance and true end of faith: It is painful to have to make them descend from the mountain into the valley, from peace into trouble; and to begin, in their short and disturbed moments of sickness, at the very gates of eternity, the entire education of a soul contaminated and proud of its error. It is the more painful, as we may little hope to see hatched under the burning fire of reprehension and alarm one of those conversions of heart which ordinarily are wrought so gently, and in circumstances so different from that in which the dying find themselves. May we, however, hesitate? And when there is but one chance against ten thousand of restoring this man to an estate of saving faith, may we be permitted to neglect this chance? And may we not venture to disturb this soul, and even to disturb it profoundly, in order to give it true tranquillity instead of false?

There is a tranquillity of another kind proceeding from the persuasion of self-righteousness in the sick man. And what righteousness? Often it is scarcely more than common honesty. Should we expect to find it in persons instructed in the Christianity which they profess? Nothing is more strange, and nothing more common. It is no less strange to see persons who call themselves Christians, and who think they are, though less persuaded of their own righteousness than the former, taking refuge in a vague idea of the mercy of God, who, they think, is too good, and is too much occupied with other matters, to observe them so narrowly. You will encounter philosophers who are accustomed to thoughts of death, and who are not afraid to die, and whose minds, fortified by sophisms more or less learned, seem impenetrable to the most pungent arguments. With others, finally, in whom an entirely material activity and an exclusively vulgar way of thinking has destroyed the moral life, or whom vice has hardened or imbruted, we can find, in a manner, no place for a soul.

There are a thousand occasions where circumstances would seem to dissuade us from making any attempt, as too evidently useless; but there are a thousand facts which prove that we can not define the limit where resources absolutely fail, and where all access is closed against the preacher of the Gospel. We ought, then, to be urgent, and persevere to the end; at the end, very often, we are waited for, and are accepted.

God, we know, can give to a moment the value of an entire life, as was seen in the case of the thief who was converted on the cross. And although every thing obliges us to think such cases very rare, and that, in general, we should place little dependence on death-bed conversions, mere possibility, in view of extreme peril, makes it our sacred duty to labor for the conversion of the sick with all our resources of heart and mind. *Spera, quia unus; time, quia solus.**

Besides, this impassibility or this security is very often affected; it is merely outward, and can not long resist us. Let us not be deceived by it.

Let us not more be deceived by that facility with which we sometimes meet. There are persons whom we would persuade to be less hasty in yielding to us; we should think them more serious if they offered us more resistance; and the docility shown us through deference, through prejudice, is a different thing from the reflecting and voluntary docility of a conscience which yields to truth itself.

We should expect to meet with many troubled souls. Among them there are those (and this, perhaps, is the most difficult case) who, having until now believed with a faith purely intellectual, thought that they were believers, and now all at once discover that they were not; who see nothing but a great void, where until now the objects of their pretended faith were floating like phantoms before them; who, having tampered with all the truths, and employed all the words of religion, have no longer any impression from them at the moment when it is most important to be able to make use of them; in a word, who at the last hour, in-

* "Hope, because there is one; fear, because there is but one."

stead of a living faith, find only a dead system. They are in a condition worse than it would have been if they had never known the truth. There are others of these with whom remorse is stronger than the promises of grace. Others there are, who, without being absolutely destitute of faith, and without being afraid of the judgment of God, have at death the fear of death itself—a fear for the most part physical, greater in some men than in others, and by which believers even are sometimes beset. We shall find, in general, more natural ease in dying among persons of small culture and a laborious life, than with learned men, thinkers, and the most highly cultivated people. The poor man passes his life but to die; his poor imagination sees nothing in death but nakedness. Finally, there are those whom the consciousness of some neglected reparation, which it was difficult, or perhaps impossible, to make, deeply agitates, or from whom some temporal engagement, some domestic care, banishes calmness and freedom of mind.

Trouble at its last stage is despair, a state into which two very different classes of persons may fall; men who have repelled or neglected the means of salvation, the more they were offered to them; and men who, having done the entire contrary, and, as it appears to them, every thing necessary to assure them of peace, see the whole frame-work of their faith crumbling as a fantastic edifice, and they ask themselves, whether all that life which they have found in religion, so real, so intimate, so serious, has been any thing more than a dream, and whether Christianity, which occupies so large a place in history, has any reality except in history. There are those also, who, without losing in any degree their conviction, find themselves punished by a sudden and deep despair, for the spiritual pride to which they had subjected themselves. This mysterious experience—despair—has more than once been suffered by the most humble and most pious faith; but in this case not prolonged, we think, to the last moment. Such persons die in comfort, and the light which shines on their last hour removes the scandal which their unexpected darkness may have given to the witnesses of their death. Without pretending to penetrate the mystery of this dispensation, we may observe, that the work of every man's conversion consists of the same elements, the proportion of which does not vary, but which may be differently distributed. In the final reckoning, the addition will not fail to be correct, and the total to be rendered. What was not in its place at first is found afterward; bitterness with many comes after joy; the order is inverted, but we must "fulfill all righteousness;" and he who may have too readily accepted the promises, must pay, sooner or later, the same price which was assessed to those who could not appropriate pardon to themselves until they had tasted condemnation. It is necessary that they should pass three days in the tomb, and descend to hell. This is always the price of the true resurrection; the date of payment only varies.

The duty of disturbing a false peace is not the most difficult, but it is the most formidable; and we must be either armed by a severe fanaticism, or by great faith and charity; moment by moment must we be guarded against our own weakness, in order to fulfill faithfully a mission so painful; painful indeed, since the success itself is formidable, and we must equally fear not producing disturbance and producing it. It may be useful to confute error as far as we can, but we shall be pre-eminently favored if God enables us to present to the soul the Gospel as a whole, with all its elements at once, so that it may not appear in its alarming aspect without at the same time assuming its consolatory character, nor have this latter aspect without at the same time retaining the former. The necessity of pardon, and the assurance of pardon; the necessity of repentance, and the blessings connected with repentance; salvation, entire, gratuitous, irrevocable, but the renunciation of all other means of safety; prayer opening heaven to the sinner, but to the sinner who prays as a sinner; the certainty of aid to every one who perseveres in asking it; these are the ideas which, intercombined always, are able to move without irritating, and with which, when no one of them is isolated from that which corresponds to it, we may be frank, inflexible, and still affecting. Sometimes, perhaps, we must use a holy violence, and snatch, as from the midst of the burning, a brand which seems about to be consumed—roughness being now the only form of charity; but the true pastor seldom finds himself placed in this stern necessity, and will doubtless exhaust all other means before he has recourse to this. And in every case the last moments are no time for summoning and threatening; a dying man, if he can hear us, should hear only words full of unction, prayers to God full of melting tenderness, supplications to himself to be reconciled to God, supplications to God to be graciously reconciled to his creature, who is about to pass away; expressions, finally, of a fervent desire and a charitable hope. If this soul is softened, if it weeps, if it prays, be content, and besides this blessing, do not ask or expect joy; the soul that empties itself, that makes itself nothing, that renounces itself, that cries to God, the soul that addresses itself to him as to an offended father, but still as to a father, may not indeed, on this side of the tomb, taste the joy of salvation; but as for you, be assured it will come, and rejoice over this weeping soul, for it shall be comforted.

We pass now to the case in which we find the soul troubled:

We must not expect that this soul will always confess itself to be troubled, or tell whence its trouble proceeds. We shall often be obliged to induce the person to tell us, or even ourselves to tell the sick, who may very well experience an effect without being able to detect the cause. And often, when he may know the cause very well, he can not make up his mind to declare it. It is as important, however, as it may be difficult, to obtain the knowledge of it; for efforts directed to any other point than the seat of the disease may aggravate the evil, while it fails of the end. Happily, the Gospel suffices for every thing, because it corresponds to every thing; and we can not present it as a whole, and in the admirable fusion of the elements which characterize it, without applying a dressing to the wound, even though we do not see it. We may thus comfort ourselves in cases in which the trouble shows itself without a distinct appearance of the cause; but we must endeavor to understand the cause, since we may then, without foregoing the presentation of the Gospel as a whole, make a more just, more direct, more personal application of it. To be telling how to adapt a remedy to each particular case, according to its nature and its cause, is to be occupied in an infinite detail: Some authors have made the attempt, but it seems to me that the very special directions which, at the outset, deprive our impressions of their liberty, and our actions of that character of spontaneity and inspiration which they ought to have, are more injurious than useful. What is important—what, perhaps, is sufficient, is to get a good understanding of the patient's state, and of the nature of his inward feelings: this obtained, the rest is left to our evangelical views, our charity, our tact, and the Divine Spirit, constrained, if I may say so, by our prayers, to intervene as an interpreter between the sick man and ourselves. The recital of the experience of accomplished ministers on this field of sorrow is more useful than a catalogue of *à priori* prescriptions.

As to the trouble which a soul heretofore indifferent finds in the presence of death, it will be difficult for us to judge of it: it is the region of mystery. It is but too certain that remorse is not repentance, that alarm is not conversion, and that the fear of death is not the fear of God. There are, it is said, souls who perceive with despair that the principle of the spiritual life is extinguished within them, and who with terrible evidence are convinced that there remains nothing in them that can love or pray: Faith comes to them at the last moment, but it is the faith of demons, resplendent with brightness, but it is the brightness of lightning. God only can know, indeed, that this soul is dead: Let us who do not know, struggle, pant with it, fight its battle, unite with it in its agony; let it perceive that there is by its side, in its last anguish, a soul that believes, that hopes, and that loves; that our charity is but a reflection, and as a revelation of the charity of Christ; that Christ, through us, has become present to it; let us give it a hint, a glimpse, a taste of the Divine mercy; let it be, as it were, forced to believe in it by seeing the reflection of it in us; let us hope against hope; let us wrestle with God to the last moment; let the voice of our prayer, let the echo of the words of Christ resound in the dying man's ear, even in his dreams—we do not know what may be passing in that interior world into which our views do not penetrate, nor by what mystery eternity may hang on one minute, and salvation on one sigh. We do not know what may avail, what one ejaculation of a soul toward God may embrace at the last bound of earthly existence. Then let us not cease; let us pray aloud with the dying man; let us pray for him with a low voice; let us commit, without ceasing, the soul to its Creator; let us be a priest, when we can no longer be a preacher. Let the office of intercession, the most efficacious of all, precede, accompany, follow all others.

Without distinguishing cases any further, let us now add some general directions regarding the spiritual treatment of the sick.

The first is to do every thing we can, in order to preclude or discard the idea that our ministry may carry a man to heaven independently of his own will.

The second is not to require a long work, not to make a long discourse, not to engage in intricate reasonings, to address the conscience directly, with frankness, cordiality, and authority.*

A third is to infuse ourselves, without our personality, into our exhortations and instructions; to put ourselves on a level with those we seek to console; to show them in ourselves a sinner assisting another sinner; to relate to them, as far as we can, the history of our soul; and, in a word, to reason with them, not from an elevation, but on the same simple footing with themselves; we shall lose nothing of our authority by so doing.

We can not too earnestly recommend patience and indulgence: We must not roughly tread on even the greatest of their errors and illusions. We may seem surprised, grieved, but never angry: Let us not forget that if, in preaching, as a whole, appeals to fear, in men who are in health, and have no thought of death as near to them, may have a salutary effect, and ought to be employed; if, even on the bed of death, we must awaken in indifferent souls a serious concern for their eternity, still, that alarm is sterile, and we can not depend upon the manifestations which it may produce.† Let us never forget that characteristically we are the heralds of good news; that these good news are sufficient for all, because they embrace all; that they chasten while they console; that they are, so to speak, a tonic as well as a tranquilizer to the soul; lastly, that the charge of the pastor in respect to the sick, as toward all, is comprised in these words of the prophet: "Comfort ye, comfort ye my people; speak ye comfortably to Jerusalem."—Isaiah, xl., 1, 2.

Expect much from prayer; I mean not only from its power with God, but from its immediate effect on the sick. We may say every thing in prayer; under the form of prayer we may make every thing acceptable; with it we may make hearts the most firmly closed open themselves to us; there is a true *charm* in prayer, and this charm has its effect also

* *Praktische Bemerkungen*, p. 79

† Page 83.

upon us, whom it renders at once more confident, more gentle, more patient, and whom it puts into an affecting fellowship with the sick man, whoever he may be, by making God present to us both.

Let us not formally tell the sick man that death is near, unless we think it the last and only means of bringing the sinner to himself; for otherwise we may have much more confidence in the genuineness and solidity of a work which has been quietly accomplished, than of one which takes place amid trouble caused by the unexpected view of death. We should, however, be able to declare to a man, not only as man, but as an individual, all his iniquities, and all the danger of his ways. Where the sin is notorious, dwell upon that: Charity, sometimes, is no longer charity, unless it assumes the form of severity. But, I repeat it, the last moment is not one for summoning and threatening: When that moment comes, we must refer every thing to submissive and tender prayer.*

The communion should not be administered to the sick unless they desire it, and then we should take care that there be no superstition mixed with the desire. We should rejoice at the expression of a desire, and should hasten to satisfy it when we are assured that it is spiritual.† At this juncture, however, and even apart from the opportunity which it affords, we must insist on necessary and practicable reparations. It is proper that others, if they are so inclined, should partake of the communion with the sick person.

Though it is well, at the beginning, that we should be alone with the sick, it is well, on many accounts, to have the members of the family, at least the most intimate of them, present at the interviews which we have with him; first, to inspire them with confidence in us, and then to profit them through our presence.

As much as possible let us avoid interfering with testa-

* KOESTER: *Lehrbuch der Pastoralwissenschaft*, p. 134. † P. 134, 135.

mentary dispositions, and have nothing to do in drawing them up, without, however, as to this, declining to give advice to a disturbed, ill-instructed, or slumbering conscience: Let us wisely use our ministry in securing reparations which are important to the repose of conscience, and which, apart from our agency, perhaps, would not be made.

Let us not neglect the relations of the sick man after his death, nor the sick man during his convalescence.*

The affliction of a family has often been the means of introducing into its bosom the truth, together with the preacher who was its interpreter. The survivors as much as the dead must be on our thoughts, that we may cultivate the field which grief has sown. We must, in many cases, be prepared for a difficult undertaking. There are idle griefs, as there are consolations which are not less so. Afflicted persons sometimes offer a kind of worship to him whom they lament, and endeavor to associate us in their panegyrics and admiration: They praise in our presence qualities in the departed which are blamable, or without moral worth; excuse what is inexcusable; make to themselves maxims, a morality, a religion, according to the impulses of their affection, and their interest in the soul of the dead: We shall find them improvising heresies for his sake, or harassing us with questions regarding his state, and soliciting from us a sentence of acquittal, even in cases in which it would be most difficult to pronounce it, if this were ever allowable. Let us not forget that grief has claims to our respect; but let us be yet more on our guard against forgetting that truth has anterior and higher claims to it; and while we express hope where there is room for hope, let us, when necessary, learn how to take refuge in our ignorance of the decrees of God and of the invisible world. We have no right to condemn any one, but

* BRIDGES: *The Christian Ministry*, p. 424; and BURNET: *A Discourse of the Pastoral Care.*

we may not, on our own responsibility, decree celestial happiness to any one.

When grief and regret alone appear in that detachment from the visible world, and in those aspirations toward the future world, which afflicted persons quite often manifest, it is important to correct their thoughts, to give another direction to their regards, and to prevent them, if possible, from making their grief a religion, and its object a god ; in a word, we should teach them to fill with God himself the heaven which they would fill with a creature. Let not the minister too readily mistake for a conversion, or the beginning of one, those emotions of apparent piety with which conscience often has nothing to do.

There are few things more painful or more embarrassing than to be required to offer consolation or condolence to individuals or families who have not evangelical views. What shall we say to them ? Shall we speak to them as they wish ? Console them after the manner of the world ? This we can not do. Forsake them ? This is still more impossible. Preach to them the Gospel ? Yes, preach, or, rather, announce it to them. After having, with a generous heart, freely sympathized with their griefs, listened to their complaints, testified a sincere interest, searched through their misfortune, of whatever kind it may be, we must make it our text, arm ourselves with it, so to speak, against them, make them to feel the emptiness of human consolation, and the necessity of seeking solid consolation beyond the bounds of time and the world, call Jesus Christ openly to the help of their misery and ours. We must not premeditate too much what we shall say, what we shall do on these occasions. The best meditation is their misfortune, the best preparation much pity. Let us go to them with tears and with a kind of joy, with the joy of a consolation of which the secret is with us : Let us go with God himself, and with the assurance that he will be with us and with them. This confidence, this committal of all to God is the chief strength and the chief light in all difficult occurrences.

II. *The Diseased in Mind.*—The case of these is not to be confounded with that of those troubled souls of whom we have spoken before (page 259): It is principally, if not exclusively, a case of sickness. As, however, it appears to be certain that moral means may be used successfully with a moral malady, the cause of which is physical, we think that the minister, in concert with the physician, may possibly effect something in this case. The influence of the moral on the physical is as unquestionable, as conceivable, and probably as powerful, as that of the physical on the moral.*

Hence we should seek to acquaint ourselves well with the idea which either occasioned or nourishes the disease; for it is generally improbable that the evil has created itself; and perhaps some secret principle of moral evil is what has produced and developed it. Let us detect this element, which it is not always easy to do, since reserve and dissimulation are far from being incompatible with states which seem to exclude the power of self-control.

We can not recommend "answering a fool according to his folly" (Prov., xxvi., 5); but we may advise against too rudely dashing away the gloomy imaginations of the patient, and we may rest assured that formal reasoning with men in whom a fixed idea produces itself with an obstinate and fatal certainty will prove ordinarily to be pains worse than lost. Expressions of affection, passages of Scripture, prayer when the patient will unite in, or, at least, permit it—in short, kindly

* "*Obsta Principiis*"—to resist at the outset, in such cases, is of very special importance. The torrent of troubled thoughts gains in force and in rapidity in proportion as it advances. We should endeavor by all means to arrive in time, to avert and restrain the strange pleasure with which a diseased mind gives itself up to gloomy thoughts.

entertaining him with what may interest or recreate him without injury to our principal object—means such as these may be used with more or less success, in the hope that God will offer some as yet unknown chance by which we may banish that fixed idea, which, born of physical evil, increases and prolongs it. The malady itself sometimes affords weapons for contending with it, which, in prudent and discreet hands, may be effectual.

Sometimes the idea makes the disease : Moral evil becomes physical evil—a disease properly so called : Let us ascertain if it has done so. If it has, an educated and enlightened pastor has resources at command, and he may expect more from the use of reasoning : But, without excluding this, I would unite it with, and subordinate it to, the use of the word of God, applied with judgment, and rather for the purpose of consolation than of proof. Let us consider that, with persons in this state, especially if they are of an active mind, reasoning which does not convince renders obstinate, confirms, in some sort, the patient in his error, and increases his mental trouble. We must not run this risk. When we meet with minds which certain religious ideas have disturbed, either as cause or occasion, we ought not to forget that the soundest and most fundamental truths may give trouble when they are suddenly encountered, or when the state of the man whom they exclusively possess favors such a consequence. When this kind of mental perturbation is caused by the unexpected onset, and, so to speak, by the shock of truth, we may be sure that it will not last. In some cases we may regard it, and so represent it to the patient himself, as an unavoidable crisis—a transition to that definitive peace which ought to be inseparable from the truth. We should likewise be reminded, as ministers, that, in the complete and faithful dispensation of the truth, an economy and a care are to be observed, without which truth may have many of the effects of error.

We should be sorry to think that to persons in whom mental disease has become a complete insanity, the spiritual aids of the ministry must be useless. With them, especially, reasoning would doubtless be useless, and even dangerous. But I think, with Harms, that when discussion is impossible, it may be useful to speak. Solitude and the absence of intercourse may irritate the disease as much as injudicious contradiction ; and, by inducing him to speak, we may obtain some insight into the patient's soul. Let us indulge the hope that, in some lucid or less perturbed moment, we may introduce into the poor wanderer's spirit some peace, perhaps some light, or may excite some favorable emotion which God may regard. "Cast thy bread upon the waters, and thou shalt find it." The mere names of the heavenly Father and the divine Mediator are very powerful, and often have effect when discourse can do nothing. A certain authority, a certain daringness is necessary ; we should be conscious of feeling strong : to use an expression of Harms, there is a kind of *magic* in the authority which faith imparts.*

Some cases may suggest the idea of *possession* or *obsession* as the cause, and I am not sure that this idea should be repelled ; but under this impression I have known those medical means to be neglected which were clearly demanded, and which, at the commencement at least, should have been used ; and as for formal exorcisms or conjurations, I think they are adapted to render disturbed persons entirely mad. Prayer and charity are the true conjuration.

A pastor should not allow himself to be unacquainted with the principal works which treat of diseases of the mind. We have a right to assume that *anthropology* has formed a part of his general studies.

III. *The Pastor reconciling those who are at Variance.*—

* "Ein Priester der nicht magisch wirkt ist gar kein Priester, und ein Prediger der nicht magisch wirkt ist nur ein halber Prediger."—Harms : *Pastoraltheologie*, tome ii., p. 73.

"Blessed are the peace-makers" (Matt., v., 9): their work certainly belongs to the ministry; which, in a religious sense, is a justice of the peace—a justice of the peace, not arbiter, as we may plainly see in Luke, xii., 14: "Man, who made me a judge or a divider over you?"

Consistently with this, we may, if we have experience, tact, and knowledge of business, propose, when necessary, measures of reconciliation; but, for the most part, we should especially recommend mutual concession and condescension, the extinction of pride and resentment, the exercise of generous qualities and religious sentiments, and give ascendency to that spirit of sacrifice which is the chief practical characteristic of the religion of Jesus Christ.

It is a delicate matter to come in as a mediator in domestic quarrels, unless we are invited:* It is best, when we can do so, to be on the side of each of the contending parties. We should fear long narrations by which each party kindles anew and feeds his hatred, and which oblige the mediator to be a very involuntary instrument and instigator of the quarrel. We should fear, also, the proposing of questions which, in a religious and moral point of view, are idle, and which, on account of the difficulty of replying to them, are dangerous—a difficulty which, when perceived or manifested, diminishes so much the reconciling authority. Still, while we should always avoid taking a side, we must not appear blind to evidence or insensible to injustice; this would also discredit us; we must always recommend humility to him who in any matter stands upon his rights and his merits.

In quarrels between man and wife, we must discard as long as possible the idea of a separation; never suggest it, and yet not repel it when the continuance of a forced connection would be only the occasion of greater sin and scandal than a separation.

There are confidential communications which it is as dan-

* Bengel: *Pensées*, § 33.

gerous and improper as it is painful to receive: Very seldom is minute and detailed information of a certain kind necessary to acquaint the pastor well with his position. Let him show a repugnance, and, if necessary, let him positively refuse to hear them, and people will be sufficiently admonished and instructed to keep them to themselves. I except the case in which it is important to know every thing, in order to prevent or remedy an evil. It is, however, necessary always that the pastor respect himself; and charity alone may persuade him to descend into the impure region of vice.

IV. *The Poor.*—The Sovereign Pastor cared for the poor, and has given, as a principal characteristic of his Church, compassion for the unfortunate, and care to restore equality by charity. The apostles, in partially devolving the care of the poor on *deacons*, did not renounce this interest, with which we every where see them engaged; the deacons, moreover, are ministers of religion; and thus the care of the poor also remains a religious ministry. There are now no deacons in the special sense, or, rather, every Christian is a deacon; as, however, nothing is regulated by this consideration, and probably never will be, what for a time has been detached from the evangelical ministry rightfully returns to it, and the pastor is a deacon.

So he will always be under all institutions, because his ministry is essentially the ministry of compassion, and this ministry can not separate itself from the sentiment which is, in fact, its foundation: For, while showing itself indifferent to the temporal miseries of men, it can not show itself moved by their spiritual miseries. Public sentiment always assigns this two-fold end to the Christian ministry.

A pastor is not only called to exercise a ministry of beneficence, but to propagate and maintain the spirit of beneficence. For this reason, he must not only give an example of beneficence, but he must promote it, and form it in all his parishioners without distinction of class, and I will even say of fortune. We ought to "bear one another's burdens" (Gal., vi., 2); and this measure, which ought to be the motto and the soul of every society, should be exemplified by the pastor before every man's door. Great, indeed, will be his success if he can make the rich receive and obey it; but he will do yet more if he can persuade the poor that it concerns them also, and that they have the means of obeying it. Associations may be well, and even necessary; but the pastor must be careful that they do not absorb personal activity and responsibility: It is needful that "the poor and the rich should meet together."—Prov., xxii., 2.

As to the direct care of the needy, the pastor ought himself to inquire into the situation and resources of each. The spirit of detail, the industry of beneficence, is what makes it truly useful; it is also what causes it to be respected; it likewise gives the beneficent man authority with those whom he comforts. We must listen with patience to complaints and narratives, endure a little ennui, enter into human nature, and remind ourselves by our own experience that, "in relating our sorrows, we often assuage them."* In this sphere of activity we meet with so many deceptions, so much baseness, we see so much of human nature under a hideous aspect, that we are in danger of losing the respect which we owe it even in its abject condition. Let the pastor put in the first rank of his cares that of elevating the spirit and the courage of the poor; of inducing him to seek his resources in himself, of maintaining and guarding the sentiment of his dignity, of showing him in his poverty all the respect to which he has a right, or which he is able to appreciate.

It is required by charity itself, and even by regard to real necessities, that we turn away from necessities which are imaginary, or which arise from indolence and selfishness. Let us beware that we do not engender poverty by the very

* Corneille: *Polyeuchte*, act i., scene 3.

pains by which we seek to destroy it. Let us acquaint ourselves with those inflexible laws which arise from the nature of things in the whole of a population, and let us have them before our mind in every particular case, since a particular case does remind us of them, and may also tend to make us forget them.

Our concern that no one should doubt our personal beneficence should not make us connive at an idea which is creditable in certain parishes, that every case, without discrimination, is to be undertaken by the pastor or his family. Let us know how to keep importunity and indelicacy in order.

Let us not appear to desire payment for aid which we may give under demonstrations of piety; nor to induce the belief that we succor the body only that we may have access to the soul. In our first approaches, let us be moderate in our religious communications.*

The good which the pastor himself can do is very small compared with that which he can do by means of others. He is the delegate of the poor to the rich, and of the rich to the poor. The first function is delicate and difficult. He must expect refusals, affronts. A sublime trait (that of a pastor who, receiving an insult from an impatient rich man, said to him, "See, this is for myself, what now have you for my poor?") should often be in the memory of pastors. We should, however, do wrong not to consider the difference of situations and antecedent demands. We must know how to withdraw in a proper manner; we must engage the rich in the details of the case which we represent to him; get him to make the investigation of this misery his own affair; ask

* Beneficence has become an art, the principal rules of which have become popular. On this subject there are important works which we must not omit reading; as, in French, the book on Charity of M. Duchatel; that of M. Naville on the same subject; *Le Visiteur du Pauvres*, by M. De Gerando; in English, *The Civil and Charitable Economy of Great Cities*, by Dr. Chalmers.

him for something better than money ; do not urge him too earnestly to give ; be content when he gives ; resigned, and not out of humor, when he does not give ; but in every case discharge this mission with as much of liberty as of modesty and delicacy. To be ashamed would be to renounce one of the most beautiful parts of the ministry, and to prepare ourselves for refusals.

[CHAPTER III.

By the Translator.

Of the Care of Souls in Times of special Declension and special Interest in Religion.

AFTER much reflection, we venture, though tremblingly, to add a chapter on this subject.

In this part of his work the author has not only transcended his predecessors, but, admirably as he had executed the other parts, he has, we think, transcended himself also : And yet there is here (what doubtless will be regarded, especially in this country, as an important omission) no distinct consideration of the care of souls, as modified justly by the two specialities in the state of the flock which we have indicated. These specialities, though perhaps more observable and more prominent under certain modes of pastoral activity, certain views of theology, and certain external circumstances, than others, have their ground in the nature of man as at best imperfectly renewed, the laws of the new life under the economy of grace, and the circumstances of trial and exposure in which churches find themselves while they remain in this world. They are not necessary ; they violate the ideal of Christian sanctification, which excludes all change except that of increase ; but probably they will continue until the triumph of Christianity is complete, and the advance of Christianity in the future be as it has been from the beginning, chiefly, as Edwards has said, by " remarkable communications of the Spirit of God at special seasons of mercy." Neither in individuals nor in masses does the spiritual life remain always in the same state ; in both it is alternately high and low, and the elevations and depressions are not unfrequently extreme and of long continuance, and it would be superfluous to prove that the care of souls should vary with these variations of their state. We can not but lament that our author's great abilities were not occupied as thoroughly with this subject as they were with the others which are included in this part, and which he has treated with such unparalleled success.

There may be specialities of other kinds in the state of a flock as such, requiring corresponding modifications of pastoral activity. The flock may be suffering severely from persecution, from war, from pestilence, from famine, from unfavorable changes in trade and business; or, on the contrary, they may be in a state of great temporal prosperity, with prospects continually brightening, by which they may be placed in severer temptation than any they might find themselves subjected to by external affliction of whatever degree or kind. It is obvious that in all such cases a demand is made on the pastor for some variations in the exercise of his ministry, in order to accommodate it suitably to the particular circumstances in which he finds himself:* Much more is he required to adapt his ministry as precisely and completely as possible to the exigencies of his flock when they are in either of the states first mentioned.

Let us not think that a flock can never find itself in the first of these states but by the pastor's fault. The principle that there is a constant proportion between the care given to souls and the life of the parish,† is not to be taken as implying that pastoral fidelity in the care of souls will infallibly and universally secure in the parish a high state of spiritual prosperity. The proportion in respect to the spirituality of the parish as a whole may even be inversely as the pastor's fidelity. "Then began he to upbraid the cities wherein most of his mighty works were done, because they repented not: Woe unto thee, Chorazin! woe unto thee, Bethsaida!

* See pages 208, 242.

† See page 238.

for if the mighty works which were done in you had been done in Tyre and Sidon, they would have repented long ago in sackcloth and ashes."—Matt., xi., 20, 21. "Now thanks be unto God, who always causeth us to triumph in Christ, and maketh manifest the savor of his knowledge by us in every place. For we are unto God a sweet savor of Christ, in them that are saved, and in them that perish: To the one we are the savor of death unto death; and to the other the savor of life unto life."—2 Cor., ii., 14–16. In general, or in a comprehensive view, the care of souls, and the actual state of religion in a parish, and we may say in a country or in the Church at large, do very observably and decidedly correspond with each other; but not so as to be inconsistent with the directly opposite state of things in particular localities and particular circumstances. The sovereignty of divine grace has subjected itself to no economy, no laws, by which its free exercise or manifestation is forestalled. A pastor, as appears from the example of Edwards at Northampton, may be rejected by his parish, on account of his inflexible adherence to what, in the exercise of a pre-eminently spiritual disposition, and after much prayer and reflection, appears to his judgment and conscience the path of duty and of wisdom in reference to the mode of exercising the pastoral care. It is, therefore, supposable that a parish may be declining in religious interest and zeal, while there is no room for the suspicion that the cause of this declension is to be found in an antecedent one on the part of the pastor, or in any fault or any neglect whatever in his ministry. Especially is this supposition admissible if there has been a high religious excitement in the parish, to which the declension has succeeded. Such an excitement as a permanent state may have been incompatible with the laws of the mind; and if a change to a lower state of feeling once have a beginning, it will naturally proceed in the same direction, unless some new influences, some new mode of agency, offer it resistance. The pastor will not be able to prevent declension by the same instrumentality which he has hitherto used, unless he use it with a different measure of force, or with modifications, with the nature of which he may not be able to acquaint himself. And it is possible that no form or manner of activity on his part might be sufficient to secure that concurrent action of the divine power, without which nothing can hinder the proper consequence of the advancing declension. The pastor, therefore, may be under the sad necessity of witnessing in his flock, notwithstanding the utmost efforts that he can make to prevent it, a progressive debility of the spiritual life. Further, the despondency which he must naturally suffer on this account may be nourished and increased by adverse means of a special kind. There is a congeniality between a state of spiritual declension and the spirit of error. As the result of backsliding in heart, there may be misgiving in not a few minds as to some of the severe truths of Christianity; the flock, moreover, may have opportunity to hear teachers of another Gospel; perhaps "of their own selves, men may arise speaking perverse things."—Acts, xx., 30. The spirit of the world, too, may reveal itself among them in forms unusually deceptive, and with peculiar recommendations: Prominent members of the flock may become decidedly worldly in their spirit and manner of life, may neglect "the assembling of themselves together;" these, and other collateral and incidental causes, may favor the downward tendency of the religious life, and the pastor's opposition to it may be altogether unavailing, or even occasion its more rapid and flagrant development.

It will be well if the pastor retain his true position, keep himself at the pastor's true point of view, continue to regard his flock in their present state with true pastoral love and solicitude, such as the chief Shepherd feels. We may well think so when we attend to a word which was spoken to the prophet Ezekiel, "Be not thou rebellious like this rebellious house" (chap. ii., 8); and to a charge given to another prophet, "Be not dismayed at their faces, lest I confound thee before them."—Jer., i., 17. Spiritual decline is a contagion, and if the pastor, with this contagion spreading around him, and becoming more and more active, may secure his soul against it, he must already have a vigorous spiritual health, and be careful in using proper means of sustaining and strengthening it. He must arm himself with firmness and patience, to avoid becoming discouraged and despondent. There is, perhaps, no severer trial of constancy than that which a pastor is enduring when his faithfulness and zeal in the exercise of the ministry are not only fruitless, but as "a savor of death unto death" to souls. There is great danger of his modifying the exercise of the ministry on a wrong principle—a principle which would vary it, so as to make it rather favor than restrain prevailing tendencies and tastes. Such a variation may seem to be strongly recommended by the fact, that even the former mode of ministration is unacceptable now, and the certain conclusion from this fact, that the same mode of ministration in a higher degree, or a different mode, tending more intensely to the same results, would be more unacceptable, and, of course, unprofitable. The pastor, seeing that the flock will not receive food of a certain kind—the kind best adapted to strengthen and increase spiritual health, is tempted to think himself justifiable, if not judicious, in providing them other kind of food—not false doctrine or false morality, but truth so softened and tempered by the manner of presenting it, or so remotely and indirectly relating to the actual needs of the flock, that they taste in it nothing that is unpleasant, nothing that seems to be in any disagreement with their present inclinations and desires. The pastor who does not suffer himself to be taken in this snare, is one most assuredly who takes good heed to keep himself in fellowship and communion with his Lord, by striving for higher attainments in the spiritual life, and especially by renewing his vocation as a minister of the Gospel. It may be impossible for him to remain a true pastor in these circumstances, faithful and approved of Jesus Christ, and having this witness in himself, "Though Israel be not gathered, yet shall I be glorious in the eyes of my Lord, and my God shall be my strength" (Isaiah, xlix., 5), without having recourse to that spiritual exercise which has been recommended in a former part of this work; without increased solitude, without much secret prayer, and fasting, and searching of heart.

But assuming that the pastor abides in the true spirit of his function, that he and the chief Shepherd are one as to the dispositions and views which control him, and that he is still a true pastor to his flock—discreet, wise, sincere, diligent, faithful in the exercise of the ministry among them—what steps, what measures, what means does his pastoral activity now embrace?

Does he employ direct efforts to make his flock sensible of their condition—to apprise them thoroughly that they are truly involved in the appalling evils of a state of allowed and progressive backsliding? Doubtless, it is his duty to aim at this: It was to a pastor, as the representative of a Church—a backsliding Church—that this word was spoken: "Remember, therefore, from whence thou hast fallen, and repent, and do the first works; or else I will come unto thee quickly."—Rev., ii., 5. There is virtually a charge to every pastor, in these solemn words, to admonish his Church, if they are backsliding from God, of their guilt and their danger: But the matter speaks for itself: A pastor may not—a true pastor can not contemplate his flock in a state of spiritual decline—can not think of them as departing from God, as deriving no advantage from his ministry, as converting the ordinances of grace, and grace itself, into stumbling-blocks and scandals—without feeling himself ready to be offered as a sacrifice, if this were the only means, or might be an effectual means, of giving them a full conviction of the evil of their state: a state from which, without this conviction, there is no hope of deliverance. They are, therefore, in some way to be awakened, to be aroused; but what is the way which should be taken?

We do not say that the pastor should not make direct statements; direct, pungent, strenuous appeals; earnest and pathetic expostulations to his flock, with reference to awakening them: But he must take heed as to the time, measure, manner of these means, lest they prove worse than ineffectual: Possibly this flock are in no degree prepared yet for being dealt with in this mode: There is, we know, a power of enchantment, of infatuation, in a backsliding spirit. The flock may have no self-consciousness as to their being in a state so alarming as such mode of dealing with them would suppose them to be in: They may have the contrary impression: They may think that it is better with them now than it was formerly; that while, in their pastor's view, they seem to be "wretched, and miserable, and poor, and blind, and naked," they judge themselves to be in a state demanding high felicitation, "rich, and increased with goods, and having need of nothing."—Rev., iii., 17.

Having which persuasion, they may regard their pastor's admonitions and remonstrances with a very high degree of disfavor, and be tempted to think him, if not really beside himself, at least deluded by a blind zeal, a frenzy of fanaticism. It may be necessary to use no little prudence, to bestow no little pains in preparing the way before we can make effectual application of this sort of instrumentality to a backslidden flock. Perhaps it may be, first of all, necessary that the pastor prepare himself specifically for the task he has to perform. His general preparation may indicate to him the expediency, the duty of a particular preparation for this very work of awakening his flock. A special anointing of the Spirit may be needful before he can become as "a polished shaft" in the hand of God for the execution of this work, imparting to him peculiar exercises of heart and mind, peculiar sympathies and desires, peculiar love and tenderness toward the souls of his flock ; in short, a peculiar intimacy of fellowship with Christ in reference to the work of saving men.

Now, after the pastor has in this way made himself ready for the work, it may be expedient for him to inquire whether there are not some few souls, at least, in his flock, whom he may, to a certain extent, associate with himself; who may be prepared, or whom he may be the means of preparing, in some measure, as he himself is prepared. The Spirit, in almost every case of declension, "reserves to himself" "a few names" at least—a few souls by whom he is not "quenched" or "grieved ;" and, perhaps while the pastor is exercised as a pastor, these souls may be at the same time exercised in their measure with that preparatory work of grace of which we have spoken. Let the pastor, then, call to mind particular persons in whose piety he has entire confidence ; let him offer for each of them a special and earnest prayer ; then let him seek them out ; confer with them on the state of the flock ; know what their views are, and how they feel in respect to it ; and if he find in them any fellowship of spirit, and any readiness to co-operate with him appropriately in measures for awakening the flock out of their sleep, then let him consult with them, in a fraternal manner, concerning measures, and, if possible, determine as to the first step to be taken.

The pastor ought not to omit efforts to obtain the aid of particular members of his flock before he begins unusual labors openly among them. If, amid the spiritual desolation by which his flock appears to him to be overspread, he should conclude there are no souls to be found in a state different from the rest, perhaps he would misjudge, as the prophet did, who supposed himself to be the only man left in Israel on the Lord's side, while the Lord had, in fact, reserved seven thousand to himself.—1 Kings, xix., 10, 14, 18. And even if his conclusions were true, he ought, perhaps, to address himself first to certain individuals—those in appearance most likely to be gained, that, by the concurrence of one or two at least, he might strengthen himself for the work before him.

What should be aimed at first? That without which all else that can be gained would be unavailing, namely, the presence of the Spirit as an Awakener. The awakening power is with him, not with the pastor and his fellow-helpers, who, by multiplying and enforcing measures apart from the Spirit, might vex, and irritate, and divide the flock, or might produce certain developments of fanatical zeal among them, but never truly awaken them: "On my servants and on my handmaidens I will pour out in those days of my Spirit."—Acts, ii., 18.

And the means of obtaining the fulfillment of this promise are indicated: "I will yet for this be inquired of by the house of Israel to do it for them."—Ezek., xxxvi., 37. "I will pour upon the house of David, and upon the inhabitants of Jerusalem, the spirit of grace and of supplications."—Zech., xii., 10. The instrumentality first of all to be employed is that whose direct aim and tendency is upward, not abroad upon the flock: Heaven is to be opened before the flock can be effectually reached. And by whom is this to be done? Instrumentally by the pastor and the two or three others whom he has now joined with himself: The flock, generally, can take no part: There may be true Christians, many such among them; but they can not sincerely offer prayer for that which they do not desire, and which they have no sense of needing: The prayer required must have its beginning with the pastor and his few like-minded aids. And the first thing which they should do in concert, after speaking to one another concerning the state of the flock, is to pray together concerning it. They should have a meeting for prayer by themselves; for as yet it must not be open to others, who can not come into it in spirit and in truth. Let the pastor appoint the meeting in his own study, and let the time, if not inconvenient, be early in the morning, before any idea of business or domestic care has had place in the mind. And let the whole hour be spent in prayer—prayer, and nothing else, if the spirit be willing enough, and the flesh not too weak. Let the brethren pray with the pastor ; and if strength does not fail, let them follow one another without rising from their knees : If there be no weariness, if the inward earnestness and importunity be sufficient to sustain the continuance of supplication to the end of the hour, it will be most accordant with the peculiar object and character of the meeting to have no interruption, and the earnestness will be deepened and increased by the lengthened exercise of it.

The next step is another meeting of the same character, but larger ; or, rather, the means of securing such a meeting. The spirit of the first meeting is, if possible, to be diffused, and the means to be used for this end are not different from those which were used by the pastor before the first meeting. Secrecy is to be observed, not because there is any thing in itself improper to be made known, but because the flock are not prepared yet to take part in the proceedings, and their character and purpose might possibly be evil spoken of: Let the pastor, with his brethren, then, confer together a moment before they separate, and let each one agree to do what the pastor did before the first meeting took place—see some one or more of the members of the flock whom he may judge most likely to welcome a visit from him, having such an object; and if, after duly and earnestly conversing with them on the state of the flock, they express solicitude, and a readiness to co-operate in measures for improving it, let them be informed that a meeting for prayer, with reference to that end, is to be held at such a time and place, and invite them to attend it. This second meeting should, if possible, take place as early as the next morning, at the same hour, and perhaps in the same room in which the first was held. And after a few words spoken by the pastor from a heart touched and filled by the Holy Spirit, respecting the design of the unusual meeting, let it be conducted as the first was; the pastor taking the lead, and designating the brethren who are to follow him, and the order in which they are to pray, one after another.

The third step, perhaps, should be another and a larger meeting, at the same place, and at the same hour of the next day. It would not be surprising if the second meeting should be many times larger than the first, and it would not be without a parallel if it should possess the same character with the first in a higher intensity. But even if this should be the case, it might not be injudicious to appoint a third meeting, to be enlarged in the same way that the first was, with the same quietness and secrecy, the same care to prevent its character from being changed. And if a third meeting should take place, it might, it probably would be as large as the pastor's study could conveniently contain, and be in spirit like the first, possibly with a yet deeper tone and intensity.

Should such be the result of these movements, here would be an incipient awakening; thus far the state of the flock would be a new and a promising state: If the whole flock were as this part is, the pastor would doubtless have cause for the hope that God was about to "turn again the captivity of Zion."—Ps. cxxvi., 1. But a change is now taking place in the character of his measures, and he may meet with unexpected difficulties if he is not on his guard, if he does not "ponder the path of his feet."—Prov., iv., 26. The meetings can no longer be held in his study; the awakening has extended too far; it must show itself openly before the face of the whole flock. What is next to be done? Shall these meetings be discontinued? The very necessity for holding them in some other place seems to forbid. Their fruitfulness has produced this necessity: They have not fulfilled their end; would it not be most unwise to discontinue an instrumentality which, proceeding as it has begun, would probably diffuse an awakening influence through the whole flock? Perhaps all would be lost which has been secured, by discontinuing them. There is danger that they will be henceforth without the peculiar influence which has heretofore belonged to them: They will be open to all who may choose to attend them, and some may come to them who partake not of their spirit—some, perhaps, who dislike, and intend to set themselves against them. Still, the pastor will probably have no hesitation, after consulting with the brethren, and providing against all violations of order, to appoint a meeting, which is to be no longer private. And, notwithstanding all difficulties and perils, he may, perhaps, secure to it the character of the others, if not improve it and advance its usefulness, by exercising prudence in the following particulars: 1. In having the place of the meeting as little public as possible, preferring some retired room to either the temple or the chapel. 2. In the manner of announcing the meeting: Let him state very explicitly the object of the meeting; let him speak frankly of the former meetings, and tell why this one has become necessary; and while he discourages no one's attendance, let him express the desire that those who shall come to it come with a determination to unite with the pastor and the others who may be present in seeking the end of its appointment, earnestly and in every appropriate method. 3. In the manner of conducting the meeting: Let there be at first, and perhaps for several times afterward, no material difference between this and the manner in which the meetings in his study were conducted: let all kneel down in prayer, after reading a few passages of Scripture, and continue kneeling and praying for the entire hour; and let the pastor designate such brethren to lead in prayer, one after another, as he may judge best prepared by the work of the Spirit in their hearts, to offer supplications for the object of the meeting. For two reasons should this manner be adhered to, at least for a time longer or shorter: (1) Because it is the manner which the deepest earnestness, absorption of the soul in desire for the object, would prefer; and, (2) Because this manner will tend to secure the proper character to the meetings, by offering no temptation to attendance on them on the part of persons whose hearts are not yet prepared to enter fully into the spirit of such meetings.

With all who attend these meetings, earnestly and intensely desiring that they may be instrumental in extending and increasing the awakening power—the pastor and all the others, it should, it must indeed, be the point of chief concern that they possess distinctively, and in as high a degree as possible, the character which is adapted, and which is necessary to secure the end. This character chiefly consists of a profound sense of the unutterable importance and desirableness of a thorough awakening in the flock, a sense involving sometimes a sympathy with St. Paul in his self-renouncing desire for the salvation of his brethren, his kinsmen after the flesh, as expressed in Rom., ix., 3, together with a sense of absolute dependence on God's sovereign grace for this result, and a spirit of importunity in prayer like that of Jacob (Gen., xxxii., 24–27) and that of the woman of Canaan (Matt., xv., 22-28). When meetings for prayer have this character, they can hardly fail to be followed by the best kind of results.

But if the Holy Spirit design to make much use of those who attend these meetings as vehicles of his influence in awakening the flock and in subsequent works, he will probably, while imparting to them these peculiar impressions and movements of soul, or, perhaps, before doing this to any considerable extent, bring them into another state of which they had no thought when the meetings commenced. Both the pastor and those who are with him may have an introverted action of mind on their own internal states, of a very peculiar character, intermingled with their thoughts and solicitudes about the state of the flock. They may find themselves engaged in a most intense examination of their personal piety, the foundations of their hopes toward God, questioning themselves most closely and severely as to the real nature of their religious affections and life. The Spirit may lead them to a most earnest renewal of their vocation as Christians, through a process of renewed conviction of sin, and mortification of corrupt desire, and humiliation of soul, in passing through which they may have a more searching, painful, deep experience, than that which was connected with their first conversion. The truth is, we are all, at our best estate, too little emptied of self, too little disgusted, too little acquainted with self; and nothing can put us at the point of view from which self is to be truly seen but a mighty work of internal humiliation, begun, carried on, and perfected by the Spirit: And it may not please him to employ us as his instruments in awakening and converting others before he has performed this work within us. The solicitude of the pastor especially, while this process is going on, is sometimes very singular: While he trembles in himself most profoundly lest his piety be unsound and his soul in peril, he is yet more concerned for the souls of his flock, and can almost adopt the words of David (2 Sam., xxiv., 17), "Lo, I have sinned, and I have done wickedly; but these sheep, what have they done? Let thine hand, I pray thee, be against me."

It is probable that the meetings in the new place will gradually become larger, especially if they retain the character which should belong to them. It would not be improper if the brethren should still seek to increase them in the mode first employed: But the mere advertisement of them will be sufficient to draw some souls to them; more, perhaps, than are well prepared to take part in them; and if the interest in them advances, the place in which they are held will become too strait for them, and it will be necessary again to transfer them to a larger and less secluded place. This should be done reluctantly, and not until the demand for it becomes very evident and very urgent.

After these meetings have thus been forced into more publicity, it may be expedient to diversify the mode of conducting them: Indeed, some change before this may have been required; but the time may now have come for material variations: Discourse from the pastor may be demanded—well prepared discourse, adapted to enlighten, to deepen, to direct the feeling of the attendants: The nature and guilt of the declension into which the flock has fallen; the evils and perils of such a state; their aggravation in the case particularly of this flock; the dreadfulness of remaining any longer at such a distance from God; these topics may now be particularly and thoroughly examined with great advantage, and the pastor ought, perhaps, to dwell upon them with tender earnestness, but also with great faithfulness, and with as much force as possible: And if the result shall be what he might probably hope for and expect, a day of fasting may seem desirable, and may be proposed; every one, doubtless, will desire it, and, with the full consent of all, it should be in an orderly manner appointed.

A fast-day, in such circumstances, properly and earnestly observed, will doubtless be of great avail. Such a day will be a natural exponent, a proper symbol, of the internal state of the souls which have been in attendance on the meetings; it will, at the same time, tend to advance that state, and thus aid also directly to extend the awakening among the flock at large. Let not the observance of the day be urged on any one; let liberty in respect to its observance be encouraged; and let those whose hearts do not strongly incline and constrain them to observe it, be prudently but earnestly dissuaded from doing so. It would not be surprising if its observance should be attended with signal evidences of the presence and power of the Spirit, and with signal results among the flock. As an instrument of extending the awakening, perhaps nothing could be of equal influence and value.

Connected with fasting, a solemn renewal of the Church-covenant may be very expedient and useful. Of this covenant their declension is a grievous violation, and, when made sensible of this, they can not but deplore their blame and reproach in this regard ; and if this covenant is not henceforth to be disowned, it ought to be renewed, and, in the existing circumstances, it would be strange, indeed, if there were any general hesitation to renew it. The principle in the exercise of which the people of God anciently renewed their covenant with Him and one another (Joshua, xxiv., 14–28 ; 2 Chron., xxxiv., 29–32 ; Ezra, x., 1–8 ; Nehemiah, ix.), has its ground in permanent equity and virtue, and there may be circumstances in which its practical acknowledgment on the part of a Christian flock is so obviously and forcibly required, that a truly enlightened, humble, and free spirit could not refuse to renew it. Still, there may be some deeply-moved souls in the assembly who refrain from taking this step, not because they would be unwilling to take it if they thought themselves prepared to do so, but from a horror of the guilt of breaking covenant with God, and from an overwhelming sense of having contracted this guilt already, and from not having as yet the witness of the Spirit with their spirits that their guilt has been forgiven. The dissent of these, however, should not hinder others from doing what they regard to be a duty and a privilege.

As the first result of these meetings and these exercises, there will probably be a new effusion of the Spirit, as a spirit of comfort and peace in the hearts of those who have been attending them : It would not be strange if they should have, for the most part, a renewal of their first love, and their first peace, and hope, and joy, in a larger measure than that which was granted to them when they were first converted. As a consequence of this, the next result, doubtless, would be a further extension of the awakening among the other members of the flock; and thus, by degrees, the flock generally may become, probably will become, awakened and revived. "When thou art converted, strengthen thy brethren."—Luke, xxii., 32. "I will run the way of thy commandments, when thou shalt enlarge my heart."—Ps. cxix., 32.

Let us not be understood as intending to say or imply that the Spirit of God limits himself to one mode of awakening and restoring a backslidden flock—the mode which we have been detailing. We know that he uses other modes: Sometimes he arouses a slumbering flock by means of alarming judgments one after another, perhaps in quick succession; sometimes he employs extraordinary preaching, continued through successive days, perhaps weeks; sometimes he breathes upon the whole flock, while the pastor is giving his entire attention to the unconverted, and laboring earnestly to win souls to Christ; sometimes the effect takes place while the pastor is presenting, in a series of discourses, the analysis and the evidences of the great verities of the Gospel, with unusual thoroughness and power; and sometimes the Spirit attests his sovereignty as to modes of influence by apparently dispensing with all mode, and by coming suddenly into his temple with his arousing and searching influences, while no one, not even, perhaps, the pastor, is seeking, or expecting, or dreaming of the Heavenly visitation. But if a pastor, against all his ordinary pains and prayers, finds the backsliding spirit still predominant among his flock, and making his ministry useless and even hurtful to them; and unable to forbear any longer, and having no help from man, no hope but from God, would pursue the means of awakening which Scripture and reason indicate as best adapted to secure the divine aid which is needed, we think he will not be misled if he takes the course we have endeavored to delineate.

The pastor, we assume, is now exercising his ministry with

encouragement and hope: There has been a renewal of religious interest in his parish; the work of God among his flock has been revived, and we are henceforth to contemplate him in new circumstances. We pass to consider the mode of pastoral activity in a season of special interest.

Let us not think that the ordinary mode will now suffice; that the speciality of the interest will make what is ordinary special; that the ordinary mode is the just measure of the pastor's strength, on the whole, and that he ought not to undertake labors which he can not continue. There may be truth in the former affirmations, but this last is not to be now a rule to the pastor. He must consider his strength, he must also remember that special labors can not be special long, and that the cessation of labor may involve in the result a proportionate cessation of fruit; still, the conclusion is not legitimate that he should content himself with his accustomed amount of activity. "You are aware of what consequence it is in worldly concerns to embrace opportunities and to improve critical seasons; and thus, in the things of the Spirit, there are times peculiarly favorable, moments of happy visitation, where much more may be done toward the advancement of our spiritual interest than usual. There are gales of the Spirit, unexpected influences of light and power, which no assiduity in the means of grace can command, but which it is a great point of wisdom to improve."* Wisdom in the pastor, when there is a fullness of spiritual power among his flock, will not permit him to work for their good only, as at ordinary times. Work now may be productive according to its amount: A month, a week, a day, perhaps, may be as an ordinary year. He must not be too economical of his strength; he must not love his life too well; his hour has come—an hour worth more, perhaps, than a life; he must fill this hour with labor, thoughtful as to consequences—as to

* ROBERT HALL: *On the Work of the Holy Spirit*, Works, vol. i., p. 450, 451.

what may be involved in the mode of his activity during this auspicious season—what may proceed from it to himself and to his flock, if he improve it as he should do—what, also, if he should not.* The pastor should not consult with flesh and blood; he should labor for his flock, in all his movements and acts, as a pastor filled with the Spirit, walking in the Spirit, walking in the footsteps of Christ and his apostles, guided by the wisdom which is from above.

An increase of labor, extraordinary activity on the part of the pastor, is a spontaneous, natural result of the internal state in which he and his flock now find themselves: It is demanded by the augmented vigor and activity of their spiritual life, and by the reciprocal influence of his soul on theirs, and of theirs on his, in this season of religious refreshing. Whenever he meets them, it is to impart to them a new energy, and to receive one from them: The inter-activity of their "mutual faith," their mutual life, results directly in a higher measure of activity in them both. The pastor would do himself violence if he should refrain from new labors: He doubtless needs self-control, pastoral prudence, firmness of will, to avoid being led into labors beyond his strength.

The preliminary meetings, if meetings of this character originated the interest, will not be discontinued; they will be changed, but the change will be only as a continuous shining of light from dawn to perfect day. They will not be discontinued: They are useful still in various ways. The prayer which is offered in these meetings has become effectual, fervent, intercessory prayer—prayer which loses sight of self in concern for others—prayer for the pastor that he may be upheld and prospered in his new labors—prayer for the

* "There is a tide in the affairs of men,
Which, taken at the flood, leads on to fortune;
Omitted, all the voyage of their life
Is bound in shallows and in miseries."
—Shakspeare: *Julius Cæsar*, act iv., scene 3.

further extension of the awakening—prayer for individuals in different states: for new converts, for troubled souls, for souls yet indifferent, etc.—prayer that excesses may be avoided, and all things may proceed in a decent and orderly course —prayer for a yet greater outpouring of the Spirit. The pastor does not neglect these meetings. As soon would he neglect to take his necessary refreshment, his necessary food. It was by meetings for prayer, from which these are not essentially different, that the dispensation of the Spirit was ushered into the world; and of the agency afterward employed by the apostles, none ranked higher than this—none, it would seem, so high. "We will give ourselves to prayer and the ministry of the word."—Acts, vi., 4. Where this order is inverted, where the highest place is given to preaching, man, doubtless, is depended on to carry on the work rather than the sovereign Spirit of God, whose influence is not given except in answer to prayer, and is given generally in proportion to the earnestness, and importunity, and boldness of faith with which it is sought by the prayers of the saints. It is by prayer on the part of members of his flock, more than by all other means, that the pastor is sustained in the pulpit, and made bold, free, wise, skillful, spiritual, powerful, happy in preaching. It gives him strength, life, and liberty in preaching, merely to think that he has been, and still is, remembered in the prayers of his flock; and if he is assured that, at the very time he is preaching, a company of souls in some private place are beseeching God to help him to liberty of thought and utterance, this persuasion, perhaps, imparts to him "a mouth and wisdom" not to be exchanged for the tongue of men and angels.

The pastor, as to the amount of his preaching, will abound beyond his usual measure. The spirit of life with which he and his flock have been baptized, is the spirit of preaching: The word has been its instrument, and it lives and subsists upon the word. The spirit begets us unto God by the word;

by the word destroys our corruptions, by the word arms us for our warfare; makes us watchful and courageous; animates, admonishes, guides, consoles, feeds us; all by the word, as applied by himself. And what the word is as to our own life, the same is it as to the use which we make of our life out of ourselves, or for the furtherance of the Gospel among those who have not received it. Our life in this outward movement, is but a holding forth of the word of Life: With reference to this our life is given to us, and it is given in vain, if this be not its fruit.—Matt., v., 13–15; xiii., 52. Indeed, that which we have received is not the true life.—1 John, iv., 2, 3. The mission of God's Spirit in this world is to Christianize it—to make all men know, love, acknowledge, serve Christ: And they are not led by that Spirit, neither are they in that Spirit's interest, who are not striving to this end. Since, therefore, it is mainly through preaching (Rom., x., 17) that the Christian life advances, every true spirit, every true life, reveals itself in activity in preaching, or the manifestation of the truth. Assuredly, wherever a true religious interest is rising and spreading in a flock, preaching, in one way or another, is advancing proportionately: If the flock have a pastor, he is not a true pastor if he be not in preaching "more abundant."

As to the form of his preaching at such a time, it will be the same as it has been, modified appropriately by the speciality of his circumstances. He will have no other Gospel to preach than that which he has preached: He will have no other gift to exercise in preaching it than that which he has received. And as to the extent, measure, and variety in which he is to use it, his guide is "the spirit of power, of love, and of a sound mind."

It is probable that he will not limit himself to preaching in public: The houses of his flock will now be offered to him, perhaps with entreaties to occupy them; and "preaching from house to house" may enter in no small measure into his plan of labor. In respect to his public preaching—its particular topics, ends, manner, times—there is, perhaps, nothing to be considered by him, after giving due regard to the speciality in the state of his flock, but these two maxims: 1. That he is in danger, from his present facility in preaching, and from the indulgence of his hearers, of becoming loose, desultory, superficial; and, 2. That, so far from yielding to this temptation, he ought to aim, more than ever, at the highest perfection in preaching. His auditory will now give him the hearing ear, a teachable heart, a tender conscience, and a self-applying mind; and he will mistake, both in reference to the best means of deepening and diffusing the interest now existing in his flock, and in reference to their permanent edification and usefulness, if he does not use the present as a most favorable opportunity for giving his flock the most thorough instruction in doctrinal, experimental, and practical Christianity. Preaching of so intellectual a character may seem inconsistent with meeting the demand for frequency; but the appearance of inconsistency vanishes when we remember that the pastor, in this "day of visitation," has received a new baptism, with reference to the exercise of his preaching gift—a baptism which "makes him of quick understanding in the fear of the Lord" (Is., xi., 3); which puts his soul into unusual affinity with the Christian doctrines, "the things of the Spirit;" which sharpens and illumines all his inward man; and that, after all, the most difficult strain of preaching, to a well-indoctrinated pastor, is not that which is most intellectual, but that which has to encounter the disadvantages of a state of moral insensibility, of declension in the religious life.

We do not think that the pastor will, on the whole, find it expedient to introduce another preacher into his parish. An occasional sermon, or an exchange of pulpits, now and then, with a neighboring pastor, may, as formerly, be still acceptable, but preaching a consecutive course of sermons by a stranger, especially if he be a man of captivating address or uncommon eloquence, may not favor the advancement of the simple and spiritual work now in progress among the flock; and, what is more to be regarded, may put the pastor, as a preacher, into a disadvantageous contrast with this more attractive, but perhaps less solid, and, on the whole, less instructive, less profitable preacher. There may be cases in which another preacher is necessary, as when the pastor's health fails; but there will probably be no gain, either to the pastor or to the flock, on the whole, by employing an additional preacher or evangelist, unless necessity seems to make the demand.

From the unusual activity of the pastor's internal state, in view of a like internal state on the part of the flock, and especially of the unconverted members of it, as to whom the present season may perhaps appear to the pastor as their "day" (Luke, xix., 42), the term of grace, the turning-point of destiny, there will be in his preaching, especially on certain occasions, an earnestness, a directness, a closeness of application to the conscience and the heart, a wrestling urgency, a tender vehemence, prolonged contestation, which might not be attainable or proper in a season of declension and coldness: And this peculiarity in the preaching may associate with itself some other unusual procedures in the care of souls now, which, in different circumstances, would not be expedient, perhaps not admissible. The pastor, after preaching, may feel constrained to second, if he can, the appeal from the pulpit, by a yet closer appeal and more particular instruction in some less public place; and to this end may appoint a meeting with such as may be willing to see him in some neighboring room, immediately after the dismission of the assembly. And here, after conversing with those who are present, whether collectively or individually, there may seem to be a demand for some further step, in order to a more thorough awakening, or more firmness of will in certain souls; and the pastor can not forbear until something more be done: What this shall be he is to determine for himself, under the direction of an apostle (Jude, 22, 23), not forgetting that, while the soul is active in conversion, and is required to exert itself to the utmost of its power (Matt., xi., 12; Luke, xiii., 24), no activity of its own will avail without the regenerating and renewing agency of the Holy Spirit.—John, iii., 7, 8; Rom., ix., 16.

The pastor will find himself unusually occupied in conversing with individuals; sometimes with some who have not yet been awakened, to sound a personal alarm in their ear; but with more, many more probably, who have been effectually touched by the Spirit, so that nothing is now more welcome to them, more earnestly desired and sought by them, than religious intercourse with their pastor. The multiplication of cases of this latter class will perhaps be so great that he may deem expedient that which at an ordinary time could have no place: We refer to what has been termed *a meeting of inquirers*, that is to say, of individuals who have so much interest in religion that they are willing to be recognized in the presence of others as earnest seekers of light and direction from their pastor.

In giving the notice that such a meeting is to be held, let the pastor be explicit in stating its object and defining its character, but let him take heed lest he make it seem needlessly repulsive to some who are but partially awakened; and let him invite all to attend it who, with knowledge of its nature, are inclined to be present; and let him even take some pains to give this inclination to souls which as yet have it not. There is awakening power in a mere notice of such a meeting; this of itself may move a soul which nothing else might move; but if the pastor, when he announces the meeting, employs some tender, earnest expressions of pastoral love and solicitude, and makes nothing to be a condition of attendance but willingness to attend, he may, in doing this, preach to some of his hearers with a power beyond that of any sermon they have ever heard from him.

The inquirers' meeting, we think, should be held in a place made convenient for conversation with small groups of individuals. After a short, pertinent prayer, let the exercises be introduced by an address to the company, collectively, in order to impress them more definitely and strongly with the peculiarity of the meeting, and in order more especially to impart to the meeting a tranquil solemnity, a calm, subdued, frank spirit. The minds of the attendants are probably more or less agitated—some with spiritual concern, too deep to be affected by any outward circumstances ; some by finding themselves in such a place in presence of others ; some by an inward shrinking from so much engagedness in religion as attendance on such a meeting implies : This agitation must, if possible, be entirely displaced by a calm, still spirit ; for the human mind, in a state of perturbation, is as incapable of receiving any just impressions of religious truth as the surface of a river to receive the image of the trees on its banks when it is ruffled by the wind. The pastor, in speaking to individuals or to groups, should be as free, as simple, as unaffectedly earnest in conversing now on religion as he would be if his theme were some subject of common life ; for the sacredness of religion is entirely misrepresented if it seem to imply any necessary association with the opposites of these qualities ; nay, if it do not appear to be absolutely inconsistent with them. Religion supposes seriousness, solemnity, a holy dread ; but it is in its very nature a tranquilizing power, until its time comes for dealing with its obstinate and incorrigible despisers.—Ezek., xxii., 14. In his conversations with individuals, let the pastor have no care to avoid being heard by those who sit by ; rather let him intend to be heard by them, for there is nothing secret here ; and what he speaks directly to one, may be no less, perhaps more, appropriate to others than to him. Questions should be asked of the inquirers, not merely for the purpose of gaining information, but also to elicit from them what may give occasion for remark. It may be well, if possible, to get a group of five or six engaged in the same conversation, and to induce them to question the pastor, and perhaps one another. And if any thing be said in a particular conversation of this sort which has any special interest, and which is of equal concern to all the inquirers, let the pastor remark on it in a familiar voice which all may hear: In this way he may give most valuable instruction, may greatly enliven and deepen the interest of the meeting, and prepare his way pleasantly in passing from individual to individual, and from group to group. When he has gone through the entire company, let him close as he began, with a short address to the whole, suggested by the general state of the meeting, as revealed to him in the course of his conversations. The meeting, we need not say, should be dismissed with prayer suited to its occasion and character.

The value of this meeting will depend much on the spirit and manner in which its peculiar exercises are conducted: The pastor should not only keep it absolutely under his own direction, but should invite no one to take part with him in conducting it, or to be present at it, except as an inquirer; and he should prepare himself for it, as perfectly as possible, by special reflection and special prayer. He will find it, if he gives it due attention, a means of great advantage to himself. It will supply him with topics for his sermons; it will be a means of edification to him: Never does the truth come home to a pastor's heart with more power of reproof, of correction, of encouragement and comfort, than when he is endeavoring to impress it on the souls of his flock by conversations with them individually.

A meeting of another character will probably enter into the pastor's plan of labor now: The new converts have become so numerous that he can not, amid all his other labors, give to each one apart the care which should be given to all belonging to this class: He may say many things most pertinent to their state at the inquirers' meeting, where he will be sure to find them as long as it is proper that they should attend it: But this time may be short; and, moreover, they will need instruction, which would be out of place at the meeting for inquiry. The advantages to the new converts, from the general influence and character of the season of special interest, are of the highest value; but they do not supersede the necessity for specific counsels and admonitions which they are prepared to appreciate, and which, on their tender and susceptible souls, may stamp an impression of sacredness and spirituality, of wisdom and prudence, of zeal and devotedness, which may be constantly reappearing throughout their whole career of sanctification to guard them against excesses and errors, and secure to them a symmetrical and complete development of the Christian life and character.

In yet another mode will the pastor's care be now employed: The evangelic life, both in the pastor and the flock, is, if we may so speak, a Christ-life—a life which, through an infinite sacrifice, entering into our fallen humanity, seeks its renewal in all individuals of the race whom its influence reaches: And as it is a life of the reason and the spirit—a life of intelligent love—a life of moral freedom, that guides itself, not by instinct or blind impulse, but by laws, ordinances, and arrangements of wisdom and prudence (Eph., i., 8), it has in this flock a system of action, a scheme or settled mode of operation; and that mode is one which prescribes to the entire flock a variety of labors and exertions, according to their respective measures of ability. To this flock, including their pastor, the words of St. Paul (Rom., xii., 6, 7, 8) are applicable: "Having then gifts, differing according to the grace that is given to us, whether prophecy, let us prophesy according to the proportion of faith; or ministry, let us wait on our ministering: or he that teacheth, on teaching: or he that exhorteth, on exhortation: he that giveth, let him do it with simplicity; he that ruleth, with diligence; he that showeth mercy, with cheerfulness." This flock, in a word, is a company of souls whom the Lord has gathered to himself as so many instruments through which his own mighty life of recovering and saving virtue may flow forth into the world, into the parts nearest in the first place, and then more remotely. And now that they have received a new and fresh baptism of the divine influence, what movements of it must there be from within themselves outward upon others who are round about them? The pastor is overseer and director of these movements, and in them all his activity, directly or indirectly, reveals itself, controlling, correcting, animating, restraining, regulating all, according as particular needs and exigences may require, in the exercise of that authority and control which pertain to his office as pastor. This flock, with their pastor, as, at the same time, ruler and chief worker, is an organized association, endued with power from above, which it is exerting in various forms and through all its officers and members, for the increase of itself and of the Church, by acquisitions from the world: It is, in short, a true Christian and apostolical system of agency for recovering and saving mankind in active and energetic operation; all the parts fulfilling their proper functions, and contributing to the efficiency and influence of the whole. Many conferences are held, many plans are devised, many works are carried on, all having the same purpose, the furtherance of the Gospel, the diffusion of the Christian life and spirit, and all under the superintendence and direction of the pastor.

We have thus delineated what appears to us to be in general (not universally, nor without variations, according to circumstances, in every case) a suitable course as to the care of souls, in its application, first, to a state of special declension, and then to a state of special interest in the religious life of the flock: Now this latter state is but the true, the normal state of the flock—a state in which the flock should remain, advancing more and more, exerting itself more and more to the last; and it can not but be that the pastor, if he retains his just state and position, should be always seeking to keep his flock in theirs, and to this end always exercising appropriately the care of souls: He will not vary his pastoral activity on the principle that a change, another declension, is, as a matter of course, to take place; he will rather proceed on the opposite principle, so arranging his plans, so pursuing his measures, so adapting his modes of influence and operation, direct and indirect—in a word, so ordering and exercising the work of the ministry in all its parts as to make it instrumental, if possible, of perpetuating and promoting the existing state of his flock. And as, from time to time, he strives to renew, to consolidate (βεβαίαν ποιεῖσθαι) his vocation as a pastor, so he will have recourse to means for confirming, establishing his flock in that grace, that spiritual prosperity in which it now finds itself: In order to this, he will probably appoint days for special prayer and fasting, and will devote much thought and time to self-preparation for the proper observance of them: He will not allow himself to look forward to another declension, except to pray and strive against it, and, by every means he can legitimately use, to prevent its occurrence, to render its occurrence a moral impossibility: He will feel that a declension would be an iniquity, an enormity; that it can not come but by means of sin; that Heaven is against it; that if it does come, a curse will come with it; and that if its futurition does, indeed, enter into the divine plan, it does so only because, according to that plan, one evil thing shall be punished by another, in order to prevent greater evil on the whole.]

PART FOURTH.

ADMINISTRATIVE OR OFFICIAL LIFE.

CHAPTER I.

DISCIPLINE.*

THIS word is almost without meaning in our ecclesiastical institutions, or, rather, in the character which the times have given them. Discipline is to ecclesiastical order what police is to civil order; but the citizen, whether he will or not, is subject to the law: Not thus with a member of the Church; and since the law of the Church has no longer the sanction of opinion, we may say that it is law no longer. The execution of disciplinary penalties has no longer a civil guarantee or external consequences. Thus the external sanction supplies nothing to the internal; in a word, discipline has nothing to rest upon. Nothing of discipline remains except what the pastor, as an individual, exercises, and what others, as individuals, are willing to accept; and we must, indeed, allow, that what little remains in these circumstances of complete freedom from compulsion is excellent in proportion as it is small.

We can not but call the attention of ministers to a peril, of which some among them have no suspicion. The remonstrances or reproofs which are a part of pastoral discipline are much more easily dispensed to the poor and the

* See BENGEL: *Pensées*, § 36.

weak than to the rich and great. We are tempted to bear heavily on some that we may press lightly on others. This is not equal. And the pastor is worthy of his mission only when he makes his authority to be felt alike by all souls, which to him are no more than souls. We must not hence conclude, however, that no difference should be observed as to manner and form. The same means have a different influence, according to the persons to which they are applied, and, with the design of maintaining equality, we may treat souls with much inequality.

Excommunication, properly speaking, can have no place in a Church which is strictly the Church of every one. The communicants themselves are the only judges. They must take care for themselves that they do not eat and drink condemnation to themselves at the table of Jesus Christ. When the Church belongs to the state, and when the severities of discipline are by general consent dispensed with, we can not dream of exercising it, at least of restoring it in its essential character, which is possible only in another state of things. The duty of the pastor is both to debar from the Lord's Supper, by private representations, the persons whom he may judge unprepared to partake of this sacred repast without danger, and to admonish them collectively from the high place of the pulpit. The same rule, and no other, applies to the officials.

CHAPTER II.

CONDUCT TOWARD DIFFERENT RELIGIOUS PARTIES.

THE first rule as to the pastor's conduct toward the religious parties which he may find in his parish, whether they be in a state of simple parties, or whether they form communities, is to preach the Gospel with sufficient simplicity, cordiality, and purity, to draw true hearts and spirits toward the form of Christian doctrine as presented in the Gospel. Such a position admonishes the pastor to be, as far as possible, a man of pure and transparent spirit. There are few cases, perhaps there are none, in which the pulpit should be polemical. Error flees before truth, as darkness before the light of day. Indeed, darkness is nothing; light alone is something. Speak the truth—this is filling a void; error is the absence of truth. Let us have little confidence in negative means: Let us not think that we have been building because we have been demolishing, or that we have edified because we have confuted. The first, most natural, and often only effect of such victories is the impatience and irritation of the conquered party. Truth is a virtue, a power; we have done every thing when we have caused it to be felt. *Virtutem viderent.**

We must give to our parishioners an example of indulgence and equity, and while, not by reasoning, but by facts, we make them sensible of the advantage which they have by belonging to our communion rather than to another, teach them to love the truth more than the Church, and the image of Christ more than their own preferences. But, doubtless, the first rule we have given is sufficient to secure this, and to

* "Let them see virtue."—PERSE, *Sat.*, iii., ver. 38.

secure, also, as benevolent and intimate relations with the *dissidents** (I use this word in a very general sense) as is compatible with the religious sympathy between them and us. Any thing beyond this, that is to say, any thing which may induce the belief that we are not really of our own party, and, so to speak, of our opinion; any thing which might give rise to the supposition that, under the pretense of belonging to one communion, we at heart belong to another, and that we are hindered from joining another only by considerations of personal interest or the fear of man, would be a scandal to our flock, and would compromise our ministry.

Taking the word *proselytism* in the most general sense, it would be almost ridiculous to ask whether proselytism is permitted to pastors; which, to tell the truth, is their essential duty and their whole work. But, adhering to the most general sense of the word, it may be asked whether there are not certain rules to be observed—a certain measure to be kept; and then it may be inquired whether this proselytism, whose object is to transfer an individual from one sect to another, is lawful and commendable.

To begin with the second question, let us say that conversion from one sect to another (ecclesiastical proselytism) never should be the immediate object of the ministry, nor of any reasonable Christian. But then we can not deny that when we labor to make a man a Christian, we labor to make him one in the sense in which we ourselves are Christians; and we must not dissemble this fact, either to ourselves or others. A man gained to our doctrine by our teaching may not feel himself obliged to forsake his own communion; that is, formally to renounce it, in order to unite himself to ours. If he is under a simple delusion, we must wait patiently until more light shall dissipate it. If the fear of man controls him, we must not connive at it, and we must express ourselves frankly on this subject, but without pressing the neophyte to take

* See BENGEL: *Pensées Pastorales*, § 41 et 42.

the step to which he is repugnant. By constantly enlightening his conscience, we shall, by degrees, create in him an imperative desire for this act of self-enfranchisement.

As to spiritual proselytism, whose end is to lead men to God, we agree with St. Paul, that we must "be instant in season and out of season" (2 Tim., iv., 2), but certainly not unseasonably. Rudeness and impetuosity are never in season, and when we do not limit ourselves to waiting for occasions or procuring them, but create them, or, rather, do without them altogether, it is hard for us not to be rude and impetuous, and consequently rather irritating than persuasive. But if we do not think it our duty to pay any attention to propriety in this matter, then we do not go as far as we should: We should stop passengers in the streets, we should invade their dwellings; introduce, to the exclusion of every thing else, the question of salvation at all times, and constantly offend to his face every human being. I think that to watch for occasions, to make good use of them, to perfect our work, is enough to occupy all our time, and that, in short, there is a greater and more extended effect in waiting in this way than in so many blows dealt right and left without discrimination or appropriateness. The longer we live, the more we think, with St. Martin, that "noise does no good, and that good is done without noise."

We must not despise the waters of Siloam, that go softly. —Isaiah, viii., 6. We must, then, neither run a venture, "nor beat the air."—1 Cor., ix., 26. But with no less care should we avoid a circuitous manner of approaching religious subjects, of leading the conversation on to the subject we have in view. There may be in this an honest adroitness, but *les ruses de guerre* have never availed any thing. Jesus Christ and the apostles never made use of them: They acted with simplicity; and in this respect, as well as others, we should take them for models.

CHAPTER III.

RELATIONS OF ECCLESIASTICS AMONG THEMSELVES.

We may distinguish the relations between clerical brethren, suffragans, and colleagues.

Without in the least degree recommending *l'esprit de corps*, or the spirit of caste, we may recommend, from regard to the interest of the ministry and of the Church, good fellowship and frequent intercourse between members of the same clerical body. If the apostle St. Paul had a lively sense of whatever affected the heart or external condition of his disciples, he had such a sense, in a peculiar degree, in respect to what concerned his companions in labor. We must be profited by others, and be profitable to others; honor one another by mutual confidence; edify one another by the spirit of peace, deference, and frankness, whether in common assemblies or in private interviews; be serious in familiarity, and suffer not confraternity to degenerate into *comradism*;* be ready to exercise an honorable hospitality toward one another; relieve the wants of a brother who is not in good circumstances, and do not leave to others all the care and all the honor of providing for his necessities; confer together as much as we can in order to profit by each other's experience; lastly, maintain among ourselves as much unity of principle, and even external unity, as may naturally consist with sincerity and liberty.

Suffragans.—The position of the suffragan in our country is not generally difficult. It may not, however, be superfluous to indicate to young ministers some principles by which they should be directed. The suffragan minister is not an

* French: *Camaraderie.*

operative, a commissioner, or a clerk; in a certain sphere he acts with sovereignty; he must, therefore, reserve to himself an inviolable sphere of independence: But in every thing which does not pertain to that sphere he should regard himself as subordinate to the will of the titular pastor—at least, remember that office has not yet been conferred on him. In cases in which the pastor does not wish to avail himself of his right, and in cases in which the suffragan has to decide for himself, he ought to consult his elder, hear him with earnest attention—being well persuaded that experience is something; that advice, which at first was very surprising, has often, in the end, appeared no less natural than judicious, and that opinions which we thought could never be disputed, have, in the end, appeared to be absurd and ridiculous. The young minister, if he is wise, will innovate but little. In general, he will not think it sufficient that a change would be useful; he must look upon it as necessary. He will not interfere, directly or indirectly, with the pastor's ministerial operations; but will, in some way, continue what has been begun, and not mix with an impulse which has been given, another impulse which, though not incongenial, yet merely because it is different, may give trouble of mind, and break the unity and solidity of the work. He will be moderate in his preaching—allowing himself few local allusions, and feeling it to be his duty to unite modesty with authority.

If it is "a good and a pleasant thing for brethren to dwell together in unity" (Ps. cxxxiii., 1), it is especially good and pleasant for those who, in the midst of the same flock, exercise the ministry of reconciliation. This unity is not so common, nor so perfect where it does exist, as we might hope and expect it to be. It is not necessary to assign the reasons of this, nor to insist on the duty of restoring and perfecting this unity, since it is evident that nothing more seriously discredits the ministry and impairs its moral power than the misunderstanding of pastors. Here is a touchstone for more than one kind of Christianity which is thought to be very pure. As long as we were alone, we thought we were doing good purely from love to it, so that we said within ourselves, *terar dum prosim.** But when we have seen others rivaling and surpassing us, and have perceived with consternation that we preferred that good should not be done at all than done by others at the great expense of our vanity; when we are surprised to find ourselves grieved by their blessings, and rejoice at their injudicious measures and their bad success, then we understand whether, in the good which we performed, we most loved the good itself or the glory of performing it. Many ministers have thus made a deeply humiliating discovery, which should have led them to see that the foundation of their Christianity and of their ministry was a deplorable weakness. Perhaps all other causes of disunion among colleagues (encroachments, jealousy of temporal advantages, discord among the families of pastors when the pastors themselves were well-disposed to each other; lastly, difference as to opinion and plan of conduct)—perhaps all these causes of alienation are of small moment compared with that which pertains to professional jealousy. But they must all be recognized, and, with the greatest care, avoided or prevented. We especially recommend frankness at the beginning of collegiate relations. Discontent and vexation may make us frank enough afterward, but to no purpose. Frankness established as a law at the outset, before all collision, will engender mutual confidence, and, better than all other means, prevent unpleasant and unedifying conflicts. The habit of praying for one another in secret with care and particularity will be most appropriate to quench the fire of jealousy and resentment. This is the first of our duties to one another.†

* "Let me be crushed, if I may but be useful."—*Edit.*

† I translate here, without comment, some rules given by Claus

Harms. Some things in them certainly deserve to be remembered. The most minute among them may give important hints.

"Meide den Bekannten von fruherer Zeit." (Avoid the acquaintances of former days.)

"Tritt nicht in das Verhaeltniss des Du und Du." (Form no very familiar associations.)

"Lass dir nicht zu viele Verbindlichkeiten auflegen." (Do not put yourself under too many obligations.)

"Fange nicht mit zu heisser Freundschaft an." (Do not hastily form too warm friendships.)

"Verschaffe dir die klarste Kenntniss von allen Beykommenheiten." (Acquaint yourself most exactly with whatever may aid you.)

"Binnen Jahr und Tag nimm keine ehrbliche Veraenderung vor." (Let some time pass before you make important changes.)

"Gehe nicht auf Verdunkelung deines Collegen aus." (Do not seek to eclipse your colleague.)

"Schlage dich nicht zu seiner Gegenparthei." (Do not join yourself to those who are opposed to him.) See the foregoing page.

"Nimm Weib, Kinder, und Gesind in acht." (Look well to your wife, children, and servants.)

"Scheue die Billets." (Avoid running up bills.)

"Lieber als Hammer sey du Ambos." (Be rather the anvil than the hammer.)—HARMS,[1] *Pastoraltheologie*, tome iii., p. 168.

[1] The originality of expression in the German often adds to the force of these counsels of Claus Harms. M. Vinet quotes them in German. We have thought it best to give the translation, though it is impossible, in doing so, not to impair their force.

CHAPTER IV.

THE PASTOR IN HIS RELATIONS TO AUTHORITIES.*

FIRST, to ecclesiastical authority, of which the pastor is a partaker. It is his duty to give his aid diligently at the assemblies of his order, to take a serious part in their deliberations, and to contribute, according to his ability, in rendering them serious.

We should beware of discussing the small questions which abound in these assemblies with the amplitude, gravity, and vivacity which belong only to great ones. There is danger, in conferences composed of ecclesiastics, of forming the habit of treating mere nothings with gravity, and of striving about distinctions of words. The *esprit de corps* is more natural in these assemblies than in any others; and the *esprit clérical*, a singular thing, finds here the more aliment in proportion as the questions which are discussed are less directly and less seriously religious. We must learn, especially if we are young, how to give place to time; and that very often the conservation of peace is of more value than all the advantages which may result from the triumph of our opinion.

Mutual discipline is a delicate matter. In all ecclesiastical constitutions it is laid down as a principle, but I should be happy to know where it is seriously practiced. It extends, in its just idea, from advice and admonition to the most penal, most positive, and most severe measures. But in the majority of ecclesiastical bodies it is never realized, except in that last and severe extremity, in which we may say it has small moral efficacy. I know not how far it may depend on

* See BENGEL: *Pensées*, § 44. It is inserted in the *Appendix*, note L, *Les Pensées de Bengel*, often cited in this course.

the *jurés** to raise above its actual level the beautiful institution of *church visits;* but I think that whatever can be done to encourage mutual frankness should be put in requisition both by the pastor who visits a church and by him who governs it. We are all, however, the *jurés* and others, bound to confer with one another in a charitable and humble spirit as to what may be respectively useful to us, and of what, very often, we ourselves are ignorant, to our great disadvantage, though it is known to all the world besides.

In our relations to the civil or municipal authority, to the state and the community, let us never forget that we are something more than functionaries of the republic, and that we are by no means amenable to the magistrate as to what concerns the essential purpose of our ministry—the teaching of the truth. But let us beware of replacing authority by pride, and let us carefully shun that bad way into which so many ministers fall, of affecting, in their relations to the authority, a spirit of discontent, of censure, and of grumbling. It would be extremely unhappy if the people should learn of us what so many learn from them, disapprobation *à priori*, the anticipation of blame as to every thing in which power is to be recognized. Servility is not more unworthy of our character than this ridiculous hostility. Besides, our relations to the political authority have nothing of politics. We are, in a certain sense, amenable to the state; but we are not state officers, and the business of the state is not ours. In a time of political fermentation or revolution, we have no other mission than that of tranquillizing the minds of men by proposing to them those great truths which, though they do not nullify worldly interests, at least subordinate all our proceedings to the grand interest of the soul and of eternity.

* The *jurés* in the established Church of the Canton de Vaud are inspectors appointed by the *classes*, or pastoral assemblies, to take the oversight of a certain number of parishes, and charged to visit them periodically.—*Edit.*

I do not mean that the pastor should feign himself ignorant of the occupations, the dangers, the fears, the prospects of the country; but the contests of opinion do not concern him; he has no part to take but that of obedience to the law as long as the law exists, and, in all cases, the part of the country and of national independence. The occasions are very rare on which the pulpit may address citizens as such, and preach to them on the actual duties which pertain to them in this character.

In general, we think we ought to counsel ecclesiastics, especially such as have the care of souls, to hold no place in political or municipal bodies. We have examined this point elsewhere.

In the administrative part of his functions, the pastor should leave nothing to be desired in respect to exactitude and punctuality. The less of taste he has for those details for which a man of his profession is bound, in fact, to have no taste, the more should he guard himself against either delaying or neglecting any thing; and it is his duty to study carefully, in their letter and in their spirit, all those institutions, all those laws and regulations which have any relation to the exercise of his functions. A pastor who would be useful, though in a spiritual respect only, should have exact knowledge and intimate acquaintance with his country, his people, and whatever, even in a material point of view, is important to the welfare of society and each of the classes which compose it.

Something might be added in relation to the laws, to the execution of which the pastor should lend his influence, and to the measures which he should use to that end.

APPENDIX.

NOTE A, page 25.

The Nature of the Priest's Office.

"THE priesthood, it is true, is accomplished on earth, but is, nevertheless, justly placed in the rank of celestial things. In fact, no man, nor angel, nor archangel, nor created power, but the Paraclete himself, has instituted this office, and chosen beings yet living in the flesh to fulfill the ministry of angels. Hence, the priest, regarding himself as established in heaven, even among the superior powers there, ought to be as pure as they. The economy which preceded that of grace was doubtless venerable and full of holy dread: Let us bring before our minds those precious stones on the priest's breastplate and shoulders; that mitre, that tunic, those golden plates, that holy of holies, that profound silence in the inner temple. And yet, comparing all these things with those of the Gospel, their glory is effaced—they appear mean. When you contemplate the Lord himself immolated and lying before you, the priest bent over the victim, and praying for all, and all sprinkled with most precious blood, believe ye that ye are yet among men? believe ye that ye are on the earth? Are ye not borne away suddenly to heaven? and then, away from every carnal thought, behold ye not heavenly things directly, and in their pureness? Who, unless he be profoundly insensate, can disregard so awful a mystery? And know ye not that no soul of man could ever bear the fire of this sacrifice; that it would devour all who should approach it, unless God himself should intervene with the powerful support of his grace? Represent to yourselves the man who yet, under the bondage of flesh and blood, personally approaches this immortal and most blessed Being, then may ye understand perfectly what honor the Holy Spirit has vouchsafed to the priest, by whom these things, and others, too, in no respect inferior to them, are accomplished."—CHRYSOSTOM, *De Sacerdotio*, lib. iii., c. iv.

NOTE B, page 27.

The Mystery of Preaching.

"PREACHING is a mystery not less awful and terrible than that of the Eucharist. It appears to me that preaching is much more awful; for it is that by which souls are begotten and quickened unto God; whereas by the Eucharist they are only nourished, or, to speak more correctly, healed. It is only by great self-renunciation that we can render ourselves worthy of this office; and after having disciplined our heart to desire nothing in this world, we must discipline our tongue to perfect silence, which, as I understand it, is the highest perfection to which a virtuous man attains: Only thus can it be prepared to speak the word of God in public, without any thought either of ourselves or others—which in prayer we can not do; for, from prayer performed according to God's will, exhortation or preaching is not to be altogether separated. And, for my part, I had rather say a hundred masses than preach once. We are alone at the altar; but in the pulpit we preach to a public assembly, where we ought to fear offending God more than elsewhere, unless we have previously labored for a long time to mortify our spirit, and that pruriency which every one has to know many fine things, which is the greatest temptation that remains to us from the sin of Adam."—SAINT CYRAN (Lettre xxxi.), *à M. Le Rebours*.

Note C, page 47.

On the speedy Assumption of the Personal Authority of the Priest.

"While inspired men thus preached Christ in entire simplicity, and added to this preaching admonition and encouragement, Christians edified themselves in their assemblies by sacred songs and pious conversation, and by listening to those from among themselves who felt constrained to preach. Those who were under this impulse were most frequently elders, whom the assemblies chose for the very reason that they had been previously chosen to this work. Other believers, who did not remain always in the community, labored thus after the manner of the apostles—so that from the beginning there was a teaching class, although their separation to this work took place gradually. We find this class already in the second and third generations of believers—that is, as early as the second century; so that the distinction between the believers and ministers in a community, or, to use the Greek expression, between the clergy and laity, was established.

"Note.—The Apostle Peter, moreover, under the word κλῆρος, comprehends, in the spirit of Judaism, the people of God or Christians (1 Pet., v., 3); the elders, however, were soon designated by this name, perhaps because they were chosen by lot, which they supposed to be a divine direction; perhaps because, as Jerome profoundly explains (Ep. ii., *ad Nepot.*), God had made himself the lot—that is to say, the heritage of the Levites; and because, in the Christian Church, the ecclesiastics occupied the place of the Levites; lastly, perhaps, because they are in a peculiar manner themselves the property of God. Immediately after the apostolic age, all those who were consecrated to the service of the Church, whether employed as teachers, or in any other office, were entitled κληρικοί, and other Christians λαϊκοι (pertaining to the people), or βιωτικοί (*seculares*, pertaining to common life), and ἰδιῶται (privati), or κανονικοί (a word taken in a different sense from that which prevailed at a later period, and coming from κανών, a list of the members of the community). The earliest proof we have of this is the following passage of Clemens Romanus, N. 40

(assuming the authenticity of this letter): *καὶ λευίτας ἴδίαι διακονίαι ἐπίκειντai, ὁ λαικὸς ἄνθρωπος τοῖς λαικοῖς προστάγμασιν δέδεται.* He here exhorts to order, in performing ecclesiastical rites, and subordinates the *ἱερεῖς* to the *ἀρχιερευς*. The distinction is yet more exact in the epistle attributed to his contemporary Ignatius, who, we know, even at that time, professed hierarchical principles. Clement of Alexandria assures us that this distinction had begun to reveal itself as early as the time of the Apostle John; and the writings of Tertullian, Origen, Cyprian, date this distinction in the second century. In Consil. Illib., the term *fidelis* is employed as a synonym for *clericus*."
—SCHWARZ, *Katechetik*, p. 11, 12.

NOTE D, page 47.

First Appearances of a Tendency to form Pastors into a Caste.

"CHRISTIANS still loved to represent their vocation under another point of view, drawn equally from Scripture and from the essence of Christianity, and fertile, like the former, in particular applications; namely, that of a Christian and universal priesthood; of an order of sacrificers, of which all Christians are members. Christianity destroyed the separation between the priest and the layman, between the ecclesiastic and the citizen: All believers in Christ, the only true High-priest, are consecrated by him to the Heavenly Father: As his brethren, they have become priests with him; united to him by faith, animated by him with the spirit of adoption, they enter freely into the heavenly sanctuary, into which Jesus has preceded them, and access to which he has opened to them. They have no longer need of a human high-priest to represent to them the new sanctuary—the spiritual and true sanctuary; or to conduct them into it, like children, by the leading-strings of ordinances, and dispense to them sparingly, and according to his wisdom, the heavenly treasures which eternal love has put equally within the reach of all. They need no one to teach them what they can now learn from the mouth of God himself; for all may be instructed of God, enlightened by the same Spirit—the Spirit of truth, and anointed by him with an internal and divine unction. There is for all the same spirit, the same heavenly life, faith, and hope; the same Savior, who alone is their Master, before whom all who would be his disciples must acknowledge themselves sinners, in order to obtain directly from him alone, and not from man, nor through the mediation of man, salvation and sanctification.

"Henceforth, with Christians, the times in which men served dumb idols, under the direction of their priests, were past; the day had arrived when all men were to be masters in religion. The great High-priest of humanity, whom Christians followed, directed them, not to senseless idols, but to the living God; and, instead of leading them, like blind men, he shed within them a light which never left them, a spirit which manifested itself by every variety of gifts. Each Christian was to receive a particular gift of grace appropriate to his individual character, and by this means to contribute, as a faithful member, to the well-being of the whole society. It was thus with the Christians a well-established principle, which was reproduced in their life, that, by faith in Christ, their sovereign High-priest, and by communion with him, they became an order of true priests — consecrated ministers of God, by the internal and sanctifying unction of the Holy Ghost, which the Savior himself shed upon them."—Citation of facts and passages, in support of this, from Justin Martyr, Tertullian, Irenæus, and Origen.

"When, toward the end of the second century, men were inclined to introduce into the Christian Church an institution corresponding to the Jewish pontificate, as if Christianity also needed a visible pontificate, and a caste of priests specially consecrated to God, those Christians who were still animated with the spirit of the primitive Church opposed themselves to this anti-evangelical measure, and the laity assumed the position that they also, as Christians, were a community of priests. And as the Oriental theosophists, who had embraced Christianity, without, however, designing to conform their habits of thought to its precepts, sought to introduce into it, in imitation of the Oriental systems, the distinction between a doctrine peculiar to the priests and an external religion suited to the people; as the Gnostics prided themselves upon possessing a knowledge superior to the belief of the multitude, who had only a faith founded on authority, and called themselves *spiritualists*, in opposition to those who attached too much importance to the letter; the Christian Church, on the contrary, laid it down as a principle that all Christians should be united in the same simplicity of faith, and through it partake of the same spiritual life; that all true Christians are necessarily enlightened by the Spirit of God, and animated with a true spirituality."

"We live already," says Clement of Alexandria (*Pædagogus*, l. i., c. vi.); "we are freed from the chains of death. To follow Jesus Christ is to have already obtained salvation. 'He who heareth my word and believeth in him who sent me,' says the Lord, '*hath* eternal life, and *shall not come* into condemnation, but is passed from *death* unto *life*.' Thus faith and regeneration are already the *true life;* for God, who produces them, works not by halves. '*Ye yourselves*,' says the apostle (1 Thess., iv., 9), '*are taught of God*.' Now we can not believe that he would leave his teaching incomplete: Consequently, he who has been regenerated and enlightened by the Spirit, is from thenceforth delivered from darkness; just as, on coming out of a sleep, a man immediately feels his thought waking up into activity; or, rather, as the operation upon a cataract communicates no new light to the diseased eye, but only removes the obstacle which prevents it from seeing, and restores freedom to the pupil, so baptism delivers from sin, which, like a cloud, intercepts the rays of the heavenly Spirit. When the Holy Spirit deigns to communicate himself to us, he gives us back that spiritual eye by which alone we can behold divine things."

"Faith," continues he, in another place, "is the only way of salvation remaining to man. The Apostle Paul declares this in the clearest manner when he says, '*Before faith came, we were kept under the law, shut up unto the faith which should afterward be revealed. Wherefore the law was our schoolmaster to bring us unto Christ, that we might be justified by faith. But after that faith is come, we are no longer under a schoolmaster.*'—Gal., iii., 23–25. Do you not, then, understand that we are no longer under that law which inspired fear, but under the founder of liberty, under the direction of the Son of God? Afterward, the apostle adds, to show that all distinction of persons is annihilated: '*For ye are all the children of God by faith in Jesus Christ. For as many of you as have been baptized into Christ have put on Christ. There is neither Jew nor Greek, there is neither bond nor free, there is neither male nor female; for ye are all one in Christ Jesus.*'—Gal., v., 26–28. "There are, then," he adds, "no distinctions in Christianity; there is no privileged class which receives truths concealed from others; there is no distinction between spiritual and carnal men (*οἱ δὲ ψυχικοὶ οἱ δὲ γνωστικοί*). On the contrary, true Christians are delivered from the yoke of carnal passions; they are equal in the eyes of the Lord, and are all become spiritual men."

"But, by a singular contrast, while Christians who were faithful to the Gospel were thus occupied in defending the rights of simple believers against the ambitious enterprises of a sect, it was, at the same time, necessary for them to sustain the equality of the Christian vocation and of its engagements against another class of individuals, who were anxious to profit by these anti-evangelical distinctions, in order to excuse themselves from leading a holy and Christian life. Under the pretext that they were not philosophers, that they had not learned to read, they thought they need not concern themselves with the Scriptures. Hence Clement says (Pædagogus, l. iii., fol. 255), 'Even though they could not read the Bible, they were on this account none the less inexcusable, because nothing prevents them from hearing the word of God. Faith does not belong to the wise of this world, but to those who are wise in the judgment of God. The word of faith, which is divine, and not the less because it is within reach of the ignorant, is no other than the word of charity.' Clement means that faith manifests itself alike in the hearts of all Christians, by works and labors of love."—NEANDER, *Denkwürdigkeiten*, etc. *Memoirs with reference to a History of Christianity and of the Christian Life*, etc., translated from the German by A. Diacon, Neufchâtel, 1829, vol. i., p. 65–74.

"Tertullian expresses himself forcibly concerning the universal priesthood of all Christians. (De Monog., c. vii.) He starts with the idea that all Christians are now what the priests were under the New Testament. The special priesthood of the Jews was the prophetic image of the general priesthood of Christians ("*Pristina Dei lex nos in suis sacerdotibus prophetavit*"). Christ has called us to the office of priests. The sovereign Sacrificer, the High-priest of the eternal Father, has united us to himself; 'for as many of you as have been baptized into Christ have put on Christ' (Gal., iii., 27), 'and thus he has made us kings and priests unto God his Father.'" —Apoc., i., 6. NEANDER, *Denkwürdigkeiten*, etc., vol. i., p. 179.

. . . . . . "Christ having satisfied the religious want which had, in general, produced the priesthood, and having, by his redemptive work, supplied the needed mediation between God and men, who felt themselves separated from God by sin, there was no longer a place for another intervention. When the apostles, in their epistles, apply to the new religious constitution the Jewish idea of a priesthood, of sacerdotal worship, of sacrifices, they design to show that Christ, having realized forever that which was the object of the priesthood and the sacrifices of the Old Testament, the reconciliation of man with God, all those who receive him by faith, enter into the same relation to God, without need of any other mediation. Consecrated to God, and sanctified by communion with Christ, they are all called to offer their entire life as a spiritual sacrifice acceptable to God; all their activity is a true sacerdotal, spiritual worship; Christians are a holy nation, a people of priests.—Rom., xii., 1; 1 Peter, ii., 9. This idea of a priesthood belonging to all Christians, and founded upon the consciousness of redemption, is sometimes expressed and developed, sometimes implied in the attributes, images, and comparisons which are applied to the Christian life."—NEANDER, *Geschichte der Apostel*, etc., translated from the German by F. Fontanès, pastor, Nismes, 1836, vol. i., p. 108, 109.

Note E, page 47.

Of the Universal Priesthood of the Christian Church.

"Christianity allows no place to a tribe of priests ordained to direct other men, as under religious pupilage, having exclusive charge to supply men's needs in respect to God and divine things. While the Gospel removes whatever separates men from God, it also calls men to fellowship with God through Christ; it takes away, moreover, every barrier which separates men from one another in respect to their highest interests. All have the same High-priest and Mediator, through whom all, as reconciled and united to God, have themselves become a sacerdotal and spiritual race; the same King, the same celestial Master and Teacher, through whom all have become wise unto God; the same faith, the same hope, the same spirit, by whom all are animated; the same oracle in the heart of all—the voice of the Spirit proceeding from the Father—all citizens of the same celestial kingdom. There were here neither laics nor ecclesiastics; but all, so far as they were Christians, were, in their interior life and state, dead to whatever there was in the world that was contrary to God, and were animated by the Spirit of God. Who might arrogate to himself, what an inspired apostle durst not, to domineer over the faith of Christians? The office of teaching was not exclusively conferred on one man, or many; but every believer who might feel himself called, might speak a word in the assembled Church for the common edification."—Neander, *Allgemeine Geschichte der christlichen Religion und Kirche*, tome i., p. 177.

Note F, page 57.

On the Dignity of the Ministry.

"Moreover, if we weigh things in a just balance, we shall find that there is no king, by whatever pomp he may be surrounded, who, as a king, is not below the dignity, I do not say of a bishop, but even of a village curate (*vicani pastoris*), regarded as a pastor. If I seem to utter a paradox, I can establish the truth of what I say. In order to this, let us but compare the functions and object of a pastor with those of a king. To what do princes give their concern? Is it not by the vigor of the laws to repress the wicked, and to preserve the upright in peace? That is, to keep the persons and the goods of the citizens of the state in safety. But how much more excellent is the object of the evangelical pastor, who seeks to establish the sweetest tranquillity in the souls of individuals by quieting and taming the lusts of the world? A king labors to the end that the state may live in peace with its neighbors; it is the endeavor of the priest that every one may be at peace with God, may have peace within, and that no one may design the injury of another.

"The prince's object is to protect the house, the field, the cattle of individuals against the encroachment of thieves. See how vile is the object of these royal functions. And what is the occupation of the priest? To protect the goods of the souls which are confided to him, their faith, their charity, their temperance, their chastity, against the violence of the devil; goods which make those happy who possess them, and the loss of which plunges them into misery. What is it that we may receive from the liberality of the prince? Revenues, appointments, titles of honor: fleeting goods—sports of fortune. But what may we hope to receive from the hands of the priest? He administers heavenly grace by the efficacious sacraments of the Church. By baptism he makes children of hell to become heirs of the kingdom of heaven; by the holy unction he gives the soul power to resist the assaults of devils; by the holy Eucharist he unites men with one another, and men with God, in order to form them into one whole; by the sacrament of penance he gives life to the dead, and of slaves he makes freemen; finally, from the breast of the Scriptures he draws daily the sustenance of saving truth, which nourishes and strengthens souls. The priest presents that spiritual beverage which truly rejoices the heart; he presents the remedy which can heal the mortal maladies of the soul, the effectual antidote of the dreadful poison of the old serpent. In a word, whatever falls under the control of the prince is earthly and fleeting; but that which engages the pastor's care is divine, celestial, eternal. Consequently, as great as is the difference between heaven and earth, between the body and the soul, between temporal and eternal goods, so great is the difference between the functions of a prince and the charge of a priest."—ERASMUS, *Ecclesiastes*, lib. i., *traduction de Roques, dans le Pasteur Evangélique*, p. 190, 191.

NOTE G, p. 116.

Of Prayer.

Prayer of Bacon.—"This invocation, the Christian simplicity of which is very touching in so great a man, afterward became," says M. Chateaubriand, "his habitual prayer when he addressed himself to study."

The Student's Prayer.—"To God the Father, God the Word, God the Spirit, we pour forth most humble and hearty supplications; that he, remembering the calamities of mankind, and the pilgrimage of this our life, in which we wear out days few and evil, would please to open to us new refreshments out of the fountains of his goodness, for the alleviating of our miseries. This, also, we humbly and earnestly beg, that human things may not prejudice such as are divine; neither that, from the unlocking of the gates of sense, and the kindling of a greater natural light, any thing of incredulity or intellectual night may arise in our mind toward divine mysteries. But rather that, by our mind thoroughly cleansed and purged from fancy and vanities, and yet subject and perfectly given up to the divine oracles, there may be given up unto faith the things that are faith's. *Amen.*"

The prayer of Bacon, which we here give, is somewhat remarkably varied in the preface of his *Novum Organum:* It there terminates in these words: "And, lastly, that, being freed from the poison of knowledge infused into it by the serpent, and with which the human soul is swollen and puffed up, we may neither be too profoundly nor immoderately wise, but worship truth in charity."—DE VAUXELLES, *Histoire de Bacon*, tome i., p. 107.

Prayer of Kepler.—"Before I rise from this table, where I have been pursuing these researches, it only remains for me to raise my eyes and my hands toward heaven, and devoutly address my humble prayer to the Author of all light: O Thou who, by the lofty lights which thou hast spread over all nature, dost raise our desires even to the divine light of thy grace, in order that we may one day be transported into the eternal light of thy glory, I thank thee, Lord and Creator, for all the ecstatic joy which I have experienced in the contemplation of the work of thy hands. I have now finished this book, which contains the chief of my labors, and I have employed in its composition the whole sum of the intelligence which thou hast given me. I have declared to men all the greatness of thy works; I have unfolded to them their evidences, as far as my finite mind has been able to comprehend their infinite amplitude. I have exerted all my efforts to raise myself to truth in the way of philosophy; and if I, a miserable worm, conceived and nourished in sin, have chanced to say any thing unworthy of thee, make it known to me, that I may blot it out. Have I not yielded to the seductions of presumption in presence of the admirable beauty of thy works? Have I not had in view my own renown among men in raising this monument, which should be entirely consecrated to thy glory? Oh, if it has been thus with me, of thy mercy and clemency receive me, and grant me grace that the work which I have completed may be the means of no evil, but may contribute to thy glory and to the salvation of souls."—BUCKLAND, *La Géologie et la Minéralogie*, etc., *traduit de l'Anglaise, par Doyen*, tome i., p. 9, note.

Prayer of De Thou.—"The historian De Thou relates, in his memoirs, that every morning, besides the prayer which each believer is required to offer, he implored God in private to purify his heart, to banish from it hatred and flattery, to enlighten his mind, and to make known to him the truth, which so many passions and conflicting interests had almost buried: We are happy to find such agreements between contemporary authors."—DE VAUXELLES, *Histoire de Bacon*, tome i., p. 107, note.

Sacerdotal Prayer.—"Prayer is the most inward and the most essential duty of the ministry; it is the soul, so to speak, of the priesthood; it is the pastor's only safety: This alone sweetens the distastes, and precludes the danger of your functions; this alone secures success in the discharge of them. . . . . But, my brethren, even if prayer were not as indispensable as it is to the success of our functions, do we not owe it to our people? Are we not charged, in our character of pastor and of minister, to pray for them without ceasing? Is it not even the most essential duty of that priesthood which establishes us as mediators between God and the people? On the prayers of the pastor God has made to depend the grace which he intends to bestow upon the flock: It is ours, my brethren, to present to him, without ceasing, the wants of our people, to solicit for them the riches of mercy, to turn away his wrath from the infliction of those scourges and chastisements with which their provocations are often punished: It is ours to deplore before him the vices with which we see our people infected, and of which our cares and our zeal can not cure them: It is ours to ask strength for the feeble, compunction for hardened sinners, perseverance for the righteous. The more boundless the wants of our people, the more lively and frequent should be our prayers: We should never appear before him without having, like the high-priest under the law, the names of the tribes written on our heart—that is to say, the names of the people confided to us; this should always be the principal subject of our prayer." —MASSILLON, *Douzième Discours Synodal, De la Nécessité de la Prière.*

The same Subject.—"Accompany your labors with your prayers: Speak of the disorders of your people to God more frequently than to them. Complain to him of the obstacles put in the way of their conversion by your unfaithfulness more frequently than of those which their obstinacy may present. Blame yourself alone at his feet for the small fruit of his ministry. As a tender father, apologize to him for the faults of your children, and accuse only yourself," etc.—MASSILLON, *Discours sur le Zèle des Pasteurs pour le Salut des Ames.*

Note H, page 182.

By the Translator.

Has the Sabbath been abolished?

What is the ideal of the Sabbath? If the Sabbath were an institution of the theocracy, like the appointment of the cities of refuge, etc., then, when the new dispensation entered, it did, indeed, pass away with the other theocratic institutions of Judaism. But the Sabbath, in its ideal, was no more judaic or theocratic than marriage. Its date was ante-judaic. The Sabbath was the day on which He who built all things ceased and rested from his work—the seventh day, which God blessed and sanctified, because that in it he had rested from all his work which God created and made.—Genesis, ii., 3, compared with Exodus, xx., 10, 11. When the Author, who was also the first observer of the Sabbath, established, under the legation of Moses, a theocratic form of government over the Jewish people, it pleased him to incorporate in it the Sabbatic institution; and by enacting laws respecting this institution with temporal or civil sanctions, to erect it into an institution of civil polity, without, however, divesting it of its original character of sacredness. The Sabbath, amid the institutions of Moses, stood in all its distinctiveness and peculiarity as perfectly as it did at its first appointment. As the civico-sacred government which the Jews had been under ceased when the new dispensation began, the Jewish appendages to the Sabbath, or the Sabbath, as far forth as it was a purely Jewish institution, now had an end. But the ideal of the Sabbath transfers us beyond the date of Judaism, and beyond all local and variable interests and communities, and, placing us at the stand-point of humanity, discovers to us, as the just sphere of the Sabbatic Law, the whole race of man regarded as possessing a religious nature, in circumstances such as man's must needs have been while an inhabitant of the earth, and subject to laws of human life appropriate to such a world and such a state as were chosen for man by his Maker.

Assuming that man was to lead a religious life on earth, we can not avoid seeing that the Sabbath, if not of indispensable necessity to this end, was at least of the highest advantage and value; and the Divine wisdom and goodness in sanctifying and hallowing it (for it was for man's sake that this was done, Mark, ii., 27), can not but be acknowledged: And to suppose that this institution, regarded in its true idea, has been abolished by Christianity, is to suppose that under Christianity—that is, under the dispensation of the fullness of the Divine favor to man, there has been an abridgment of privileges in a very comprehensive, if not an all-comprehensive, respect. Indeed, it seems impossible to think that Christianity, without a constant miracle, could attain its purpose, if the Sabbath, such as it was from the beginning—the Sabbath in its original ideal and influence—should be denied to it. Was, then, the Sabbath abolished by Christianity?

"Jesus Christ," says M. Vinet, page 42, "instituted very little; he inspired more." He abolished as he instituted. He employed no direct legislation against the peculiarities of Judaism, the shadows of the good things which were to come in with the Gospel: He left the shadows to themselves, after the "very image of the things" had manifested itself, except when the shadows sought to displace this image. The shadows very reluctantly, but slowly and gradually, retired, and the Christian verities availed themselves of the advantages which were afforded them by the dispensation of liberty to which they belonged; and as Christian institutions were needed, they made their appearance, sometimes by the special agency of the disciples, and sometimes spontaneously, or, as it were, of a natural birth or growth. In one way or another, the new wine was provided, or provided itself, with new bottles as they were needed.

The law of the spirit of life in Christianity, in its action in reference to the Sabbath, followed its own appropriate mode: It needed, as a sacred day, a different day of the week from that which had been observed as a Sabbath under the former dispensation: It did not legislate *out* the seventh day; it did not explicitly and magisterially legislate *in* the first day: As the new life had its beginning and its fountain in the resurrection of Christ, it was natural, assuming it had need of a sacred day, that it should take the first day of the week: It did this, it would seem, spontaneously or naturally, and not by means of any legislative or instituting act, whether immediately on the part of Christ himself or through the agency of the apostles. The first day, without any expression of discontent with the seventh, without forbidding expressly the observance of the seventh, naturally, quietly, unobjectionably assumed the place to which it was called by the wants and exigences of Christianity. But did it take this place less under the divine sanction, and less by the action of the divine will and the divine Spirit, than it would have done if a law had been passed appointing it to this place, with all the authority and force with which the seventh day was installed as a great fundamental institution of Judaism? Though it came in with the spontaneity and freedom which pertained to the essence of the new life, let us remember it was this new life as it dwelt and developed itself in the apostles — inspired, and, in reference to the work of the apostolate, *infallible* men — that, as with the swelling flood of the sea, advanced the Lord's day to the sanctity and honor of the sacred day of Christianity. It is impossible that there should be any tokens of majesty, sacredness, authority divine and inviolable, more unambiguous, more decisive, more commanding, than those by which the religious observance of the first day of the week is sanctioned and enforced.

So our author thinks: "Sunday was not added to Christianity; it was born of it: Sunday is a summary of Christianity. . . . Internal necessity is the true law, the best authority for Sunday; it speaks more strongly to us than a written ordinance. . . . Nothing binds so much as Christian liberty and conscience—this has consecrated a day; it ought, then, to be holy." This would seem to be putting the authority and sanctity of the Lord's day, as a day of sacredness, on ground as high and as holy as we could desire for it. Its observance as a sacred day is binding, is necessary, is the natural offspring of Christianity, without which there would soon be no Christianity. We rejoice in this view of the subject, from this most vigorous and profound thinker, the more, because men of high name and station have recently advanced different views, which we can not regard as favorable to Christianity. The Archbishop of Dublin, for example, puts the authority of the Lord's day on the same ground with that of Holy Thursday, Christmas, and other days which the Church has thought proper to appoint as sacred ones in the exercise of the power of the keys, or the power of binding and loosing, granted by Christ to his first followers, and through them to their successors. In contradistinction to this, M. Vinet's view of the ground of the sacredness of "Sunday" places it in perfect independence of ecclesiastical legislation, identifies it with the very essence of Christianity, and thus gives it a position into which no other day can be introduced without sacrilegious usurpation. Still, even he asserts that the Sabbath is abolished: *Le Dimanche*, the Lord's day, is not a Sabbath. That institution, which was ordained by the Maker of the world, for the benefit of mankind, before the generations began, and without the appropriate influence and advantage of which the spiritual life, in such a world and in such circumstances as ours, can not be perpetuated—did Christianity, indeed, abolish this institution by setting aside that system of Judaism which, for its own purposes, appropriated the Sabbatic principle and invested it with secular authority? Did an institution, having its ground in the spiritual nature and necessities of man, pass away with a mass of institutions, the ground of which was local, temporary, and, after its day had passed, illegitimate, and impossible to be retained? Did Christianity abolish an institution as old, as radical, and as necessary as marriage, because it was its lot to be taken, for special reasons, into company with the shadows and symbols of Moses' law?

This question may be thought to be unimportant, since the sacredness of Sunday, the Lord's day, is put into such high and commanding relief by the doctrine of our author. Indeed, according to this doctrine, the Sabbath, in its essential idea, is not abolished; it is retained; it is advanced into more full and perfect power and life: Nothing is abolished but the laws of Moses respecting the Sabbath: This was, indeed, a small thing; nay, it was a good and a necessary thing, that these laws should have been abolished. Had they remained to regulate the observance of the Sabbath under the

Christian dispensation, they would have militated against the whole genius and purpose of that dispensation: But not less hostile to these would have been the setting aside the influence and sanction of the exact idea, and the intrinsic law and life of Sabbatism. Not without reason was true piety, under the Old Testament, resolved into Sabbatism—the keeping of a Sabbath. There was more than a mere symbol in Sabbath-sanctification; there always has been more; there always will be more: When all the shadows and all the changes of time shall have found their end, Sabbatism will remain, as comprising the substantive and immutable piety of the heavenly state: *απολείπεται* ΣΑΒΒΑΤΙΣΜΟ'Σ *τῶ λαῶ τοῦ θεοῦ.*—Heb., iv., 9. All will be Sabbath forever in heaven: that is to say, the piety of saints, such as it is when it exercises and expresses itself in the form of genuine Sabbath-sanctification—this piety perfectly developed under this form, as it will be in heaven, gives us the ideal, and is most completely identical with the very essence of the piety of heaven. And if the most perfect exhibition of the piety of heaven was needful or desirable in advancing the cause of Christianity, it were strange, indeed, that Christianity should deprive itself of this advantage, as it certainly has done, if it has strictly and absolutely abolished the SABBATH.

It is the change of the day, nothing besides this,* that has suggested the idea of abolition: But not to assume with some a position not tenable, that the day has not been changed, except to change it back to that which had been observed from the beginning until the time of Moses, we ask whether there be any thing in the identical twenty-four hours between the termination of Friday and the beginning of Sunday which would involve the abolition of Sabbatism, if any other hours than these should be taken in their stead? Would there not be in this case a most gratuitous application of the principle, *the letter killeth*—a principle which, as much as any other, may be termed a fundamental one in hermeneutics? If Christianity retains the whole of the Sabbatic institution, except the sanctification of these identical hours—if, with all the fullness and power of its mighty life, Chris-

* Gal., iv., 10, and Col., ii., 18, do not refer to this subject.

tianity has declared itself in favor of exactly that essential thing which constituted the all in all of Sabbatism at the beginning, except that, for high and necessary purposes, it has assigned to it a place in the run of the week different by one day from that which it first held—if this is all that Christianity has done in modifying the ancient Sabbatic institution—if, with this one exception, it has advanced the idea of Sabbatism, together with all the particular ideas which this comprises as entering into the unchangeable and eternal essence of piety, far, immeasurably far, beyond its original sphere—is there any warrant, any justification, for the use of such language as this : Christianity has abolished the Sabbath?

If fidelity to the truth does not require this affirmation, we think it should not have been made. Words are things. Luther, in order to express in the strongest manner his abhorrence of legalism, employs these terms in regard to the observance of Sunday: "Keep it holy, for its use' sake both to body and soul! But if any where the day is made holy for the mere day's sake—if any where any one sets up its observance upon a Jewish foundation, then I order you to work on it, to ride on it, to dance on it, to feast on it—to do any thing that shall reprove this encroachment on the Christian spirit and liberty." For the observance of Sunday, in Luther's conception, there was no ground of obligation excepting expediency: no inviolable law of God required it: So he taught with all the power of his mighty tongue. His end was good: So, with his views of the sacredness of Sunday, he was, perhaps, right in teaching: We say he may have been right in teaching as he did if Sunday truly have no other ground of sacredness than expediency, according to man's ideas of expediency. M. Vinet had no such conceptions as to the foundation of Sunday sacredness; but in saying that the Sabbath is abolished, it is to be feared that he opens the door, by possibility at least, to the legitimation, to an indefinite extent, of Luther's teaching on this point. If we say the Sabbath is abolished, do we not virtually make expediency the rule of Sunday sanctification, unless, indeed, we assume Whately's position, that Sunday should be kept from regard to ecclesiastical prescription or recommendation. M. Vinet rests the sacredness of the Lord's day on the same foundation on which Christianity itself rests: herein he is right; but that which has a firm foundation may still need law to inform, to regulate, and direct it; and, taking mankind as they are, to remove the authority of positive law from religious institutions, to place the claims of these institutions to our regard on any other ground than that of the peremptory authority and inviolable command of God, is a virtual desecration of them.

NOTE I, page 185.

By the Translator.

On Liturgies.

THE question whether the spirit of the evangelic life or Christian dispensation desires or needs a Liturgy in worship; whether this spirit prefers or consents to bind itself to forms of prayer, prescribed or imposed by ecclesiastical authority or prudence, we would appeal, for a new examination on its merits, against the disposition which is made, or is sought to be made of it, by predominant sentiment. Whether it be from the new appearance of formalism, or from desire for a more chaste and cultivated manner in conducting public worship, or from defect of the spirit of free prayer in these times, or from all these causes combined, there are indications, not to be mistaken, that a preference for the stated use of Liturgies is prevailing to some extent in denominations which have hitherto thought it, among themselves at least, inexpedient: And as the tendencies of this preference in these denominations seem to us unfavorable to the interests of Christianity, on the whole, we should scarcely be true to ourselves if we should leave our author's remarks on Liturgies without at least indicating our judgment.

Let us not misapprehend our author on this subject. Though he says, when speaking of the performance of the service, "Le ministre est lié à la Liturgie qui ne lui appartient pas, qui est la voix même du troupeau et à laquelle il ne fait que prêter sa voix individuelle," he had said before, "Des paroles à la fois humaines et préscrites ne me semblent pas réaliser l'idéal d'une Liturgie : Si la parole humaine devait s'y mêler, je l'aimerais mieux libre et individuelle." Taking both these passages together, and interpreting them as we feel bound to do, without making our author inconsistent with himself, we obtain, as M. Vinet's judgment, on the whole, that, while the officiating minister, as the minister of a flock that has prescribed to itself forms of worship, is to be tied to the Liturgy of the flock, and not to use his own voice except as that of one individual thereof, there is, nevertheless, in this mode of worship, something inconsistent with the ideal of a Liturgy. "It appears to me," he says, "that the ideal of a Liturgy can not be realized in words at the same time human and prescribed. If human words are to be admitted, I prefer that they should be free and individual." As there are "human words" in all extant Liturgies, it is M. Vinet's impression that the ideal of a Liturgy is realized in no Liturgy; that is to say, if we understand him, that liturgical worship, such as it is every where in fact, involves more or less of inconsistency with the just idea of worship. This he might believe, and yet, on the whole, think this mode of worship expedient—expedient as being less objectionable than free prayer.

And yet free prayer he thinks more congenial with the ideal of a Liturgy than prayers precomposed and prescribed by man. In the nature of free prayer as such, there is nothing incongenial with this ideal: In prescribed forms, on the contrary, the ideal can not be realized: Free prayer, then, has this advantage, and it is surely no unimportant one, that, in its just and complete exercise, the ideal of worship may be realized: It will be realized if those who offer free prayer are not in fault; it can not be in the other mode of worship. If, then, it be feasible to have free worship, unobjectionable as to manner and spirit, or just in proportion as this is feasible, the preferableness of free worship is unquestionable.

Dismissing for the present the question as to this feasibility, we return to the other point—the incongeniality of Liturgies with the spirit of Christianity—the ideal of Christian worship: With such views of this spirit as our author has so forcibly and beautifully expressed, it was impossible for him not to have felt the incongeniality, the inconsistency of which we speak. He could not but feel that the spirit of Christianity, especially in its primitive manifestation, was entirely inconsistent with such an interference with spiritual liberty as the authoritative prescription of a human Liturgy would have been. History had acquainted him with the fact that there was no such interference;* but, independently of history, he knew this by *à priori* evidence—he knew it, we may say, by intuition. The early Christianity would, in his apprehension, have denied itself if it had submitted to the imposition of a prescribed and stereotyped Liturgy.

But, though we have no need of historical evidence, we ought not to forget this fact of history, namely, that there was no appearance of liturgical worship in the Christian Church until Christianity had become degenerate and corrupt. Liturgies were unknown in the purest times; in their beginning, their increase, and through all their changes, they were the work of uninspired men's hands; their origin is unknown: "They seem to me," says Dr. Owen, "to have had but slender originals; their beginnings were small, plain, brief; their use arbitrary; the additions they received were from the endeavors of private men in several ages, occasional for the most part;" their apology was necessity, arising from the introduction of men "into the office of the ministry who had not gifts and abilities for the profitable discharge of the work of the ministry;" the times of their greatest abundance and prosperity were the ages of darkness; and, in Dr. Owen's judgment, they had the chief influence in promoting the degeneracy of the Church before the Reformation.†

It has seemed to us an invincible objection to the general use of

* The following is the account given by Tertullian of the manner of worship in his time: "Illuc (that is toward heaven) suscipientis Christiani manibus expansis quia innocuis, capito nudo quia non erubescimus, denique sine monitore quia de pectore oramus."—*Apol.*, cap. 30. Justin Martyr's is as follows: *Ἄθεοι μὲν οὖν ὡς οὐκ ἔσμεν, τὸν δεμιυργὸν τῶν δὲ τοῦ παντὸς σεβόμενοι, ἀνενδεῆ αιμâτων καὶ σπονδῶν καὶ θυμιαματῶν ὡς ἐδεδάχθημεν λὲγοντος λόγω ευχὴς αἰ ευχαριστίας εφ' οἰς προσφερὸμεθα πᾶσιν ὅση δύναμις αἰνοντες.—Apol.*

† Owen's Works, vols. iv. and xix. London, 1826. Dr. Owen has with great care examined the question before us, and the study of his powerful treatises we would earnestly recommend as especially seasonable at the present time.

Liturgies, apart from their intrinsic incongeniality with the spirit of Christianity, that they are unfavorable to the object of Christianity in these two respects:

1. The extension of the Gospel. Liturgies suppose churches already organized, power in the people to read, &c., difficulties which, we think, can not be embraced in any judicious plan for evangelizing the heathen: How could Brainerd have conducted public worship among his Indians had he been compelled to use a prayer-book?

2. Particularity in the offices of public devotion: Liturgies can not anticipate the various occasions and circumstances which demand distinct reference and mention in prayer. The life of prayer consists, in a great degree, in its suitableness to times and providences, and in particularity of petition. Herein Liturgies must needs be deficient: The state of the flock and the aspect of affairs are continually varying, but the Liturgy does not vary. The words, for general purposes, may be suitable; but they must be always read as they stand; and the new exigences rising up daily, and demanding distinct notice at the throne of grace, must be passed over with a generality of expression, which covers many other things as well as them. Surely that can not be the best way of conducting public worship which, in its very nature, has so great an inconvenience and defect.

There are, however, objections against free prayer which ought not to be overlooked. The chief objections are these two:

1. Extemporaneous or free prayer produces confusion in the minds of the worshipers. "The congregation, in extemporaneous prayer," says Dr. Paley, "being ignorant of each petition before they hear it, and having little or no time to join in after they have heard it, are confounded between their attention to the minister and their own devotion. Their devotion is necessarily suspended till the petition is concluded; and before they can adopt it, their attention is required to what follows. Extemporary prayer can not, for this reason, be joint prayer. Joint prayer is that in which all join, and not that which one alone in the congregation conceives and delivers."*

* Works, vol. i., p. 314.

This argument confutes itself by proving too much. It proves that all that portion of mankind who can not read can take no part in public prayer. It proves that when the disciples prayed for Peter (Acts, xii.), and lifted up their voices together in prayer after the return of Peter and John from the council (Acts, iv.), they did not *unite* in prayer on these occasions. It concludes, moreover, as much against a joint hearing of the word as against joint praying. Truth from the pulpit can not be acquiesced in by the hearers until after its announcement is completed. It must be heard before it can be considered; but how can it be considered, since the discourse runs on, and a subsequent announcement is continually calling off attention from a previous one?

The truth is, that this argument rests on difficulties which are wholly imaginary. The supposition that the attention of the hearers is suspended—that they are confounded between their own devotion and attention to the minister, &c., is groundless. The movements of the human mind are quicker than this argument assumes them to be. The mind takes in the most of what is said, whether in prayer or preaching, without any measurable lapse of time. Even in argumentative discourse, the attention of the hearers keeps pace with the speaker, and sometimes anticipates him. Discourse may, indeed, be so ordered as to confound attention, but it need not, and should not be.

2. The imperfection of extemporaneous or free prayer. It is often incomprehensive, omitting many things which ought to be in public prayer: It is often loose and inconsecutive: It is often full of faults as to diction: It is often delivered in a hesitating, stammering manner, &c., &c. In reply, we say, in the first place, that faults here are to be set over against faults—the faults of free prayer against the faults of Liturgies; recollecting, moreover, this difference, that the faults of liturgical worship are, for the most part, inseparable from it, while the faults of free prayer may, perhaps, be corrected: In the second place, that advantages, too, are to be compared with advantages; to lose those of free prayer would be to suffer a loss which were worse to the Church than all

the faults of this mode of worship many times multiplied. What could compensate the Church for the loss of all that benefit which she has received and is to receive from the exercise of the gift of prayer in public, on the part of holy men filled with faith and the Holy Ghost, and furnished by him specifically for the performance of this important part of divine service? We add, thirdly, that if free prayer be imperfect, the door to perfection is open to it; whereas the Liturgy must not be changed, while the need of a change in some things is, by many who use it, admitted and deplored. The character of free prayer will vary, of course, with the various gifts and graces of ministers, and the various measures of aid afforded them by the Spirit at the time of prayer, and there may, of course, be instances in which the faults of performance will be unusually great; but not to insist that the reading of the Liturgy may vary with the reader's gifts, so that, in some instances, the faults of performance may be almost equivalent to faults in the Liturgy itself, the absolute uniformity of liturgical worship may be more hurtful, as we believe it to be in fact, than all the faults which are incidental to the other mode, and which, we should not forget, may, to a great extent, be corrected by general proficiency in piety, and by suitable pains directed particularly to that end. It is inconsistent with the idea of free prayer to be directly studious as to either expression, or order, or thought at the time of offering it; but there is a way of making proficiency in the exercise of this gift, and a minister who neglects the cultivation of it disregards the charge of the apostle (1 Tim., iv., 15), in regard, at least, to one part of his work, and one of no inferior importance.

We have not meant to say, we do not think, that the spirit of life and liberty in prayer can make no use of forms. In its full realization, it is indeed above all forms; but in its inferior spheres it may sometimes serve itself of forms with great advantage; and in such a Liturgy as that, for example, which is used by Episcopalians, the best extant, it may, occasionally at least, find itself much more in its proper element than in free prayer itself, as it is too often performed.

In conclusion, let us say that while we have no desire that liturgical worship should be abolished; while we suppose it probable that worship in the Christian Church, on the whole, is better than it would be if this mode of worship formed no part of it, we can not but lament that any denomination which prefers this mode should not combine free prayer with it, and give its ministers some degree of liberty in regard to it: And that, on the other hand, we greatly regret to see, in the denominations in which free prayer has been conscientiously preferred, any dissatisfaction with it on account of the faults which are incidental to it, and any appearance of a desire to introduce forms.

Note K, p. 231.

On the Use of the Catechism.

"Declension in the Christian faith has had no more direct cause, no more evident symptom, than the absolute substitution of the Catechism for the Bible in the religious instruction of children: And the revival of Christianity in Protestant countries has, on the whole, been produced and characterized by the preference given to the Bible above the Catechism, not to the exclusion of the Catechism, but limiting it to its only reasonable use, which is to supply the reader of the Bible with a summary of biblical truth. When the Bible shall have its place in the religious instruction of children, there must needs be a revision of the Catechism; and he only will perform this office well who shall have taught Christianity first from the Bible: And we think we may guarantee that this kind of manual will then be conceived and prepared differently from the best of those which have been hitherto in use. But what is of the greatest urgency, is to bring those poor children to the fountain, and also to let them drink at it, who, until now, have had administered unto them drop by drop, as if it were a medical potion, the water of life, which, by its passage through such long and old tubes of human manufacture, has been rendered insipid, and has even become corrupt.

"After it shall be discovered that many Catechisms which have been authorized and consecrated by long use were made in violation of logic and common sense, presenting the Christian doctrines in an incoherent state, which destroyed their true meaning, and in a state of contradiction, wherein some are made to annul others; in brief, after Catechisms shall have been made as good as possible, it will be no less necessary to remove them from the place which they have usurped, and to make holy Scripture the chief Catechism. But it does not hence follow that we are to put the Bible into the hands of children; this would be neither useful nor proper. And the idea has hence occurred of extracting textually every thing which it is necessary to know in order to be a Christian; that is, to extract from the Bible whatever is intelligible to a child. This, in fact, is the plan on which this divine Book has been conceived: It is a river, we are told, in which an elephant may swim, and a ford which a child may cross without drowning. The question is not whether we shall swim or walk, but whether we shall get across; and the child must cross as well as the adult. Now, to become a Christian, or, according to the expression of the Gospel, *to enter into the kingdom of heaven,* we must return to infancy—we must become a child. I admit that the infancy must be a voluntary one, and that it is only as such that it is of any value or utility; even a child himself is not a true Christian until he has ceased to be a child in the proper sense of the word; he must become one of choice and of reason; but it is nevertheless true that, in order to become a Christian, we must accept the verities of the Bible in the sense and in the simplicity in which a child apprehends them."—A. Vinet: Article sur *L'Histoire Sainte, extraite de le Bible,* par M. Morel.

Note L, page 339.

Thoughts of Bengel upon the Exercise of the Ministry.

Taken from his Life by Burk: Pamphlet published by M. Vinet in 1842.

I. "A Pastor should be divinely assured in respect to his occupation—that is to say, his vocation to the ministry of reconciliation, as well as in respect to the truths which he preaches; he should be able to produce the certificate of his spiritual birth; he should be firmly resolved to promote the glory of God; to live for Christ, and to serve him; to gain heaven for himself, and for many others with him.

II. "A pastor should give himself entirely up to his work; should throw himself bravely into the midst of the conflict; and, whatever may happen, should never allow himself to be cast down. In order to this, he must consider:

1. "That the third Sunday after Trinity has never passed without having given occasion for joy in heaven over a sinner gained by the preaching of the Gospel; and that this single grain of wheat, even after a long delay, is for him who gathers it a rare refreshment.

2. "That crosses in life help us to know ourselves better, humble us before God, and make us pray with greater fervor for the manifestation of that Spirit, before whom doubt is silent and quieted.

3. "That those who have received, who believe, who publish the message of grace, have no less need than others of the patience of God. How long has he to wait before they produce any thing in conformity with his will? How much wisdom from him is necessary in order to extract any thing good from so much weakness and so much impurity? And shall they themselves be impatient?

4. "That it is not the pastor's fault if he be born in a disastrous time in which it is very difficult to do good; in a time when injustice having trampled upon the weak, and devoured the substance of the poor, it is no wonder if his preaching remains without fruit; in a time when authority itself, though recognizing the evil, hardly takes the trouble to remedy it, and sees, without dismay, the great crushing the weak.

5. "That God (Ezek., ix., 4) set a mark upon the foreheads of all those who deplored the prevalence of public sins, that they might prevent the chastisement which was coming.

6. "That a pastor is strengthened by what others achieve for the kingdom of God, when he humbly rejoices over the good which has been done without him. He thus makes the works of others his own, while he escapes the danger of self-complacency.

7. "That even when souls are not positively gained by truly evan-

gelical preaching, they are, nevertheless, somewhat softened and prepared by the clear knowledge of spiritual things. H. Franeke testified, after long experience, that the parishioners of a courageous pastor are always in the end more tractable and gentle.

"When God grants a richer harvest to a pastor, it does not always follow that this pastor is more acceptable to him than others. Surgeons have various instruments: some they use daily, others very rarely, and only for particular cases: They do not prefer one of these instruments to the others. It is only the last stroke of the axe which fells the tree; but if one man gives fifty strokes, another thirty, a last only two, who can tell which of the wood-cutters has been most useful, and which blow most contributed to prostrate the tree? It is thus in regard to the work which is accomplished in souls.

III. "A pastor should be like the hen who takes her chickens under her wings, and sometimes even lets them mount upon her back. We can not force confidence and freedom; charity alone can call them forth: Friendly intercourse often does more good than much reasoning and many sermons. When heated by the sun, the traveler spontaneously unbuttons his coat. A single pigeon that voluntarily enters the pigeon-house, is worth more than a great number which have been forced to enter. It would be well for all if the habit of familiarly asking questions and friendly conversation prevailed. I believe that this might be successful even with the unconverted.

IV. "The pastor should not altogether avoid intercourse with the people of the world; but he should guard himself against partaking of their sins. By bearing witness, in our familiar intercourse, to the same truths which we solemnly teach from the pulpit, the mind receives more impression than it allows us to perceive. Many of the seeds we sow are lost, but still something remains. When it snows, and the ground is wet, the snow, as it falls, seems to be absorbed into the earth; but, by constant falling, it forms,in the end, a white covering: *sparge, sparge, quam potes.*

V. "There is reason to be concerned about a pastor when he does not seek the company of true Christians. His occupation degenerates by degrees into a common trade; and there are many who exercise it for their own convenience, as men do any other trade, or who allow themselves to seek the good things of this world—although, truly, we can not cite many examples of rich pastors. Faithful souls are the pastor's hand; himself is the eye; the hand may bear, may push, may raise, and render itself very useful to the eye.

VI. "Experience teaches that many souls may be savingly reached by preaching; but the work of grace can be fully accomplished in them only by means of individual treatment; hence great importance should be attached to private labors. The pastor often obtains more fruit from his visits than from his public preaching. He should always show himself equally well disposed to go wherever he is called; and those whose spiritual necessities draw them to him, should, by his hearty welcome, feel themselves encouraged to open themselves to him with perfect freedom: He should show pleasure in meeting neighbors in the house where he is visiting.

VII. "The principal rule to be observed in the direction of souls is to do nothing of our own will, and every thing that we know to be according to the will of God. We should approach those souls of which we have some hope in their calmer moments. To those who rebel and harden their hearts we must always present the word of God. We must endeavor to prepare the way in an agreeable manner for the subjects of which we wish to speak, beginning with indifferent things, and gradually leading the way to replies without formally asking questions. When we have occasion to see people every day, it is well to wait for a favorable moment. But if occasions are rare, or if we should only have one opportunity, we must guard against suffering it to escape without bearing our witness. If such persons were to die suddenly, it would be a great cause of anxiety to the pastor that he should have neglected to testify the Gospel to them; and, in a contrary case, how greatly would he rejoice in having been faithful! Moreover, we should not yield too much to anxiety; it is productive of much harm. We should act in concert with God, not with ourselves; so that we might afterward be able to say, 'I have done, O God, according as thou hast commanded.' Then, certainly, we shall receive a divine answer in the time of need. A single word, a look, a ray of light, may work great things in a soul when we have found its true point of concern, and the right moment. It was one day said to a man whose wife was ill, 'You have now a sanctuary in your house.' These words sank into his heart, and did him much good. To be able to use happy words, which hit directly, is a great gift.

VIII. "When souls are to be gained to God, we should despise nothing; however few they may be, we should convince them that we think it of great importance to lead them to the Lord.

IX. "Despair absolutely of no one. If we see a fault in any one, make it known to him, and endeavor to lead him to correct it: And, whether we succeed in this or not, let us endeavor to discover or to develop whatever good there may be in him.

X. "I think it very important not to heap together indiscriminately arguments and motives, mingling the weak with the strong, to make up a number. They only injure one another. It is better to produce only one decisive argument and adhere to it.

XI. "There are souls which, in proportion as we urge them and seek to penetrate into them, seem to offer less footing, and escape from us like a subtile vapor. We must wait, keep ourselves tranquil, and be willing to delay some time before we see the fruits of our ministry. The state of *passivity*, of which Tauler and others speak, is too little known to those who so much wish to precipitate their own activity and that of others. Often, in such a state, more reflections pass through the soul in a single moment than, in other states, in many months; and this advantage is much surer and more durable than a forced and factitious success. There are souls for which it is well, because of the temptations of the evil world, that they remain until death undeveloped, or in the state of a bud, and do not reveal themselves and enter into the kingdom of life until at the moment of departure. Let those remember this, for their consolation, who are charged with the care of souls. We are to do what can be done kindly, freely, and with a joyful heart, and leave the rest to the Chief Shepherd, saying, with Moses, 'Is it, then, I that have begotten this people?'

XII. "It is very necessary that the pastor should have the gift of discernment. Where there is a genuine life, it sustains itself. But when the pastor is always wishing to arrange and prepare souls, they allow it to be done for them, and fall into indolence. The patriarch Abraham (who lived in the fourth century of the Christian era) left persons to themselves after having led them on to say, 'I believe in God the Father and his Son Jesus Christ.' Christ himself said to his disciples, 'It is expedient for you that I go away;' and the eunuch of Queen Candace was left alone as soon as he had been baptized. If I had a tree at which I was always cutting and digging, I do not believe it would prosper any the more on that account. As a child just beginning to walk is never so sure to fall as when we exclaim to him, 'Do not fall,' so it is when we wish to obtain from souls by force *actus reflexos* (great efforts, in order to have a distinct knowledge of their state of grace and of their progress in sanctification). There are souls whose whole business consists in *actibus directis* (free action proceeding from faith and love). These are those who advance best; and if we should awkwardly push them forward, we should only intimidate them, or turn them aside. There are others, doubtless, who need to be urged; hence we should ever ask and seek a discerning mind.

XIII. "What is the essential thing in the pastorate? It is what is so often called in the Psalms *jaschar*—uprightness; it may be compared to a straight line, in which there is nothing oblique, nothing double; which avoids heights and depths, and is the road that leads most directly to the end.

XIV. "Dear pastors! let us fill our hearts with love for Christ. It is this love which makes us serene, courageous, active; it makes us penetrate into the true state of a soul, and discovers to us the road in which we should lead it. We should establish closer relations with our parishioners, remind ourselves constantly that we have before us men like ourselves. What do we do in times of pestilence or other public calamities? We mingle and are confounded with the crowd for the common welfare, without remembering the vain distinctions of rank and talent. If we act thus toward a man, we may hope to make him in a manner our prisoner, and to dispose of him as we wish.

XV. "I would leave to each soul the particular foundation of its faith; even if the premises be feeble, provided the conclusion be just, that is sufficient. It is as with a child who tries its first steps across the chamber, and holds on to its own dress; if it advance, we freely allow it this imaginary help. With how much delicacy should man be treated! If the cords be stretched too tight, they will relax again the more quickly, and the soul will incline to that side which we wished to make it avoid.

XVI. "As to private meetings, it is desirable that, under the pretext of public order, we should not disturb good souls in those exercises of which they have need; and that at those hours in which others assemble to amuse themselves, it should be allowed to them to assemble for their edification. I see here, also, a *swarm* from the parent hive—a good swarm, which we must shelter with care, instead of allowing it to go astray.

XVII. "I can not understand the desire to forbid meetings. Should we, then, require every one to be pious for himself alone? It is as if, seeing some persons setting out together on a journey, I should recommend them not to walk in company, but to keep themselves a gunshot apart.

XVIII. "Disease supposes life: Wherever a spiritual malady is found, there must be also spiritual life. The ungodly are perfectly dead. Why should the pastor reject or treat severely children of God because there is something in them to reprove? Should we not rather take means to join ourselves with them, and to offer them the remedy which they need?

XIX. "There are persons who value meetings too highly, and who appear to think themselves better because they take part in the exercises. But neither are they the only pious ones, nor are even all of them pious. There are excellent souls who do not go to meetings; and in meetings, as elsewhere, there are some hypocrites. The same man does not take the same view as a spectator and as a judge. Destroy not the work of God. Do we not allow each one to pursue his own course in ordinary life? We should be more indulgent in little things, that we may have the more right to insist upon the great things. We should not be too ready to comfort those who are despised by the world because of their frequent attendance on meetings; this contempt may be good and salutary for them. If my servants were coarse and rude to my daughters, I should at first say nothing, for these servants may spare me somewhat of paternal discipline.

XX. "In these times there is so much *lukewarmness*, that it is not possible to establish between the pastor and his flock that mutual acquaintance and that intimacy which can only exist in a church of which all the members are converted: This favorable moment has not yet come. Many things are needed in order to create a true community: There should be experience and much knowledge. A community should have the spirit of discernment, and members capable of leading others; otherwise it would seem that we were met together only to trouble each other. Let us take care that brotherly love does not become a farce: Alas! this is very common; we are hypocritical toward each other; we seek to please each other; we neglect reproof, admonition, the encouragement of charity. There are people who, having neither humility nor charity, nothing of the spirit of Christ, are yet distinguished by their zeal in forming associations and meetings: Is not this playing a farce? In a community of brothers there must be communion of prayers, and laws to which all are subject, without, however, binding the individual to time and form; for the tighter the knot is drawn, the nearer it is to breaking. There are persons who continue because they have begun, and in order not to draw upon themselves the reproach of inconstancy. The more spiritual exercises and intimacies increase, the more we should guard against the spirit of imitation. What should we think of two travelers, each of whom had his own road, and was even required to make that road for himself, if one should constantly tread in the footprints of the other? Can they not walk near enough to each other, and yet follow each his own road? We should not force each other, but all together should be impelled by the inspiration of the Lord. But there are undoubtedly persons who constantly withdraw from the presence of the Lord, and fall into their own ways. These people continually become more and more cold and idle in their Christianity; they need incessantly to be followed, and allowed no repose. He who does not truly believe can not maintain himself, and must backslide.

XXI. "Let him who can not prevent reigning sins groan much on their account before God, and render from time to time a serious and calm testimony against them, and not be disturbed whether he be listened to or not: The pastor should take example from certain persons who protest against the violation of their rights, although they know very well that their protestation will be useless; he should continue to bear witness to the truth, even when the people do not seem to attend to it; something of it will always return to him in time, and meanwhile he will have satisfied his conscience: A river continues to flow, whether we draw water from it or whether we throw a stone into it.

XXII. "As to what is evidently contrary to the law of God, the preacher should show the evil of it with all the seriousness and clearness which are necessary, in order to be understood by every one. He should not let himself be deterred by the fear of men. Besides, the world will allow bitter truths to be spoken to it. It is true that the grief and humiliation caused by reproaches often turn into anger; but afterward we are ashamed of our anger, we come to ourselves and recognize the truth. Undoubtedly, all reproof should be made with prudence, and in order to this:

1. "We should guard against evidently useless enterprises; our credit depends upon this: After great fighting with the air, the finest triumphs do not regain us the good opinion of men.

2. "We should not cherish as a personal offense the irritation caused by truth. All that touches us only should glide over us.

3. "We should try to seize the right moment; nothing irritates more than a stroke which has missed its mark; though we do not feel its effect, we recognize the intention, and know that it was meant for violence.

4. "When we have knowledge of a person's old sins, we should

not speak to him of them; we should wait and see if he fall into them again: this we should consider a flagrant offense; but we should not stop at one isolated fact; we should have regard to the general state of the individual.

5. "We should show impartiality, charity, and compassion. To have succeeded in making a sinner feel that we do not, as men, place ourselves above him, is to have done much toward gaining his heart.

6. "We should show as much mildness as possible in our exhortations. A golden *no* is often better received than a brutal *yes*.

7. "We should not treat all men indiscriminately as flagrant sinners; it would be the way to teach others a secret phariseeism; each one being able to say to himself, 'I have not yet gone so far; I, however, have better views; my conduct is not so bad,' etc.

XXIII. "In respect to the things which may be ranged among the *Adiaphora*, as the play, the dance, etc., it often happens that we exaggerate and stretch the cord too tight. We should not judge others according to ourselves; we can not give them our eyes, nor our manner of seeing. People have often been brought up in such a way that their heart is like leather, even, indeed, like wood. If I had to choose between the natural gayety and the sorrow of an impenitent heart, I should give the preference to the first; it is an image, false, it is true, but an image of the happiness of God; the other is the opposite of it. We give the name of sins to things which are only a simple form of life, and which have sometimes the advantage of preventing the explosions of sin, properly so called. Undoubtedly, these things do not take place in heaven, but when repentance comes, it is not the remembrance of them which causes the most grief: This is lost in the general regret for a life of vanity. The taste for worldly pleasures is the natural result of an unconverted state, and is quenched of itself in conversion. We should not, then, be too exacting; we should not condemn the taste for the dance and amusements of this kind with too much bitterness and a too legal spirit; we should not establish absolute rules, but refer people more to their own consciences, teach them to listen to these, and induce them to avoid those things which they enjoy only with an internal uneasiness. Job had his children in his power; he did not, however, forbid them to feast together, but he prayed for them. This is what we should do for our parishes most assiduously, and particularly in times of public rejoicing; this never remains without fruit, while the law engenders wrath.

"It does not follow, from what we have said, that we should not take advantage of occasions to tell our parishioners our way of thinking on these subjects; we should show them that, in carrying the use of their liberty to excess, without considering that by doing so they may fall into sin, they act like those who, walking along the bank of a river, constantly place their foot as near the water as possible, while yet they endeavor to keep it always on the edge and never let it go in. They should take care that these vanities, these luxuries and follies, do not deprive them of their part in heaven, and, even here below, the share of happiness which this life may offer; they should consider that the pleasure which they take in these things is a certain mark of the unregenerate state of their heart, and that they will see all things with other eyes when God shall work in their heart by his Spirit, etc.

"The pastor should also guard against judging all his parish from the noise and disorder made by certain bad characters. If, standing on the bank of a pond, we should hear nothing but the croaking of frogs, we should not imagine that there are no fish in it.

XXIV. "Not only in the pulpit, but in particular interviews, and whenever the occasion for doing so presents itself naturally, should the pastor insist upon the duty of renouncing the world; but he should not think himself obliged to correct, at one stroke, all the evil with which he may meet. Let him be directed, in this respect, by the inspirations of the Spirit of God: At one time we may keep silence, and groan before God; at another we may feel an internal impulse, which gives us the power and liberty to communicate the like to those with whom we have to do. If we feel ourselves pressed to exhort and to reprove, we should do very wrong not to do so immediately and directly, and not adjourn the discharge of this duty to some holiday, some visit of compliment or condolence; we should also do very wrong in taking a circuitous way to arrive at our end. If we reprove, let it be done directly, without artifice, with a cordial frankness: Let us not be cunning; experience has proved that this method closes hearts instead of opening them.

XXV. "We owe respect to a parish, and we shall be wanting in respect if we do not set it the example of an exact observance of laws, which, moreover, is the most persuasive way of preaching order and regularity. Even in external matters which concern the Church, we must show *accuracy*, regularity, and precision. From want of exactitude in our manner, our hearers would too readily conclude that our doctrine also was inexact. How can they believe that we have fixed principles in our instruction if we have them not in our functions? We do not mean, however, that, in preaching, respect for forms should hinder us from subjoining, after having said amen, this or that good thing which may come to our mind. In the case of Macarius, we find that often a homily was interrupted by some question from an auditor, and that he would reply to it, even when it had but little connection with the subject. I should like to see this simplicity still prevailing in our worship.

XXVI. "From the nature of my functions, I have not been often called to the sick and the dying; but the little experience that I have in this part of the ministry authorizes me in affirming what follows:

"It is by prayer that the pastor will most surely obtain spiritual wisdom, a tender compassion for the sick, and a precise view of what he should do. Let him read, or take for his subject what is best relished by the sick man, and let him apply it to his particular case, without asking him at first if he has always depended much upon these truths: It is better to lead him on gradually to a free confession. Much is gained when the sick man comes of his own accord to compare his present experience with his former ways. Where hypocrisy is not manifest, it is not prudent to overturn every thing, and to make the soul think that we take no account of any of the movements which grace has wrought in it, and of which it has still the remembrance. Let us rather seize the feeblest footing that it may offer us, in order to raise it up: Increasing light always leads to a more complete recognition of the defects and the darkness of the past. In this manner we acquire more facility in leading the sick man on to those individual applications which have so much importance. In the case of very notorious sinners—of ravishers and voluptuaries, for example—there is often despair; and we are obliged to begin by showing them that, though their case is a serious one, there is still ground of hope. This despair sometimes induces them to say, "I am lost; I belong to the devil," which gives us occasion to make them consider their state of sin in general and in detail, and also to lead them to the free grace of God: According as it may seem to us most suitable, we should dwell more on one point than another—on repentance, or on faith, or on devotion to the will of God. We must beware of saying too much. In visiting very sick persons, we may have two opposite experiences: there are some who find that the pastor's visit does them good, and is agreeable to them; others are wearied by it: we should study different cases with care, and conform ourselves to the necessities of the sick man; know when it is best to be silent, and when to speak. If the sick man shows himself inaccessible when we wish to make him confess his state of sin, we must anticipate him by prayer, and put into his mouth what we wished him to have spoken of himself. A man willingly allows himself to be accused when he is placed face to face with God by prayer; it is not so easy to induce him to relate his sins before men, particularly when there are all sorts of persons present to hear him.

"There are sick persons, particularly among the old, who consider suffragans and young pastors as people of very good intention, undoubtedly, but who have too little experience of life to know that the evangelical law is not always to be taken according to the letter. We should strive to remove this prejudice by turning away their attention from the instrument, and fixing it upon immutable and eternal truth. It is well to make them understand that our only concern with them is the salvation of their souls, since we have nothing to gain by preaching to them in one way rather than in another.

In private communions especially, we have a good opportunity for unfolding all the treasures of the love of Christ. But we must strongly oppose the *opus operatum* mistake, which attributes merit to external works, and particularly to the external participation in the sacrament: we must combat this, whether we address ourselves to the past, the present, or the future; and before, during, and after the communion, insist upon the sick man's seeking his peace nowhere but in the grace of God in Jesus Christ.

"The pastor should strive, as much as possible, to lose no opportunity of doing good. He should accordingly address those who may be present before or after death, and make them well understand that his exhortation, however strong it may be, can not save the sick man independently of the state of his own heart; that it is not enough to acquiesce generally in what is said to him, if he do not agree with it in the inward feelings and desires of his heart: Many souls do not experience this spiritual hunger; probably many die impenitent. This, however, should not be applied to those who pray and lend their ear to the word of God. The baptism for the dead, or over the dead, of which St. Paul speaks, should be understood, if I mistake not, as referring to conversions to Christianity shortly before death. "To pluck out of the fire" is the action of recovering a soul which is in the most imminent danger, and with which we are obliged to use the most violent means, since we should only waste time in mild and tranquil representations. The words of Jesus, "There are few chosen," instead of discouraging the pastor, should redouble his zeal and earnestness. I believe, nevertheless, that death-bed conversions are rare. Either the sick man has had more grace in him than he has allowed to be seen, and the last moment brings to light this hidden grace, or else he leaves this world in the temper in which he has always been. It should, however, be observed, that there are poor people who, from want of culture, can not express that which is in them. God loves to reveal such souls upon their death-bed; he does not allow his children to depart entirely *incognito*.

"The impenitent who would put off conversion to the last moment should be admonished that at death one can not be sure of rendering a free and honest testimony; for if, at this last moment, he interrogate his conscience, it is very probable it will answer, "Thou wouldst not have done this hadst thou been well."

"We sometimes find persons who are constantly mourning, without being able to say why; we should not be scandalized at their not being able to express what they feel; we must let them weep, and exhort them to pour out their heart before God, through Jesus Christ; he will hear and understand them.

"We should remember also, by the bed of the dying, that there are some who are disturbed by the want of pardon from an offended person, and should procure for them this word of reconciliation, after which they may die in peace.

XXVII. "We add to these rules of Bengel for the visitation of the sick a few of his own words, addressed to the sick.

1. "He said to a man whose state was desperate, 'Dear friend, penetrate into the love and the light of God; know how to use the privilege which Jesus Christ, the well-beloved, acquired for the rebellious children of his Father; let the spirit of grace be mighty in your weakness; and let it draw from you those sighs which bear our souls even into eternity, where we are called to be with that great Forerunner who has entered thither for us, and for all those who have followed the right road. I recommend you to God: let us pray for one another.'

2. "Mademoiselle de St. ——, ill of a consumption, showed him her emaciated arms, and complained that God had not yet called her away. Bengel replied to her: 'You are like one of my pupils, who wished, at vacation, to go away before the time; he was obliged to stay until the last lesson. You believe that you have nothing more to do here below; but you may be sure that it is, to a Christian, a good preparation for eternity, when, having packed away every thing, and thinking himself ready to depart, he is still obliged to wait for the signal of his Master. By patiently submitting yourself, you render to God a sacrifice acceptable to him.'

3. "Bengel was present with several other Christian friends at the bed of the pastor Grammich, to whom, at his request, this song was sung:

'Cendre, froide et muette,
Dans ta sombre retraite
Dors en paix, jusqu'au jour
Où le Seigneur qui t'aime
T'emportera lui-même,
Vivante et rajeunie, au bienheureux séjour.'

Bengel repeated to the sick man each of the most touching expressions of this song. Then he spoke to him of the glory of the city of God, 'which must indeed be beautiful,' said he, 'since it is written, *God is not ashamed to be called their God; for he hath prepared for them a city.*' Then the sick man, impressed with the majesty of God, felt himself profoundly humiliated by his own misery. He groaned, he tossed himself in his bed, and confessed his sins. Bengel said to him: 'It is indeed necessary that the servant ask pardon.' The sick man did so, with many tears; then Bengel continued: 'If we confess our faults and our misery, God will not reckon with us; he acts royally; he remits to us ten thousand talents at a time.' Finally, the sick man recovered his serenity, and kept it to the end. When they took leave of one another, each placed his hand upon the other's head, and they blessed each other abundantly.

4. "In regard to a person attacked with a mental malady: 'I like very well,' said he, 'to listen to these persons; they often retain something of what is said to them; and then here is a great advantage for studying human nature. But when the melancholy is so great that the sick man opens neither his mouth nor his heart, I beseech and advise him to repeat my words aloud: There is a great power in the voice.'

XXVIII. "As to disputes between husband and wife, ... we must show them how much advantage they give to the devil when they cease to combat him in order to oppose each other. . . . . . As a general rule, the pastor will sometimes do well to undertake the particular treatment of a divided household, and conduct it in a studied manner, as in the case of a cure to be accomplished. We can not efface a large spot by lightly rubbing it once. Formerly, much more was written on particular sins; now we are content to lay the foundation, believing that the rest will come of itself. We forget that very often we may uproot a whole tree by drawing it only by a single branch. There are souls with whom all would be in order if one sin were removed. Do not be wearied, then, pastors, in distributing the Word abundantly. That atheism, which is always spreading itself more and more in society, and which consists less in the gross impiety of certain persons than in a general negligence of all serious thought concerning the living God, is combated with success only by an assiduous, minute, and complete exposition of the divine truth.

XXIX. "When we endeavor to excite the rich to benevolence, it is desirable, also, to take occasion to remind the poor of the duty of justice and fidelity; else the poor and the rich will complete our words greatly to their detriment in reproaching each other bitterly with their mutual wrongs. Would it not be better to lead both to seek the Lord together, and to induce those who have too much to give to those who have not enough? Perhaps it is because we are contented with preaching to the rich that they seek, in the conduct of the poor, pretexts for not succoring them.

XXX. "The pastor should give the greatest care to the first of his parish, I mean the children; and to the last, that is, to the dying. To the first, because it is from them that the most fruit may be expected; and to the last, because he has but a very short time to acquit himself of his ministry toward them.

XXXI. "The communion administered to persons so differently disposed must necessarily give much anxiety to a conscientious pastor. If I be asked whether it would not be better not to give the communion than to give the body of our Lord to all indiscriminately, I reply, that there is a difference to be made between the defense of the truth in theory and the defense of truth in practice! The first is more or less independent of the variations of the worldly scene, and is accomplished, more or less, in spite of all circumstances. The second is more difficult from its nature, and has, in every age, been subject to abuse.

"When a pastor seriously doubts whether a person who presents himself at the sacred table be worthy to commune, he should, before the communion day, speak in private to this person, explain to him the gravity and the responsibility of the action which he undertakes, and then let him act according to his will. Let the palisade be raised before the door of the temple, not around the altar. The pastor must be able to dispense the Lord's Supper with fullness of joy, as if he were communicating to all his sheep all the virtue of the blood of Christ—as if he felt himself strong enough, with these sacred pledges of mercy, to raise all the souls at once to heaven.

"The holy communion is a means of conversion for many; the officials should then, according to the knowledge which they have of the situation of the communicant, address to him the words of the institution, with all the gravity and emphasis which may be necessary, in order to make a proper impression upon him. But I can not approve of placing the utility of the communion in its being the means of conversion—a doctrine, properly so called, for this precisely is not its end.

XXXII. "The doctrine of the efficacy of prayer and of the internal word is very important; but without great prudence in the manner of teaching and applying it, we run the risk of falling into the deceit of the heart, and of tempting God. The words of St. John, 'They shall all be taught of God' (vi., 45; Heb., viii.), should not be taken in the sense that no one needs the instruction of another. If it were so, why should the apostles have taught? These words indicate the pre-eminence of the New Testament over the Old. In the former, God was obliged to use force with the Israelites; the New is characterized by a spirit of liberty which opens the mind. When a man receives the spirit promised in the New Testament, all becomes easier to his comprehension, and he acquires a facility in spiritual things which others only acquire by long studies. The passage in 1 John, ii., 27, is applicable to false doctrine, with which the Christian need not be made acquainted. To know whether certain souls may be aroused without the intervention of the evangelical ministry, or whether the entire Church can be sustained and perpetuated without it, are two different questions.

XXXIII. "The mystics date from the fourth or fifth century. The

Aristotelian philosophy, and afterward the scholasticism which was derived from it, being cultivated with ardor, sincere persons, in order to escape the disputes of the school, withdrew into themselves. Each mystic had a certain ray of light, but that was all. He understood nothing of the economy of God, nor of his ways in general. These men were wrapped up in themselves, and were no longer any thing to society. They lived in times of obscurity; they were happy themselves, but contributed nothing to the happiness of others. While the scholastics attached value to nothing but speculation and reasonings, they, as well as the Platonists, valued only sentiment, and a blind and silent disposition of the heart. The mystics must, however, confess that what they have of good they could have found nowhere but in the pale of the Church.

XXXIV. "It is suitable for a country pastor to pursue, together with his pastoral labors, some particular studies relating to the ministry, in order not to fall back always upon himself; he should know what is passing elsewhere in the kingdom of God, so as to be, in time of need, encouraged, aroused, humbled, and instructed."

The *Thoughts of Bengel on the Exercise of the Ministry*, translated by M. Vinet, have appeared in the *Life of Bengel*, by Burk, under the title of *Pastoral Grundsaetze* (Part ii., chap. ii., art. 2). M. Vinet has omitted, in his translation, the sections III., IV., XII., XIX., XXIV., XXXVII., XXXVIII., XLI., XLII., and XLIV., of the German work, although he refers to the three last in the Notes of his *Pastoral Theology*. The references to the retained paragraphs, corresponding to the divisions of Burk, we have thought it our duty to indicate here only because of the omissions. Section XXVII. of the original work corresponds to section XXII. of the translation; section XXX. to section XXV.; section XXXIII. to section XXVIII.; and section XXXVI. to section XXXI. The parts omitted relate chiefly to local usages, or to questions which are now no longer discussed, as they were in the time of Bengel, who was born in 1687, and died in 1752. —*Edit.*

THE END.

ERRATA.

Page 69, 3d line from the bottom, for "Troizième" read "Treizième."

Page 123, 15th line from the top, for "now said" read "to say."

Page 131, 11th line, leave out "of man."

Page 211, seventh line from the bottom, for "rebels" read "provokes."

Page 272, 2d line from the top, remove parentheses from "souls."

Page 273, 9th line from the top, for "used" read "use."

Page 297, 5th and 6th lines from the top, for "them" read "it."

Page 371, 2d line from the top, for "Franeke" read "Francke."

Upham's Life of Faith:

Embracing some of the Scriptural Principles or Doctrines of Faith, the Power or Effect of Faith in the Regulation of Man's Inward Nature, and the Relation of Faith to the Divine Guidance. 12mo, Muslin, $1 00.

Upham's Life of Madame Adorna;

Including some leading Facts and Traits in her Religious Experience. Together with Explanations and Remarks, tending to illustrate the Doctrine of Holiness. 12mo, Muslin, 50 cents; Muslin, gilt edges, 60 cents.

Upham's Life of Madame Guyon.

The Life and Religious Opinions and Experience of Madame Guyon: together with some Account of the Personal History and Religious Opinions of Archbishop Fenelon. 2 vols. 12mo, Muslin, $2 00.

Upham's Principles of the Interior or Hidden

Life. Designed particularly for the Consideration of those who are seeking Assurance of Faith and Perfect Love. 12mo, Muslin, $1 00.

Sacred Meditations.

By P. L. U. 48mo, Muslin, gilt edges, 31¼ cents.

Thankfulness.

A Narrative. Comprising Passages from the Diary of the Rev. Allan Temple. By the Rev. C. B. Tayler. 12mo, Paper, 37½ cents; Muslin, 50 cents.

Book of Common Prayer:

Elegantly printed, according to the revised Standard adopted by the General Convention, in the following varieties of binding and size:

Standard 4to. A splendid volume, suitable for the desk. Turkey Morocco, gilt edges, $10 00.

Standard 8vo. From the same stereotype plates as the preceding. Sheep extra, $2 00; Calf extra, $2 50; Turkey Morocco, gilt edges, $5 00.

Royal 8vo. Hewet's Illustrated Edition. Turkey Morocco, gilt edges, $6 00.

Medium 8vo. Double Columns. Sheep extra, $1 25; Turkey Morocco, gilt edges, $4 00.

12mo, Sheep extra, 62½ cents; Roan extra, 75 cents; Turkey Morocco, gilt edges, $1 75.

18mo, Roan or Sheep extra, 75 cents; Calf or Turkey Morocco, gilt edges, $1 75.

24mo, Sheep extra, 35 cents; Roan extra, 40 cents; Calf or Turkey Morocco, gilt edges, $1 25.

32mo, Roan or Sheep extra, 40 cents; Calf or Turkey Morocco, gilt edges, $1 25.

Pearl, Roan or Sheep extra, 40 cents; Pocket-book form, gilt edges, $1 00; Calf or Turkey Morocco, gilt edges, $1 25.

Saurin's Sermons.

Translated by Rev. R. ROBINSON, Rev. H. HUNTER, and Rev. J. SUTCLIFFE. New Edition, with additional Sermons. Revised and corrected by Rev. S. BURDER. With Preface, by Rev. J. P. K. HENSHAW. Portrait. 2 vols. 8vo, Sheep extra, $3 75

Hall's complete Works:

With a brief Memoir of his Life, by Dr. GREGORY, and Observations on his Character as a Preacher, by Rev. J. FOSTER. Edited by O. GREGORY, LL.D., and Rev. J. BELCHER. Portrait 4 vols. 8vo, Sheep extra, $6 00.

Barnes's Notes on the Gospels,

Explanatory and Practical. Designed for Bible Classes and Sunday Schools. With an Index, a Chronological Table, Tables of Weights, &c. Map. 2 vols. 12mo, Muslin, $1 50

Barnes's Notes on the Acts of the Apostles,

Explanatory and Practical. Designed for Bible Classes and Sunday Schools. With a Map. 12mo, Muslin, 75 cents.

Barnes's Notes on the Epistle to the Romans,

Explanatory and Practical. Designed for Bible Classes and Sunday Schools. 12mo, Muslin, 75 cents.

Barnes's Notes on the First Epistle to the Corinthians,

Explanatory and Practical. Designed for Bible Classes and Sunday Schools. 12mo, Muslin, 75 cents.

Barnes's Notes on the Second Epistle to the

Corinthians, and the Epistle to the Galatians, Explanatory and Practical. Designed for Bible Classes and Sunday Schools. 12mo, Muslin, 75 cents.

Barnes's Notes on the Epistles to the Ephesians,

the Philippians, and the Colossians, Explanatory and Practical. Designed for Bible Classes and Sunday Schools. 12mo, Muslin, 75 cents.

Barnes's Notes on the Epistles to the Thessalonians,

Timothy, Titus, and Philemon, Explanatory and Practical. Designed for Bible Classes and Sunday Schools. 12mo, Muslin, 75 cents.

Barnes's Notes on the Epistle to the Hebrews,

Explanatory and Practical. Designed for Bible Classes and Sunday Schools. 12mo, Muslin, 75 cents.

Barnes's Notes on the General Epistles of

James, Peter, John, and Jude, Explanatory and Practical. Designed for Bible Classes and Sunday Schools. 12mo, Muslin. 75 cents.

Barnes's Questions on Matthew.

Designed for Bible Classes and Sunday Schools. 18mo, Muslin, 15 cents.

Barnes's Questions on Mark and Luke.

Designed for Bible Classes and Sunday Schools. 18mo, Muslin, 15 cents.

Barnes's Questions on John.

Designed for Bible Classes and Sunday Schools. 18mo, Muslin, 15 cents.

Barnes's Questions on the Acts of the Apostles.

Designed for Bible Classes and Sunday Schools. 18mo, Muslin, 15 cents.

Barnes's Questions on the Epistle to the Romans.

Designed for Bible Classes and Sunday Schools. 18mo, Muslin, 15 cents.

Barnes's Questions on the First Epistle to the Corinthians.

Designed for Bible Classes and Sunday Schools. 18mo, Muslin, 15 cents.

Barnes's Questions on the Epistle to the Hebrews.

Designed for Bible Classes and Sunday Schools. 18mo, Muslin, 15 cents.

Neal's History of the Puritans;

Or, Protestant Non-conformists; from the Reformation in 1517 to the Revolution in 1688; comprising an Account of their Principles, their Attempts for a further Reformation in the Church, their Sufferings, and the Lives and Characters of their most considerable Divines. Reprinted from the Text of Dr. Toulmin's Edition: with his Life of the Author, and Account of his Writings. Revised, corrected, and enlarged, with additional Notes, by J. O. Choules, D.D. With Nine Portraits on Steel. 2 vols. 8vo, Muslin, $3 50; Sheep extra, $4 00.

Noel's Essay on the Union of Church and State.

12mo, Muslin, $1 25.

Abercrombie's Miscellaneous Essays.

Consisting of the Harmony of Christian Faith and Christian Character; the Culture and Discipline of the Mind; Think on these Things; the Contest and the Armor; the Messiah as an Example. 18mo, Muslin, 37½ cents.

Jarvis's Chronological Introduction to Church History:

being a new Inquiry into the true Dates of the Birth and Death of our Lord and Savior Jesus Christ; and containing an original Harmony of the four Gospels, now first arranged in the Order of Time. 8vo, Muslin, $3 00.

Butler's Analogy of Religion,

Natural and Revealed, to the Constitution and Course of Nature. To which are added two brief Dissertations: of Personal Identity—of the Nature of Virtue. With a Preface by Bishop Halifax. 18mo, half Bound, 37½ cents.

Hawks's History of the Protestant Episcopal

Church in Virginia: being a Narrative of Events connected with its Rise and Progress. With the Journals of the Conventions in Virginia. 8vo, Muslin, $1 75.

Jay's complete Works:

Comprising his Sermons; Family Discourses; Morning and Evening Exercises for every Day in the Year; Family Prayers; Lectures; Lives of Cornelius Winter and John Clark, &c. Author's enlarged Edition, revised. 3 vols. 8vo, Muslin, $5 00 · Sheep extra, $5 50.

Jay's Morning and Evening Exercises for the

Closet, for every Day in the Year. With Portrait. 8vo, Muslin, $1 25; half Morocco, $1 50.

Summerfield's Sermons,

And Sketches of Sermons. With an Introduction by Rev. T. E Bond, M.D. 8vo, Muslin, $1 75.

Spencer's Greek New Testament.

With English Notes, critical, philological, and exegetical Indexes, &c. 12mo, Muslin, $1 25; Sheep extra, $1 40.

Lewis's Platonic Theology.

Plato against the Atheists; or, the Tenth Book of the Dialogue on Laws, with critical Notes and extended Dissertations on some of the main Points of the Platonic Philosophy and Theology, especially as compared with the Holy Scriptures. 12mo Muslin, $1 50.

Gieseler's Compendium of Ecclesiastical His

tory. From the Fourth Edinburgh Edition, revised and amended. Translated from the German by Samuel Davidson, LL.D 8vo.

Blair's Sermons.

To which is prefixed the Life and Character of the Author, by J. Finlayson, D.D. 8vo, Muslin, $1 50.

Bunyan's Pilgrim's Progress.

With a Life of Bunyan, by Robert Southey, LL.D. Illustrated with 50 Engravings, by J. A. Adams. 12mo, Paper, 50 cents; Muslin, 75 cents.

The Sacred Philosophy of the Seasons.

Illustrating the Perfections of God in the Phenomena of the Year. By Rev. Henry Duncan, D.D. With important Additions, and some Modifications to adapt it to American Readers, by F. W. P. Greenwood, D.D. 4 vols. 12mo, Muslin, $3 00.

Theology Explained and Defended,

In a Series of Sermons. By T. Dwight, LL.D. With a Memoir of the Life of the Author. With a Portrait. 4 vols. 8vo, Muslin, $6 00; Sheep extra, $6 50.

Waddington's History of the Church,

From the earliest Ages to the Reformation. 8vo, Muslin, $1 75

Lord's Exposition of the Apocalypse.

8vo, Muslin, $2 00.

Brown's Dictionary of the Holy Bible.

Containing an Historical Account of the Persons; a Geographical and Historical Account of the Places; a Literal, Critical, and Systematical Description of other Objects, whether Natural, Artificial, Civil, Religious, or Military; and an Explanation of the appellative Terms mentioned in the Old and New Testaments: the whole comprising whatever important is known concerning the Antiquities of the Hebrew Nation and Church of God; forming a Sacred Commentary, a Body of Scripture History, Chronology, and Divinity; and serving in a great measure as a Concordance to the Holy Bible. With the Author's last Additions and Corrections, and further enlarged and corrected by his Sons. Also, a Life of the Author, and an Essay on the Evidence of Christianity. 8vo, Sheep extra, $1 75.

Brown's Pocket Concordance to the Holy Bi-

ble. 32mo, Roan, 37½ cents.

Hunter's Sacred Biography;

Or, the History of the Patriarchs. To which is added the History of Deborah, Ruth, and Hannah, and also the History of Jesus Christ. 8vo, Muslin, $1 75.

Milman's History of Christianity,

From the Birth of Christ to the Abolition of Paganism in the Roman Empire. With Notes, &c., by James Murdock, D.D. 8vo, Muslin, $1 90.

Milman's History of the Jews,

From the earliest Period to the present Time. With Maps and Engravings. 3 vols. 18mo, Muslin, $1 20.

The Old and New Testaments Connected,

In the History of the Jews and Neighboring Nations, from the Declension of the Kingdoms of Israel and Judah to the Time of Christ. By Humphrey Prideaux, D.D. With the Life of the Author. Maps and Plates. 2 vols. 8vo, Sheep extra, $3 75.

Turner's Sacred History of the World,

Attempted to be Philosophically considered, in a Series of Letters to a Son. 3 vols. 18mo, Muslin, $1 35.

Vol. I. considers the Creation and System of the Earth, and of its Vegetable and Animal Races, and Material Laws, and Formation of Mankind.

Vol. II., the Divine Economy in its special Relation to Mankind, and in the Deluge, and the History of Human Affairs.

Vol. III., the Provisions for the Perpetuation and Support of the Human Race, the Divine System of our Social Combinations, and the Supernatural History of the World.

The Incarnation;

Or, Pictures of the Virgin and her Son. By Rev. C. BEECHER With an introductory Essay, by Mrs. HARRIET BEECHER STOWE 18mo, Muslin, 50 cents.

Paley's Evidences of Christianity.

A View of the Evidences of Christianity. 18mo, half Roan 37½ cents.

Paley's Natural Theology.

With illustrative Notes, &c., by Lord BROUGHAM and Sir C. BELL, and preliminary Observations and Notes, by ALONZO POTTER, D.D. With Engravings. 2 vols. 18mo, Muslin, 90 cents.

Paley's Natural Theology.

A new Edition, from large Type, edited by D. E. BARTLETT Copiously Illustrated, and a Life and Portrait of the Author. 2 vols. 12mo, Muslin, $1 50.

Neander's Life of Jesus Christ:

In its Historical Connection and its Historical Development Translated from the Fourth German Edition, by Professors M'CLINTOCK and BLUMENTHAL. 8vo, Muslin, $2 00; Sheep extra, $2 25.

The Land of Israel,

According to the Covenant with Abraham, with Isaac, and with Jacob. By A. KEITH, D.D. With Plates. 12mo, Muslin, $1 25

Evidence of Prophecy.

Evidence of the Truth of the Christian Religion, derived from the literal Fulfillment of Prophecy; particularly as illustrated by the History of the Jews, and by the Discoveries of recent Travelers. By A. KEITH, D.D. 12mo, Muslin, 60 cents.

Demonstration of Christianity.

Demonstration of the Truth of the Christian Religion. By A KEITH, D.D. With Engravings. 12mo, Muslin, $1 37½.

The Mysteries Opened;

Or, Scriptural Views of Preaching and the Sacraments, as distinguished from certain Theories concerning Baptismal Regeneration and the Real Presence. By Rev. J. S. STONE. 12mo, Muslin, $1 00.

The Novitiate;

Or, a Year among the English Jesuits: a Personal Narrative. With an Essay on the Constitutions, the Confessional Morality, and History of the Jesuits. By ANDREW STEINMETZ. 18mo, Muslin, 50 cents.

Duer's Speech,

Delivered in the Convention of the P. E. Church of the Diocese of New York, on Friday, the 29th of Sept., 1843, in support of the Resolutions offered by Judge Oakley. 8vo, Paper, 12½ cents.

Biblical Legends of the Mussulmans.

The Bible, the Koran, and the Talmud. Compiled from Arabic Sources, and compared with Jewish Traditions. By Dr. G. Weil. 12mo, Muslin, 50 cents.

Scripture Illustrated,

By interesting Facts, Incidents, and Anecdotes. By Rev. C. Field. With Introduction, by Rev. J. Todd, D.D. 18mo, Muslin, 50 cents; Roan, 60 cents.

The True Believer;

His Character, Duty, and Privileges, elucidated in a Series of Discourses. By Rev. Asa Mahan. 18mo, Muslin, 50 cents.

Mosheim's Ecclesiastical History,

Ancient and Modern; in which the Rise, Progress, and Variation of Church Power are considered in their Connection with the State of Learning and Philosophy, and the Political History of Europe during that Period. Translated, with Notes, &c., by A. Maclaine, D.D. A new Edition, continued to 1826, by C. Coote, LL.D. 2 vols. 8vo, Sheep extra, $3 50.

Turner's Essay on our Lord's Discourse at Capernaum,

recorded in the Sixth Chapter of St. John. 12mo, Muslin, 75 cents.

The Sufferings of Christ.

By a Layman. 12mo, Muslin, 50 cents.

The Heart Delineated in its State by Nature,

and as renewed by Grace. By Rev. Hugh Smith. 18mo, Muslin, 45 cents.

Smedley's History of the Reformation in

France. Portrait. 3 vols. 18mo, Muslin, $1 40.

Gleig's History of the Bible.

With a Map. 2 vols. 18mo, Muslin, 80 cents.

Zion's Songster;

Or, a Collection of Hymns and Spiritual Songs, usually Sung at Camp-meetings, and also at Revivals of Religion. Compiled by the Rev. Thomas Mason. 32mo, Sheep, 25 cents.

Luther and the Lutheran Reformation.

By Rev. John Scott. Portraits. 2 vols. 18mo, Muslin, $1 00.

Sunday Evenings.

Comprising Scripture Stories. With Engravings. 3 vols. 18mo, Muslin, 93¾ cents.

Beauties of the Bible:

Selected from the Old and New Testaments, with various Remarks and brief Dissertations. Designed for the Use of Schools and the Improvement of Youth. By Ezra Sampson. 18mo, Muslin, 50 cents.

www.ingramcontent.com/pod-product-compliance
Lightning Source LLC
La Vergne TN
LVHW020113110826
845151LV00001B/148

* 9 7 8 1 4 2 5 5 4 3 5 2 5 *